An introduction to
national income analysis

An introduction to national income analysis

Second edition

Wilfred Beckerman

Fellow and Tutor in Economics,
Balliol College, Oxford

Weidenfeld and Nicolson
London

© 1968 by Wilfred Beckerman
First published 1968
Second impression 1969
Paperback edition 1972
Second edition 1976
Second impression 1978
Weidenfeld and Nicolson
11 St John's Hill London SW11

ISBN 0 297 77059 4 Cased
ISBN 0 297 77060 8 Paperback

Printed and bound in Great Britain by
REDWOOD BURN LIMITED
Trowbridge & Esher

Contents

v

CONTENTS

Preface to the second edition

Two entirely new chapters have been added to this second edition of this book. These are Chapters 3 and 7, which are about the relationship between national product and 'welfare' and what is often known as the 'quality of life', and the distribution of income. These two topics have been the subject of so much discussion during the last few years that it seemed undesirable to exclude them from a general textbook on national income analysis. At the same time the original chapters have been preserved intact in the interests of what had been the object of the first edition of this book, as originally described below.

There are many economics textbooks where mathematical techniques are being widely used nowadays and the increasing availability of textbooks on mathematics for economists or on mathematical economics has provided a most valuable addition to the student's (and the teacher's) scope for checking how far he had really understood some aspects of economic theory that he had previously, perhaps, grasped only in a rather vague manner. But the object of this book is not quite so ambitious. It is to introduce the technique of numerical – as distinct from abstract mathematical – exercises, of the most elementary nature possible (from the mathematical point of view) into an area of economics that is not usually treated in this manner, namely national accounting.[1] Many teachers of economics have encountered good students who have read the basic texts on national accounts without difficulty but who, when faced with a simple question,

[1] The book *Exercises de Comptabilité Nationale* by G. Vibert, Dunod, Paris, 1965, is of a rather special kind, being more a manual of practical exercises addressed primarily to persons who will be engaged on practical work with French national accounting estimation.

such as how national product is affected by the sale of a second-hand car, will give an incorrect answer. Since national income accounts are concerned with numbers, it seemed desirable that they should be taught with the aid of numerical exercises. I was originally introduced to this way of teaching national accounting by Professor Brian Tew, when I was a member of the Economics Faculty at the University of Nottingham over fifteen years ago, and I have at last got round to writing a book along these lines. Professor Tew would have done it much better. I have also been influenced and helped by those who read parts of the manuscript, notably J. L. Nicholson (particularly on 'the quality problem'), E. F. Jackson, C. T. Saunders, G. Stuvel, R. D. Portes, Paul A. Lee and Lawrence Whitehead. The remaining defects in all the chapters are, of course, entirely my responsibility.

Another person to whom I am greatly indebted is Milton Gilbert who first made me realise that national accounting was an interesting subject and an important tool of applied economic analysis, not a special brand of theology. In fact, one theme that I have tried to emphasise in the early chapters of the book is the dependence of the choice of national accounting conventions on the particular questions that economists are investigating and the particular working hypotheses that they use, *at present*, in the course of arriving at answers. After the first four chapters, in which the basic national accounts framework is explained, therefore, I have tried to show, in Chapter 6, the relationship between the picture of the economy that emerges from this framework and the main areas of economic theory. This may have the purely pedagogic value of presenting the national accounting framework as a link between the different main fields of theory with which the student is confronted. Too often the student obtains the impression that, say, the theory of demand and of public finance are in separate compartments which do not closely link up anywhere in the course of more practical applied macro-economic analysis. In presenting the subject in this way I hope that the student will see more clearly that the main areas of economic theory can be regarded as theories about certain aspects of the operation of the different sectors in the economy that are distinguished in the conventional social accounting frameworks. Chapters 8 and 9, on macro-economics, are designed partly to illustrate the applications of the 'model' of the economy that has been built up in the preceding chapters on the national accounts and partly to emphasise the distinction between purely accounting relationships and identities, on the one hand, and, on the other hand, relationships that describe aspects of the way that the different sectors in the economy behave.

These two chapters do not constitute an adequate elementary exposition of the process of short-term fluctuations in the level of output and incomes in an economy since no allowance is made in them for monetary phenomena, such as the money supply and the rate of interest. This is largely because such a treatment, in the context of the present book, would logically require an extension of the system of accounts set out in the book to include the financial sectors of the economy, which would be beyond the scope of the book. In any case there are now numerous excellent introductory texts available on macro-economics which concentrate on the operation of macro-models of the economy rather than on the related accounting framework and the meaning of the figures that are bandied about so much in public discussion of general economic issues.

The last two chapters (10 and 11) are concerned with the problem of what is meant by a change in national product or income (or by a comparison between the income of one country and that of another) and the problems of measuring such changes or income differences. No attempt has been made to use numerical exercises for this part of the book since it seemed to me that the sheer computing labour that the examples would have to involve would be out of proportion to the benefit that the students would derive from the exercises.

This book is aimed chiefly at first-year University students who have probably not had any serious formal instruction in national accounting concepts, though some of the chapters are also probably within the reach and interests of students at the pre-University level. It may also be useful to more advanced students who have hitherto rather ignored national accounting or who feel the need for supplementary reading on the topics covered in Chapters 10 and 11, namely on the measurement of changes in national product, the 'quality problem' and so on. The numerical examples do not require any mathematical knowledge beyond that taught in all schools by the age of about thirteen. For this reason there are no numerical examples to Chapter 6 since useful exercises to this chapter – in which input–output tables are introduced – would require knowledge of elementary matrix algebra, and I have not assumed this knowledge.

This is not supposed to be a full-scale textbook on national accounting, though the discussion of the basic concepts in the early chapters may go beyond what is customary in general textbooks on economics. For the reader who wishes to go further or to study a more rigorous and technical treatment of national accounting theory there are excellent scholarly books of a more specialised character, such as those by G. Stuvel and I. Ohlsson.[1] Other books carry much further than does this book certain areas of the subject. For example, R. Marris's *Economic Arithmetic* contains a much more detailed explanation of the official British national accounts statistics as well as a very thorough discussion of the economic theory of index numbers. Ruggles and Ruggles, in *National Income Accounts and Income Analysis*, not only emphasise the very important relationship between the national accounts and the accounts of individual enterprises but also provide extensive illustrations of the concepts from actual data on the US economy.

W. Beckerman

[1] G. Stuvel *Systems of Social Accounts*, Clarendon Press, Oxford, 1965, and I. Ohlsson *On National Accounting*, National Institute of Economic Research, Stockholm, 1961.

Chapter 1

What national income accounts are about

In any economy countless transactions are being conducted all the time – housewives are buying their daily needs, firms are paying wages and buying machinery, taxes are being paid, second-hand cars are being sold, old-age pensions are being received, imports are arriving and exports are going abroad, etc., etc. For purposes of any rational analysis of the way the economy is behaving these millions of transactions have to be classified in some systematic manner. One cannot even begin to examine questions such as whether national product is rising or falling unless one knows which of the various transactions form part of national income and which do not. (In fact, not all those transactions listed above enter into national product, and the reader who is not quite sure which ones are being referred to here is the class of reader to whom this book is most addressed.) But, of course, there are an unlimited number of ways that the transactions can be classified. For example, one could classify transactions according to size, or the age of the persons involved, or any other system provided the system of classification was such that the classes into which the transactions were divided were exhaustive and mutually exclusive.

However, no system of classification is likely to be suitable for answering all the questions that one might encounter in the subject concerned, and for certain issues that arise in economics it may be necessary to classify transactions on a special basis devised for purposes of that particular issue. For example, to study the equality of income distribution, it is necessary to classify incomes according to the size distribution of incomes. But the basic classification that is now generally adopted in the national accounts has been influenced largely by the desire to see how the level of national income is determined in the short

1

and the longer run. To design a classification system for this purpose meant, of course, taking some view as to what makes national income change. In selecting a system of classification for purposes of analysing any phenomenon, one must start with some theory of what are the important distinctions that have to be drawn between different categories to be classified, and what are the important relationships between them.

For example, in the analysis of the causes of lung cancer, if it is required to see how far lung cancer is related to smoking one obviously wants to begin by classifying cancer victims according to how much they smoke. At the same time, if it is thought that the type of smoking involved is also important one would want to have a sub-classification according, say, to whether it was cigars or pipes or cigarettes that they smoked. There would be little interest in having a classification by the price of the cigarette, or by the particular brand unless there was reason to believe that different brands had different impacts on cancer. In other words what classification system one adopts depends on what view one takes as to the important factors to be isolated in explaining the phenomenon under examination.

The first problem, therefore, in setting up a system of classification for national accounts is to decide what are the important categories of transactions from the point of view of the main questions that economists ask about the operation of the economy, such as 'How fast, if at all, is the economy growing?' or 'What makes it grow and how can we get rich quicker?' In fact, the very rapid progress in the last thirty years or so in national accounting has come about largely as a result of the major breakthrough by Lord Keynes in the theory of what caused fluctuations in income in the 'short-run' (i.e. from year to year or over the course of a few years), since this had been the most important practical question economists were asking. Although the national income concepts in Keynesian theory had – albeit though with different interpretations of their precise role – been occupying the centre of the stage in discussions of the causes of fluctuations in economic activity for several decades already, the power and conviction of the Keynesian theory based on these concepts certainly provided the major boost to the development of national income accounting. The elements of this 'theory' – i.e. this view of the way that the level of income was determined – will be developed in a subsequent chapter of this book. But in order to explain why the particular system of national accounts classification that will be set out in this book has in fact been adopted, it is necessary at this stage to give a preview of this theory.

The main outline of the short-run theory of income determination that is now generally accepted is roughly speaking as follows (see Chapters 8 and 9 for fuller explanation). National income is in 'equilibrium', in the short-run, when the demand for goods and services is equal to the supply of goods and services. But not all the incomes earned from selling goods and services go back to constitute demand for goods and services, since people *save* some of their incomes. The equilibrium condition will only be satisfied, therefore, if this saving is offset by some other injection of demand. Thus, the flow of incomes and expenditures in the economy will be affected by the extent to which 'leakages' in this flow are matched by new injections into the flow. It is rather like a pipe through which water is circulating; if there is a leakage in the system somewhere the amount of water flowing through it will fall unless there is a corresponding re-injection of water somewhere else. In the circular flow of incomes, it is 'savings', in the widest sense of the term, that constitutes the 'leakage' – i.e. the failure to spend all incomes generated in the economy on consumption of home produced goods. In order that the flow be maintained, this leakage must be offset by 'investment'. The way this works, and the precise definition of savings and investment in this context, will be examined later in this book. The essential point here is simply that this theory provides a starting point for the classification of activities, namely between consumption, saving and investment. However, as in the case of the cancer problem, further sub-divisions may be desirable, corresponding to the sub-division of smoking between pipes, cigars and cigarettes (and many other sub-sub-categories). In the case of the economic transactions, it is also important, for purposes of answering other important economic questions, to have additional classifications of the transactions, sometimes as sub-classifications of the basic aggregates of consumption and investment, and sometimes as quite separate classifications of the whole system of transactions.

For example, the manner in which some of the important aggregates, such as total investment or consumption, behave, and hence the way they affect the overall level of income, may depend on who makes the decisions about those particular items. The behaviour of, say, investment probably depends to some extent on whether one is referring to fixed investment, such as factories or machines, or to changes in the economy's stock of raw materials or semi-finished goods, since the former are likely to be determined, in a more deliberate manner, by longer-run considerations. For somewhat similar reasons – namely, the difference in motivation – it may often be useful to divide total consumption into private and public consumption.

Economists are interested, of course, not only in short-run fluctuations in economic activity, but also in the longer-run growth of the economy, the efficiency with which resources are allocated, the structural changes in the economy, and many other questions. For analysing these (and other) questions it may be necessary to classify transactions according to the outputs of the different industries in the economy, or the shares of wages and profits in total national income, the regional pattern of output, and so on. Innumerable other examples can be given of the needs for special kinds of classification to answer special problems. Thus although, on the whole, the usual national accounts classifications adopted are based mainly on the major categories of transactions that are important from the point of view of the fluctuations in the economy, these major categories are further broken down into sub-categories in a way likely to be important both for the analysis of the way in which the major categories are determined and, as far as possible, for the analysis of certain other standard important questions about the economy that arise. Quite different classifications may be required, of course, for other problems. But in this book, we shall be concentrating on the former type of classification, this being the one that is the subject matter of national income analysis.

Since a classification system is only useful insofar as it is an aid in answering certain questions, it is futile to discuss the relative merits of one classification system rather than another in the abstract. Some systems may be more useful than others in answering certain questions but less useful for answering other questions. It is vain to seek for a system that will answer all the interesting questions that might be asked. How many interesting questions any particular accounting system can answer is itself an open-ended question to which there can be no answer. Discussion of the relative merits of different systems is only useful, therefore, if it is in the context of specific questions. And even then the extent to which any accounting system is appropriate and useful for answering any specific question is, of course, a matter of judgement, which is why there is an arbitrary element in many of the decisions that have to be made in drawing up a classification system for national accounts. At the same time, once the principles of the system have been selected they have to be applied as logically and consistently as possible. The rules of any game, such as football or bridge, may be somewhat arbitrary, but once they have been selected a failure to apply them uniformly would lead to chaos and confusion. Much of the discussion of national accounting concepts is about the correct logical application of principles that have been accepted. But some of the discussion tends to be concerned with the basic principles that should be adopted, which is a more arbitrary matter, and about which there can be no definite answers. It is important to distinguish between the two types of issue. Although definite answers should not be expected to what are essentially matters of judgement, this is no excuse for a failure to apply the rules that have been adopted in a logical and consistent manner.

Finally, it must be emphasised that there is constant evolution and change in the questions that economists are asking, in the institutional structure of the economy, and in the working hypotheses that economists use for purposes of analysing the behaviour of the economy. In accordance with these changes so it will be necessary to modify and adapt the classification system used for national accounting. It would be useless to persist with a classification system, for example, that no longer corresponded to the institutional and social categories of society, or to the latest knowledge about how the economy operated and so about which relationships were important for analytical purposes. Since the science of economics is in a very primitive state at present and there is little firm empirical information about the way that the economy works it is to be expected that the appropriate national accounts classification will, as the years go by, be subject to far-reaching modifications. There is nothing final or sacrosanct about the particular framework presented in the following chapters.

Chapter 2

What is national product?

1. Productive and non-productive activities

As indicated above, in order to analyse what determines the growth or the stability of the national product, it is desirable to have a clear idea of what transactions contribute to it. For this purpose it is necessary to distinguish clearly between (a) those transactions that relate to 'productive activities' – that is, activities which contribute to the flow of goods and services – and (b) other transactions, which are simply means of re-distributing, among the different members of the community, the goods and services produced in the economy. These latter transactions are called *transfer payments*, indicating that, by contrast with the productive activities, they are simply transfers of purchasing power and are not the counterpart of any addition to the current output of goods and services. This distinction between productive activities and all other transactions is absolutely central to the basic concepts of national accounting, and a failure fully to grasp this distinction, which is encountered in the most surprising places, is often responsible for important errors in economic diagnosis. One reason for this failure is that the dividing line between what is and what isn't a productive activity is not all that clear since it is essentially arbitrary.

A very clear case of a 'transfer payment' is the payment of old-age pensions, since it would be generally agreed that these payments are not made in return for the provision of some productive activity. Old-age pensioners do not have to produce any goods or services in exchange for their pension; in many countries they merely have to be old. Hence the inclusion of the pensions in national product would imply a very strange use of the term 'product'. But a transfer payment, such as an old-age pension, is analogous to, say, a father giving some pocket money

7

to his son. The father's wage or salary represents a payment for his own productive activity, but if he then chooses to transfer some of his wage to his son or to his grandmother, without their providing any productive service in exchange, one should not include this as a payment for something that has been produced in the economy. And if the father transfers some purchasing power to other people's grandmothers, instead of his own, through the mechanism of tax payments and old-age pensions paid by the State, this does not affect the principle that these are transfer payments which merely re-distribute purchasing power without adding to the total flow of goods and services to be transferred.

But although the example of old-age pensions may be clear enough there are other transactions in the economy about which there is more room for dispute. For example, Soviet economists regard many transactions as transfer payments on the grounds that although payment is made in return for a service (such as entertainment), and, hence, is not unrequited in the same way as an old-age pension, the services provided are not regarded as *productive* services. Such a decision is obviously a value judgement. As we shall see later in this chapter, the dividing line between what is and what is not a productive activity is necessarily arbitrary in any system of national accounts, including the systems adopted by nearly all the Western countries. The point to note at this stage is simply that, given some definition of what are productive activities, all other current transactions must be regarded as transfer payments and hence must not be included in national product.

Being essentially arbitrary, different countries have different conventions regarding the distinction between transfer payments and other payments. Even in a given country, where certain major questions of principle may have been settled, convention will still play a part. For example, instead of relying on pocket money from his father, the schoolboy may have to wash his father's car or deliver newspapers. In both cases there is a *quid pro quo* of services for money, but in the former case the car-washing is not included in national product, on arbitrary grounds (that it is a leisure activity and so not absorbing a scarce resource); whereas the paper-delivery service might or might not be included in national product, according to the particular conventions of the country concerned, which will depend largely on whether the relevant data could be collected anyway.

Another way of looking at current transfer payments is to consider that, in general, the money flows in the economy are in the reverse direction to the flows of 'real' goods and services. For example, apart from capital transfers such as gifts or loans, the payment of money by Mr A to Mr B will usually correspond to a flow of goods (or services) from Mr B to Mr A. In most of this book we shall be analysing these money flows and their classification, and shall pay little direct attention to the corresponding real flows in the reverse direction since (a) it will usually be obvious what these are and (b) it is only possible to add them up in money terms, anyway; one cannot add two oranges to three apples in any other way for purposes of valuing their total contribution to national product.

There are two types of exception to the general rule that the money flows correspond to real flows in the reverse direction. First, some money flows do not correspond to any flows of goods and services. These will be transfer payments. Secondly, some flows of goods and services are not matched by any money flow. For example, part of the wages of the armed forces (and of other employees) is 'in kind' – namely in the form of goods such as their food, lodging and clothing for which they make no payment. In these cases, where the goods and services concerned are to be included in national product it is necessary to *impute* a value that they would have had if they had entered into a market transaction in the normal way.

These two types of exception to the rule that money flows reflect real flows constitute – as will be seen below – the two main areas in which there is scope for difference of opinion as to what should be included in national product. That is to say, much of the disagreement about what should enter national product concerns *either* transfer payments *or* the extent to which one should impute values for goods and services that do not pass through the market and therefore have no corresponding money flow.

2. Intermediate products and final products
The classification of all transactions into those that represent productive activities and those that do not is the most important

distinction to be made in deciding what transactions are to be included in national product. But it is not enough for purposes of estimation, and one cannot simply add up the value of all transactions in productive activities in order to arrive at total national product. Before one can say which productive transactions can be added together to arrive at total national product a second vital distinction has to be made. This is the distinction between transactions in (a) intermediate products and (b) final products. The former are, as the name implies, the result of productive activities, but they are products that are used in the production of other productive goods or services. Final products, by contrast, are required, roughly speaking, for their own sake.

For example, the production of steel is generally accepted as a productive activity. So is the production of automobiles. But suppose that £100 of steel is sold to automobile manufacturers and is used to produce £500 of automobile. Now, if the £500 of automobile is included in the value of national product one cannot add in also the £100 of steel incorporated in it, since this would be adding the steel twice over; first when it was produced and secondly when it is included in the value of the automobile. In the end, all the economy is getting is the £500 of automobile. It is not getting that *and* the £100 of steel; the latter was sacrificed in order to produce the £500 of automobile. In this particular example, the sale of the steel is what is known as an *intermediate transaction*, since the steel itself is an *intermediate product*. The sale of the automobile, by contrast, is known as a *final sale* or a *sale to final demand*, and the products so sold constitute part of *final product*.[1] Thus, one way of estimating national product is to find the sum of the goods and services that enter into final product. *Final product*, again as the name implies,

---

[1] Strictly speaking, one should not talk about final and intermediate *products* but about final and intermediate *transactions* or *sales*. What matters is not any specific character of the goods but whether or not they are sold for purposes of being used up in the course of further production. For example, fuel may be an intermediate product in general, but it may also be sold to final demand – e.g. if sold for domestic heating. It is for this reason that it is more accurate to talk about 'sales to final demand' or 'final sales' on the one hand, and 'intermediate sales' on the other, rather than final products and intermediate products, as if products could be classified in this way irrespective of how, and to whom, they are sold. Nevertheless, as it is more convenient, if less rigorous, to follow the conventional terminology we will do so here.

consists of goods and services that are purchased for their own sake – they are what the economy finally wanted and obtained – whereas *intermediate products* are those that are required only to be used up in the course of producing other products. If the sales of intermediate products are added to the sales of the final products, this would constitute 'double counting'. If one counts the whole value of the automobile in estimating national product one must not count in the steel as well. Alternatively, if one wants to count in the steel one must only count in the automobile after deducting its steel content.

It should be clearly understood that the reason for not adding together transactions in intermediate products and final products in order to estimate total national product, is not at all the same as the reason for excluding transfer payments from the calculation. The latter are excluded on the grounds that they are not payments for productive activities to start with, and so are simply not part of national *product*. The 'intermediate' products, however, are part of national product, but they are used up in the production of other goods and services and so should not be counted twice. Just as one cannot have one's cake and eat it, one cannot proceed as if one has got both the automobile and the steel when, in fact, the steel was used up to produce the automobile.

A good example of the difference between the two quite distinct reasons for excluding certain items from the estimate of national product is the treatment of certain government expenditures on transport. As has been mentioned, Soviet national accountants exclude the services of law and order, of passenger transport, and of many other public and private services from the estimate of national product on the grounds that the services concerned are not *productive* services and hence do not contribute to national product in any way. In the Western world some economists would also prefer to exclude the same services from the estimate of national product, but on the grounds that instead of being part of final demand, as conventionally defined, they are really *intermediate* transactions which are just as necessary for the production of the rest of national product as is steel for the production of automobiles. Hence, it is argued, if they are added to the rest of final demand in arriving at total national product they are being counted twice, like the steel in the automobile. Thus the proponents of this view agree with the Soviet national accountants that these services should be excluded from the estimate of national product, but the reasons are conceptually quite different, and, as will be seen later, would have different effects on the measure of the contribution to national product of various sectors in the economy.

To understand this last point, and similar issues, it is necessary to consider in slightly more detail how, given one's definition of what are productive activities and one's classification of which of such activities are used up in the course of other productive activities, national product may actually be measured. For this purpose we will consider a simple economy, with no government sector and hence no problem of whether the output should be valued inclusive or exclusive of indirect taxes.

3. Three methods of measuring national product

(i) The expenditure method
Consider the following economy in which the only transactions are:

(i) Industry A sells raw cotton to Industry B for £50;
(ii) Industry B sells cotton cloth to Industry C for £80; and
(iii) Industry C sells cotton shirts to final consumers for £100.

It is assumed that there are absolutely no other transactions in the economy at all. For example, there is no trade with the rest of the world, no changes in stocks, no purchases of any raw materials by Industry A, and so on.

The total of all transactions shown above is £230, but this would be a very curious way of measuring the total amount of goods that the economy is getting out of all its activity. For it can be seen that in the end – i.e. after materials have been passed about from one industry to another – all that the economy is finally getting is £100's worth of shirts. This then is the correct value of national product. The figure of £230 that would be obtained by adding all the transactions at every stage is much in excess of the true value of what the economy is really obtaining for its activity, for the simple reason that it involves counting certain elements of output two or three times. It is a *duplicated* total that involves double counting. For example, the value of the cotton cloth sold by B to C for £80 is also embodied in the value of the shirts sold thereafter for £100. One cannot, there-fore, in calculating national income or product, take the £100 *and* add to it the £80's worth of cotton cloth that is already embodied in it, as this would amount to counting the value of the cotton cloth twice. Also, if the chain of production were split up further – e.g. by separating out the dyeing of the cloth into a distinctly separate activity – the same method would yield a total greater than £230, though there would have been no real change in the amount produced.

In short, a simple way of seeing at a glance from such a list of transactions what the national product is is simply to ignore all the intermediate inputs and to look at the figure of what the 'final product' or 'final demand' of the economy is, for that provides an unduplicated figure of what, in the end, the economy got out of all its activity. This particular estimate of national product is known as the value of *expenditure on national product*. In a less simplified economy, there will be many items that were sold to 'final demand' – shirts, food, automobiles, and so on. Hence the measure of national product by the 'expenditure' method consists of adding up the value of all such 'final products' or sales to final demand – i.e. all goods and services that are not used up in the production of some other good or service.

(ii) *The output method* (or *'production' method*, or *'industry of origin' method*)

This second method of estimation amounts to calculating what each separate industry added to the value of final output. This is known as the 'value added' by each industry. As the term 'value added' implies, it is the value added by each industry to the raw materials or other goods and services that it bought from other industries before passing on the products to the next link in the whole chain of production.

In the above example, Industry A bought nothing from other industries – i.e. it purchased no 'intermediate' inputs – and sold its output for £50. Hence the whole of the £50 constitutes value added by this industry alone. Industry B, however, had to buy this £50's worth of output in order to sell its product for £80, so that Industry B only added £30 to the value of the goods

13

concerned – i.e. value added in Industry B was £30. Similarly, Industry C only added £20 to the value of the goods concerned, having purchased intermediate products for £80 before selling its output for £100. The sum of all three industries' value added is £50 plus £30 plus £20, which is equal to £100, the same figure, of course, that one obtained directly by looking at the value of the final sales to consumers. With this method, the intermediate inputs are not ignored, but since only the value added embodied in each activity is included in the final total, there is still no double-counting.

The equivalence of the two methods of estimation – from the point of view of expenditures on final product or of value added by industry – is, of course, inevitable whatever the particular figures that we may like to insert in this particular economy, and the reader is invited to check this himself by varying the example. But it will be fairly obvious, for example, that if, say, the value of final shirt sales had been £120 (and there were no change in intermediate transactions) this increase in the value of final demand would have been accompanied by an increase in the value added of Industry C by £20, so that either method would still have led to the same total figure of national product, namely £120. Similarly, if, say, Industry B's sales had risen by £10, with the same input of £50 from Industry A, but Industry C still sold only the same value of shirts (£100), then, from the point of view of expenditure on final product, national product has remained unchanged at £100, and, from the point of view of value added by industry, there has been an increase in the value added in Industry B of £10, but this has been offset by a decrease in the value added of Industry C by £10. This inevitable arithmetical identity of the two ways of estimating national product simply follows from the common sense conclusion that the sum of what the economy gets out of all its activity in the end must be equal to the sum of what all the individual industries contributed to it. In a less simple economy, there will be many chains of connected, and inter-connected, productive activities, and national product will equal the sum of the value added in all of them. Tables that show national product broken down into the contributions made to it by individual industries instead of by the various items of final expenditure are generally referred to as showing national product by *industry of origin*.

(iii) The income method

There is a third way of looking at the value of national product – and, indeed, of calculating it – namely in terms of the incomes accruing to the basic factors of production used in producing the national product. Without entering here into a discussion of what exactly constitutes the factor of production 'capital' for example, for present purposes one may classify all basic factors of production into two categories, namely, labour and capital. Labour can be defined to consist of all the human contribution to output, whether by an employee or an employer, so that it includes 'entrepreneurship'; and capital will be all the rest, so that it includes land, and sub-soil resources such as mines, as well as man-made capital such as machinery or roads. All payments of incomes originating in the production process can be classified into the payments to these two factors of production; labour receiving wages and salaries, and capital receiving the remainder, which can be defined as profits (though, in fact, some of these profits may be transferred to certain members of the community in the form of interest payments of dividends). That is, labour and capital may be defined for purposes of simplification as the two basic factors of production that, in the end, must receive the incomes generated in the economy.[1] Other payments are made by firms in the course of production, such as payments for raw material inputs, etc., but these do not receive any 'income', and the firms supplying these inputs in turn pass on their net value added to the factors of production labour and capital used in producing them.

Thus, out of the value added by each industry, payments have to be made to the two factors of production. Not all profits are necessarily distributed, of course, but even if they are not, they still belong to the particular profit receivers involved in that particular industry.[2] Consequently, the sum total of all factor payments must equal the sum total of value added by industry, which in turn, as we have seen, equals the value of sales to final product. Thus, retaining the economy described on page 12, we

[1] If land is defined as a part of capital – as we have defined it here – rents will be regarded here as part of profits.

[2] If profits are not distributed they still 'belong' to the shareholders since the latter's equity in the business concerned will have increased. For example, the reserves of a company are included amongst its liabilities on its balance sheet.

might, for example, distribute in factor incomes the value added of each industry as follows:

(£s)

value added	industry	distribution of value added	
		wages	profits
50	A	30	20
30	B	20	10
20	C	10	10
TOTAL 100		60	40

Now, even if the statisticians cannot obtain data on the net output of each industry, they may be able to obtain estimates, at a national level, of the total wages and other incomes received. For example, these may be available from income tax returns. Hence such data may enable national product to be estimated even if there are no statistics of final expenditures or of net ouput by industry. Thus, we now have that national product may be measured by three methods, namely, the value of all the final sales of what has been produced in the economy, the sum of value added (or 'net output') in each industry, and the sum of incomes received by all the basic factors of production. Again, it is common sense that the income of the economy should be equal to the value of what that economy actually produced.

Another way of looking at the three ways of measuring national product is the frequently used analogy with a system of pipes through which liquid circulates. For this purpose it is useful to introduce here the terminology of the *productive sector*, which produces goods and services and pays out the incomes generated, and the *household sector* which represents the receipts of incomes by private individuals and their expenditures of these incomes on private consumption. The circulating flow will then consist of the flow of payments from the household sector to the productive sector for its final product, and then the payment of the resulting value added to the household sector in return for the contribution to production which it has made, thereby closing the circle. The three different ways of measuring national product then appear as merely three different points at which the flow of money round the whole circuit is measured. The size of the national product is represented by the width of the pipe, but this width can be measured at different points. If measured at the point where the money is flowing into the productive sector then it is the expenditure method that is being used. If measured at the point where the money leaves the productive sector then it is value added that is being measured. If measured at the point where the income recipients receive the incomes then it is the income method that is being used.

Whilst in principle all three methods of estimating national product should give the same answer, in practice they will usually not do so. This is chiefly because most of the statistics that national accounts statisticians have to use have not been collected primarily for purposes of national product estimation. They have usually been collected by various government departments for their own particular purposes. For example, most statistics about personal incomes are collected by special Ministries in connection with the payment of taxes; import statistics are collected in connection largely with the payment of import duties and foreign trade policy; output statistics are collected largely in connection with the desire to supervise or develop individual industries. Other statistics, such as those relating to food expenditures or to health or education or employment may be collected in connection with the government responsibilities for certain social conditions or with the need of Ministries to show to the legislature that they have spent public funds in the manner authorised.

The national accounts statistician has to try to piece together a complete picture of the national product as best he can with the aid of such data as have been prepared for quite different purposes. Whatever method he adopts, therefore, always contains a large element of estimation – not to mention guesswork – and hence always involves a certain margin of error. It would only be by chance, therefore, if different methods gave exactly the same result. In fact, the different methods are generally used in conjunction with each other – some components of national product being best estimated by one method and other components by another method. They constitute partial checks on each other, and it is usually not possible to say that the final total of national product shown has been exclusively reached by one method rather than another. The basic reason for the errors involved in national income estimation is thus that national accounts are, in principle, a consolidation at the national level of the individual accounts for all the firms and individuals in the economy. Since the statistician does not possess all these accounts (most of them do not exist) he cannot be expected to produce a completely accurate national total for them.

Figure 2.1

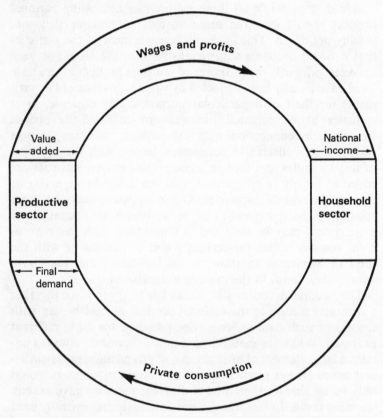

EXERCISES 2.1

In the economies described below only the transactions shown take place and no other transactions (e.g. no changes in stocks). The only sales to final product that take place are sales to private consumption (e.g. shirts, food). In exercises 1 to 4 inclusive, show what is the value of national product, and what is value added by industry of origin. (Note: A, B, ..., etc., are industries.)

example:
A sells for £60 to B;
B sells for £100 to C;
C sells for £120 to private consumption.
answer: final sales = sales to private consumption of £120;
      therefore national product = £120.

Value added by Industry A = £60;
Value added by Industry B = £40 (£100 minus £60);
Value added by Industry C = £20 (£120 minus £100);
    Total national product = £120.

1   A sells for £20 to B;
    B sells for £40 to C;
    C sells for £60 to private consumption;
    D sells for £20 to private consumption.

2   A sells for £50 to B;
    B sells for £40 to C and for £20 to D;
    C sells for £60 to D;
    D sells for £100 to private consumption.

3   A sells for £30 to B and for £20 to C;
    B sells for £10 to private consumption and for £30 to C;
    C sells for £120 to private consumption.

4   A sells for £50 to B and for £50 to private consumption;
    B sells for £80 to C;
    C sells for £100 to private consumption.

5   In the economies described above all value added is allocated between wages and profits, the share of wages in total value added by industry being as follows:
    Industry A: share of wages = 50%;
    Industry B: share of wages = 30%;

Industry C: share of wages = 80%;
Industry D: share of wages = 60%.
What is national income in the above exercises broken down into total wages and profits in each exercise?

6 A sells for £50 to B;
B sells for £80 to C;
C sells all his output to private consumption.
National product is £180.
What is private consumption and what is C's value added?

7 A sells for £40 to B and for £20 to C;
Consumers divide their expenditure equally between B's goods and C's goods.
National product is £100.
What is value added in B and C?

8 A sells all his output to B;
B sells for £80 to C;
B's value added is equal to A's.
How much does A sell to B?

9 A sells to B for £20;
B, whose value added is £40, sells half his output to C and half to D. C sells all his output to D. D, whose value added is £30, sells all his output to final product for £130.
What is C's value added?

10 A sells to B for £60, and distributes his value added equally between wages and profits;
B sells all his output to C, and C sells all his output to final product;
B's wage bill equals A's wage bill, and total wages in the whole economy equal total profits.
National product is £140.
What is the value of B's sales to C if
(a) B's profits equal C's profits?
(b) B's profits equal A's profits?

11 A sells all his output to B and B sells all his output to C;
A's wage bill is one-half B's wage bill and one-third C's wage bill.

National product is £180.
Value added is equal in all three industries.
Total profits are twice total wages.
How large are profits in each industry?

4. The 'production boundary'

The above exercises will have helped to underline the fact that the sum of incomes generated in the economy or of the contribution of each industry to the income or output of the economy is always identically equal to the value of expenditures on the final product of the economy. For this reason, such expenditures on the final output produced by the economy are often referred to as 'income generating expenditures', to distinguish them from other expenditures, such as transfer payments or payments to non-nationals, that do not generate any net addition to the income of the economy as a whole. As we have seen, the relationships examined above between the final expenditures and value added or incomes in the economy can also be represented graphically in the form of a picture of the circular flow of incomes in a simple economy in which, as in the above examples, final output comprises only consumer goods. This notion of the circular flow of incomes will be seen later to play a central role in the analysis of the way in which leakages in the flow and re-injections into the flow influence the equilibrium level of the flow. But meanwhile it can be used to serve an additional purpose, namely of illustrating the very important concept of the 'production boundary'.

In the following diagram, two blocks are shown. The one on the left, which can be described as the 'productive' sector block, represents the economy from the point of view of its productive activities and the right-hand block, which can be called the 'household' sector, represents the economy from the point of view of its activities as consumers of the final output produced by the productive sector. Alternatively, the left-hand block groups the citizens of the economy in their capacity as active producers who receive incomes for the part they play in adding to output, and the right-hand block groups the same people in their capacity as ordinary people spending these incomes on their various private wants, such as food, clothing, etc. The 'production boundary' is the line round the productive sector.

Everything that crosses the line either leaves or enters the productive sector.

Figure 2.2

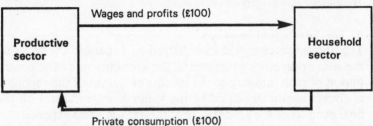

The particular arrows drawn in on this diagram represent the money flows in the economy, *not* the flows of goods and services – which will be in the reverse direction, of course. In this economy final expenditures by consumers are £100 and the whole network of transactions may have taken the following form:

Industry A sold for £40 to Industry B and distributed the value added as £30 to wages and £10 to profits;

Industry B sold for £60 to Industry C and distributed its resulting £20 of value added as £10 in wages and £10 in profits;

Industry C sold for £100 to private consumers and distributed its £40 of value added as £20 to wages and £20 to profits;

Thus total wages amount to £60 and total profits amount to £40, the sum of the two being, of course, equal to the £100 spent by consumers on the final output of the economy, namely the consumers' goods sold by Industry C.

It is obvious that if consumers had only spent, say, £80 on the products of Industry C and no other changes in the transactions are introduced, then national product falls to £80, corresponding to the fall in C's value added to £20, and C will be able to distribute only £20 altogether in wages and profits, so that total wages and profits would also amount to only £80. Thus the two arrows would have to be amended to indicate a flow of only £80 from consumers to the productive sector and only £80 would be shown as the flow of incomes from the productive sector to the household sector.

We have already seen on page 13 that national product is equal to the value of the final sales of the productive sector. In this simplified economy, these comprise only the sales to private consumers (if any) by each industry, so that the value of these sales is enough to tell us what national product is without bothering any more about all the *intermediate* transactions that may be going on (such as sales by A to B or by B to C). Thus, if we define the line drawn round the productive sector in the diagram as the 'production boundary', we can say that national product must be equal to the value of the goods that cross this boundary, and given the value of such transactions (in the diagram shown this is the £100 of private consumption) national product is determined irrespective of what transactions are taking place inside the production boundary. Whatever these transactions may be, we know that the value added by them and the incomes generated by them must be equal to the value of the goods that crossed the production boundary.

Hence, the whole question of what constitutes national product can be regarded as a question of what transactions cross the production boundary – or, alternatively, what is final product? Expenditure on total final output has been seen to be identically equal to total value added in the productive sector.[1] Hence the *definition* of what constitutes total final output must also determine the *definition* of what can be included in the value added of the productive sector. The two magnitudes must necessarily be equal, and so insofar as the definition of final expenditures determines the value of these final expenditures it must also determine value added in the productive sector and hence must determine what is to be included in the productive activities of that sector.

In other words, once final output has been defined then we will have implicitly defined the two other categories of transactions referred to earlier, namely (a) the intermediate products that are used up directly or indirectly, inside the production boundary, in the production of final output; and (b) the transfer payments, which lie outside the production boundary altogether. In the above numerical example, the activities of A and B are

---

[1] As the reader can check for himself, however, by means of arithmetical examples, expenditure on any particular component of final output is not necessarily equal to the value added in the industry supplying that particular component. For example, the value of final clothing sales is not necessarily equal to the value added in the clothing industry.

productive activities, but, being intermediate products that contributed to the production of C's output, they take place inside the production boundary and do not cross it. Transactions that take place completely outside the production boundary are simply *not* productive activities. Thus, the definition of what constitutes sales to final demand, or what crosses the production boundary, implicitly defines whereabouts in the scheme of accounts these other two classes of transaction must lie.

Another way of looking at this is as follows. In any economy countless types of transaction are taking place. Some of these are not regarded as productive at all and, among the rest, many of them are connected in a chain of production – iron ore used to make pig iron, pig iron used to make steel, steel used to make machines and automobiles, the machines used to make other articles, etc., etc. At some point in this productive process a line is drawn which is called the 'production boundary', and all goods and services which cross this line are defined as 'final product' – i.e. as goods and services that are not used up in the production of further goods and services. Defining this line means defining which goods cross it. Having done this *everything else is defined by implication*. All productive goods and services used up in the process of producing the final goods are 'intermediate products', which lie within the production boundary, and hence result from productive activities. All activities lying outside the production boundary – i.e. all transactions that are neither for final goods nor for goods and services used up in the process of producing final goods – are transfer payments. The value of the goods and services defined as final product is equal to national product, and this also defines – since they are identically equal – national income or national expenditure. As an exercise in consistency of definition the whole operation is neat and straightforward. The only trouble is that the crucial decisions, namely deciding (a) which goods and services are productive and (b) of these, which are final products, is basically somewhat arbitrary.

5. The arbitrary nature of the production boundary
Different views on what are the important questions that one wishes to ask about the economy, or on what are the important

relationships and categories of decision-maker in the economy, may imply different views as to what constitutes national product. There can be no absolute validity about a classification system. Consequently it is not surprising, in view of the great scope for differences in the interpretation of economic phenomena, to find that official national accounting conventions differ to some extent between countries. As a result of the need for internationally comparable data for various purposes (such as estimating the contribution of member countries to the budget of organisations such as the United Nations, invaluable work was done after the war to standardise the national accounting conventions of most of the countries of the world, and these standardised rules naturally had a big effect on the way that countries developed their national accounting practices for their own domestic purposes. But many countries, nevertheless, while preparing national accounts estimates for international organisations that conformed – in principle at least – to the internationally accepted conventions, still prepared the accounts on a different basis for their own purposes when they felt that their national systems were superior with respect to the questions that they were asking and in the light of their own views as to what were the important relationships in their particular type of economy.

The most important differences in national official practice are those between the Western countries and the Soviet bloc countries. On the whole, as already indicated, the crux of the difference lies in the different treatment of services, particularly the services of government and service industries (such as entertainment or passenger transport). In the Soviet system, many services that are generally included in national product in Western countries are excluded from national product – i.e. they lie outside the production boundary. However, there is no complete uniformity of doctrine on these points among either the Soviet countries or the Western countries. France which, naturally, does not conform with either the Soviet or the normal Western concepts, includes service industries in national product but excludes certain government services. Among the other Western countries, there are many other numerous differences, though the only one of real importance is the Scandinavian countries' different treatment of repairs and maintenance of machinery.[1] And in the Soviet bloc there are differences in treatment; for example, in 1959 the Hungarians switched from excluding passenger transport from national product to including it.

The differences between the Soviet and Western concepts of what is a 'productive' activity, or what activities take place within the production boundary, amounts to a difference in answering the first question that national accounts is designed to answer, namely 'How much does the economy produce?' The Soviet view so far has been that, in answering this question, one is interested primarily in material output and those services that are employed in the production and distribution of material goods. Services such as entertainment services or personal services such as those of hairdressers are regarded as being merely ways in which the resources created by national production are used. To some extent this view is a hangover from an interpretation of Marxist theory (following some observations of Adam Smith) to the effect that such activities are non-productive. Whether or not one accepts this view, it has to be recognised that there may be something to be said for the argument that, in some countries, economic development policy is primarily concerned with the expansion of material product and very little interested in how the incomes that are originated in the course of producing material product are subsequently distributed among various services. If this view is adopted then payments for most services can quite justifiably be regarded as lying outside the production boundary and, therefore, as constituting transfer payments.

In Western national accounting conventions, however, the only payments that are regarded as transfer payments are those for which there is clearly no *quid pro quo* in the form of the provision of some goods or service. Thus, in making such payments, the payer is not acquiring any *'scarce' goods and services that might otherwise be used for some other purpose.* The direct effect of transfer payments is simply to change the distribution of power to purchase the economy's output of productive goods and services. Examples of transfer payments in Western

[1] The Scandinavian countries tend to include much more repair and maintenance work in final product than the rest of the Western countries, who count most of this as intermediate product.

economies are the old-age pensions that have been referred to already, grants to students, and tax payments.

As we have already seen, some Western economists would prefer to exclude from final demand certain government services, not on the grounds that they are not the fruits of productive activities, but on the grounds that they are intermediate inputs into the rest of the productive machinery. This reduces national product, of course, in that, on the one hand, final demand is lower and, on the other hand, value added in some other sector must be reduced by the additional input. Thus, an element of arbitrary judgement can also enter into the question of which, among productive activities, are intermediate products and which are final products. For most activities, of course, there is barely any room for differences of opinion. For example, nobody would dispute that the lubricating oil used up in running a machine is an intermediate product that is not used for its own sake. But when it comes to certain services there is considerable room for differences of opinion.

It is sometimes argued, for example, that the services of the police are necessary in order for the economy, as we know it, to function at all. Another practical example is the treatment of personal transport charges. When a firm pays for the transport of, say, the raw materials that it requires, this is generally agreed to be an intermediate input into that firm and is deducted (along with other intermediate inputs) from its total receipts in estimating the value added in that firm. Otherwise one would obtain an exaggerated picture of what that firm has, in fact, added to national product. (Anyway, the value added by the suppliers of the transport services is already counted in the value added of the transport industry and so one must not count it again in the value added of the firm using the services.)

But some would argue that when employees have to incur heavy expenses for transport to their place of work this, too, should be deducted from *their* value added (i.e. their incomes from wages and salaries), since these transport charges are just as much expenses that have to be incurred in order for them to be able to make their contribution to national product as are the transport charges incurred by the firms in obtaining raw materials. As it is, such personal expenditures on passenger transport to work are treated like any other *passenger* transport

27

in the Western concepts, namely as *final* goods and services, not as an intermediate input into labour which have to be deducted in arriving at the true value added of labour. But the view that they should be treated as inputs is not necessarily illogical. It may, however, be rather anti-humanistic to treat human beings like machines or raw material inputs, which incur transport costs and maintenance and so on in order to be delivered in good working order at the required point of production. Furthermore, if one takes the view that certain services are an indispensable input into the productive system – in the sense that, without them, production would be reduced – and that they should hence be excluded from the final output that the economy has available in the end to use how it wishes, why stop at transport charges? The same line of argument could be used in support of the above-mentioned view that the services of law and order are also essential inputs into the productive system.[1]

Without wishing to enter into these somewhat theological issues, it might be pointed out that production would also be difficult if people did not eat and have some means of protecting themselves from the elements, so that advocates of this line of argument should also accept that most of expenditures on food, clothing and fuel be regarded as intermediate inputs, necessary for the maintenance of production, rather than as final output of goods and services that society can enjoy as the fruits of its productive activity. In the end, if all 'final products' were re-garded as either adding to the stock of wealth or as just keeping the productive system going, then the whole economy would be included inside the productive sector. Even the household sector would be included, since it would be simply one more industry converting inputs of food, clothing, shelter, recreation and so on, into another intermediate product, labour, which would be inputs into other productive sectors. This problem of how far one is justified in saying that there are some 'ultimate' outputs of the economic system, which are required for their own sake

[1] The French exclude government from their concept of national *production*, but include it in their concept of national *product*, on the grounds that the latter concept is prepared in the interests of international organisations (see M. Malinvaud *Initiation à la Comptabilité Nationale*, Institut National de la Statistique et des Études Économiques, Presses Universitaires de France, 1964, page 27).

is an important one which has many ramifications. These are not merely in the context of how to define national product, but also in the field of cost–benefit analysis, particularly for special projects, such as education, and in welfare economics.

But whatever the pros and cons of defining specific items as final product rather than as intermediate inputs into the productive sector, the practice in most Western economies is to include all government services as final output and therefore as part of national product. If such services were to be regarded as intermediate inputs, as some writers suggest, national product would be lower by the amount concerned. This would also, then, have implications for the value added in different industries, though the effect on the value added in *individual* industries would not be the same if the services are excluded on the grounds that they are intermediate products as it would be if the services are excluded on the grounds that they are not productive activities to start with.

The different effects of the two reasons for excluding certain transactions from national product can be illustrated by a simple numerical example. Suppose that the only transactions in the economy are as follows:

A sells goods to B for £50;

B sells to final demand both £60's worth of goods and £20's worth of services.

Total national product is £80. Final sales are clearly £60 plus £20, since, unlike A's sales to B, B's sales are not part of a chain of inputs into other activities. Equally, value added in A is £50 and in B is £30 (£60 + £20 − £50), giving a total of value added of £80, which is, of course, equal to the value of final sales. But suppose now that the Soviet national accountants wished to exclude the sales of services from national product on the grounds that these did not represent productive activities. Then these £20 simply disappear from the value of final sales – *they do not cross the production boundary as they lie outside it*. National product is now only £60, this being all that is left of final sales. And value added in B is now only £10 (£60 − £50), whereas value added in A is left unchanged at £50.

But suppose that the services concerned comprised passenger transport and police services used by the economy as a whole. Now some Western economist would regard them as perfectly legitimate productive activities, but as activities that should really be regarded as intermediate inputs, on the grounds that without them the economy as a whole could not operate as it does. They must not, therefore, be counted twice. National product would be reduced to £60, as in the Soviet system since final sales comprise only B's sales of £60 of goods. *The £20 of services do not cross the production boundary; they remain inside it.* But, unlike the Soviet system, A would have to share with B, to some extent, in the corresponding adjustment to value added since both A and B would have to be debited with some of the intermediate input of £20 (their use of the £20 of service that originally crossed the production boundary when sold to final demand).

The reader may well ask how it is that one can reduce the estimate of national product in this way, since in both cases somebody did actually receive some income from the sale of the services, so that if services are excluded from national product for one reason or another, how is the corresponding income made to disappear? The answer depends on which reason was used for excluding the services from national income. If the Soviet reason is used, then the incomes received for the services become transfer payments, like old-age pensions or fathers' giving pocket money to their sons, and so do not form part of the income that is paid out of value added and which contributed to national income. If the services are excluded on the grounds that they are intermediate inputs into the economy then value added in all sectors will be reduced by some amount. The sum of value added after either adjustment is £60, which is in both cases equal to the adjusted figure of final sales, but according to which reason is given for eliminating the sales of services from national product, the distribution of the value added between A and B is altered.

Another respect in which the definition of what are productive activities is somewhat arbitrary arises out of the treatment of illegal activities. All illegal activities are excluded from national product (though not all legal activities are included). This may be largely for the statistical convenience of excluding items about which data would be difficult to collect, rather than on strict logical grounds. For example, if a robber coshes somebody on the head and steals his wallet, this is certainly only a transfer payment. But it is less clear why – apart from statistical con- venience – one should exclude the incomes of liquor vendors in countries where the sale of alcohol is illegal. Hence, in com- paring different countries or the same country over time, it has to be recognised that what is legal and what is not may change. When prohibition was abandoned in the USA, national product rose, since expenditures on liquor became legal so that they had to be added into national product whereas hitherto they were excluded. The same applies to some forms of gambling in Britain, which only recently became legalised. But the arbitrary nature of the dividing line between what is and what is not legal is obviously not a matter that is determined by economic criteria, but depends more on society's fickle and changing social attitudes.

There are many other problems of where exactly the dividing line between productive and non-productive activities should be drawn, notably in connection with certain unpaid activities, such as those of individuals who produce their own food (in their gardens, say), or the activities of housewives. A famous national accounts paradox (pointed out initially by Professor Pigou) is that if one were to marry one's housekeeper national product would fall. The reason for this is that whereas the services of a housekeeper are paid and are included in national product, housewives' services in the home are not so included (whether they are paid or not).

6. Transaction in 'second-hand' goods and financial assets

We may define national product as the unduplicated value of the flow of goods and services produced by the nation in the time period concerned (usually a year). At other points in the chapter, too, we have insisted on the *current* character of the output of the national economy. It follows from this that a whole class of transactions can be eliminated from national product without even taking into account whether they represent productive activities or not. This is the class of transaction that represents solely transfers of capital assets from one holder to another.

For example, if Mr X sells his old automobile to Mr Y, this should not be added to the national product of the time period in which this sale took place, for it is not an addition to the flow of goods and services produced by the nation during that time

31

period. The reason for this is very simple and obvious, namely, that it has already been counted once when it was produced. If, after that, one were to count it again every time it changed hands, there would be no limit to the level to which national product could be raised. Mr A could sell it to Mr B, who could sell it to Mr C who could sell it back to Mr A and so on. Raising national product would be just too easy. Where an asset such as a house or a car is sold for the first time after completion, it is included in the national product of the year when the sale is made. But if it is re-sold in a later year it clearly cannot be part of what the nation produced in that later year as well.[1]

From the national accountant's point of view all that happened when a second-hand object changes hands is that there has been a change in the composition of somebody's balance sheet of liabilities and assets. For example, the balance sheet of the seller of a second-hand car will show a fall in his holdings of durable goods and an increase in his holdings of cash. At the same time, the person who buys the car may show a fall in his cash holdings matched by a rise in his holdings of durable goods. Adding the two together, of course, one finds no change at all.

This last point throws some light on the treatment of financial transactions such as sales of stocks and shares. Again, these can obviously not form part of national product; it would be too easy to raise national product by simply passing the shares back and forth faster and faster. This would not correspond to any increase at all in the goods and services actually available for use by the community (ignoring indirect effects). For the stocks or shares simply represent titles to the ownership of part of the capital stock of the country.

One important qualification has to be made to the statement that transactions in second-hand capital assets cannot add to national product. This is that any margins or profit that the dealers in such transactions obtain is a legitimate part of national product since they are being remunerated for their services in transferring the assets from some place where they were no longer wanted to a place where they were wanted. The incomes from, say, second-hand car dealers are thus part of value added in the appropriate sector, and the part of the

[1] If, when it is re-sold, the price is different, this will constitute merely a capital gain or loss, not a flow of current output.

purchaser's payment for the second-hand car that represents the dealer's margin is part of consumer's expenditure.

7. Domestic product versus national product

So far we have discussed the question of where to draw the production boundary in terms of *which* activities lie inside it. But there is another sense in which the location of the boundary has to be settled, namely around *whose* activities it is to be drawn. In particular, one can talk about either (i) the production on the domestic territory of a country or (ii) the production of all the residents of that country. These will not necessarily be the same, for some of the production in a country may be produced with the aid of assets that belong to residents of other countries.[1] Hence a distinction is made between what is produced within the domestic territory of a country, which is known as *domestic product*, and what is produced by the residents of the country (i.e. including the return on the overseas assets that they own), which is known as *national product*. In a country in which a large part of the capital is owned by foreigners – such as in certain Middle East oil-producing countries – the assets so owned by foreigners may be making a large contribution to *domestic product*, but as a significant part of this will not enter into national product of the same country, the difference between domestic and national product in such countries may be substantial.

This difference between national and domestic product which may, of course, be positive or negative, is known as *net property income from abroad*. A country which has, over the long run, been the recipient of foreign investment rather than an investor overseas, will tend to have to pay out more to other countries as earnings on the investments in the country owned by foreigners than it will receive from abroad from its own returns on its own investments abroad. In this case, its net property income from abroad will be negative and its national income will be smaller than its domestic income.

---

[1] Technically, the 'residents' of a country may include persons whose activity is carried out abroad, so that national product of a country will include the value of activities of its ships and aircraft wherever they operate. However, it will exclude the activities of foreign diplomatic personnel stationed on its territory.

8. National product at market prices and at factor cost

Two other alternative concepts of national product that are frequently encountered are national product at market prices and national product at factor cost. The need for this distinction arises as follows. Consider again the simple economy introduced on page 12 in which A sells to B for £50, B sells to C for £80, C sells to final consumers for £100. We have seen that national product was £100, being also the sum of the value added, or incomes earned by the factors of production in each 'industry'. Suppose now that the government imposed an indirect tax of 10% on the goods sold by C to final consumers and that this was passed on in the form of a price rise of 10%, so that the value of the final sales would now reach £110. National product, valued at the prices actually paid in the end, would then be £110, whereas the factors of production would still only receive £100 – the difference being the £10 of indirect tax collected by the government. These two alternative valuations of national product are known as national product at market prices and at factor cost respectively. That is, the market price valuation of national product, as its name implies, is the valuation at the prices actually paid on the market and so it is the valuation that includes all indirect taxes levied on the products. National product at factor cost, as its name implies, excludes all such taxes since it relates to the factor incomes – or factor cost – created in producing the goods and services concerned, and the addition of some indirect taxes cannot directly add to the amount of the basic factors of production employed in the production of the goods.

Governments do not only affect the market prices of goods by imposing indirect taxes; they also often grant subsidies that enable goods to be sold at prices below their factor cost. For example, the real cost of producing a bushel of wheat in terms of the ultimate factors of production used to produce it (the labour and the capital) may be $2.00 a bushel, but the government may grant to producers a subsidy of 50 cents a bushel so that the wheat may be sold for only $1.50 a bushel. In this case the market price valuation will be *less* than the factor cost valuation.

In most economies there is a variety of both indirect taxes and subsidies.[1] Hence, in the end, national product will be greater at

[1] Strictly speaking it is impossible to draw a hard and fast distinction between *indirect* taxes, such as sales taxes, purchase taxes, tariffs and the like, and

market prices than at factor cost only if, on balance, the indirect taxes are greater than the subsidies (which is usually the case).

Indirect taxes and subsidies can be regarded as a special form of transfer payment. Like any other transfer payment they do not affect (directly) total national income or the actual product of the basic factor of production. But, unlike other transfer payments, they are treated as crossing the production boundary. These two statements are reconciled by the fact that they cross the production boundary twice – once going in (e.g. as an indirect tax added to the price of the goods bought by, say, consumers) and once again going out (when the firms pay out these taxes to the government). When they cross the boundary the first time, on their way in, they raise the value of national product at market prices. But by going out at the other end, as it were, they leave the amount available for 'national income' unaffected. In a sense, the productive sector is merely acting as a tax-collecting agent for the government. Subsidies, of course, simply flow in the reverse direction, leaving national income unaffected but reducing the value of final expenditure at market prices.

EXERCISES 2.2
1 What is the immediate direct effect on national product of the following transactions (other things remaining equal; and assuming no dealers involved)?
(i) Mr X buys a new car for £1,000;

---

direct taxes such as taxes on income or on corporation profits and so on; but for present purposes only the former, which directly add to (or subtract from) the value of a transaction, are relevant. The subsidies, being simply negative taxes, are also subject to the same difficulty of deciding which ones should be treated as negative indirect taxes that lead to a difference between the 'market price' and the 'factor cost' valuation of national product and which ones are simply current transfer payments from the government to certain groups in the community (such as farmers, or consumers of school-meals). The usual convention is to define as indirect taxes those that do not depend on the income or wealth of the person paying the tax (e.g. the purchase of taxed alcohol) and which can also be avoided, at the purchaser's discretion, by simply not entering into the transaction concerned. In the context of international comparisons, the latest internationally agreed conventions have abandoned the market price basis and concentrated on comparisons at (factor cost) 'purchasers' prices – a somewhat misleading term.

(ii) Mr X buys a new car for £1,000 which he finances partly by selling his old car for £300;

(iii) Mr X buys a cheaper new car for only £500 and, with the other £500 he buys shares;

(iv) Mr X changes his mind and instead of buying shares (in the last example) Mr X, who still buys the £500 new car, gives the other £500 to his wife. She spends £300 of this on a new fur coat and remaining £200 on a piece of antique furniture;

(v) Mr Y sells his house for £10,000, has a new house built at a cost of £8,000, pays £1,000 income tax to the Inland Revenue, and gives £1,000 to his son. The latter squanders £800 of it on food, drink, tobacco, clothes and books and the remainder goes to pay off old debts.

2 Transactions in an economy are basically as follows:
Industry A sells to Industry B for £50;
Industry B sells to Industry C for £80;
Industry C sells to final demand for £120.

What is total national product at market prices and national product at factor cost, if the transactions are modified as follows (each one separately) and assuming that all indirect taxes or subsidies are 'passed on'[1] fully as price increases or decreases respectively unless otherwise specified?

(i) an indirect tax of 60% is imposed on the products of Industry A and it is entirely passed on as price increases throughout the economy;

(ii) as for (i) but an indirect tax of one-third is also imposed on the product of Industry C (i.e. on the value of his sales including his allowance for the higher price he had to pay as a result of (i));

(iii) an indirect tax of 20% is imposed on the products of Industry A which adds the tax to its price (to Industry B). But Industry B cannot pass on the price increase and absorbs the whole tax;

(iv) a subsidy of £20 is given to Industry B which enables it to reduce the value of its sales to Industry C from £80 to £60,

---

[1] By 'passed on' here, what is meant is that the selling price is raised so that the exact amount of the tax paid, and no more or less, is added to the value of the sales. Assume that the quantity sold is unaffected.

and Industry C reduces the value of its sales to private consumption from £120 to £100.

3 The government decides to abolish the subsidy it had been giving for school milk, which must be paid in full by parents in future. What will be the direct effect of this on national product at market prices if (i) the subsidies had been treated, as with most subsidies, as being paid by the government to the productive sector which made a corresponding reduction in the price it charged to consumers for the product concerned and (ii) if (as is the case in Britain) consumers are treated as spending the full cost of milk but receive the subsidy themselves directly as a form of transfer payment to them from the government, and (iii) if the government were regarded as having bought milk to the value of the subsidy and as having, then, given it away free to the household sector? (It is assumed, in all cases, that the amount of milk consumed is unaffected.)

4 Transactions in an economy are basically as follows:
A sells to B for £60;
B sells to C for £40 and to final demand for £90;
C sells to final demand for £30 and to D for £50;
D sells to final demand for £70.
What is total national product at market prices, value added by industry and national product at factor cost if the transactions are modified as follows (each one separately), and assuming that the indirect taxes or subsidies are fully 'passed on' in price increases or decreases respectively unless otherwise specified?
 (i) an indirect tax of one third is imposed on D's products;
 (ii) an indirect tax of 10% is imposed on the products of B, who is able to pass it on in his sales to C but cannot raise the price of his sales to final demand;
(iii) a subsidy of 10% is given to C's products.

Chapter 3

GNP, welfare and 'the quality of life'

1. Limitiations of the GNP concept

During the last few years there has been increasing criticism of the conventional measurement of national product on the grounds that it is a poor measure of 'welfare' in some sense or other. The reasons for this increasing dissatisfaction with the GNP measure are not hard to find or understand. During the postwar period all the advanced industrialised countries of the world experienced historically unprecedented rates of economic growth, so that *per capita* real incomes soon reached levels that were way above those of the prewar period. Yet this remarkable rise in prosperity, as conventionally measured, did not seem to be accompanied by a corresponding rise in people's sense of wellbeing.

This is natural, to some extent, simply because people have difficulty in recalling the intensity of the hardships that many of them suffered in the prewar years on account of widespread poverty. Also many people resent the manner in which established features of life, to which they had become attached, change in the course of economic growth. At any point of time the older generations tend to say that the world has gone to the dogs and that life is nothing like it was 'in the good old days'. At the same time increasingly large proportions of current generations were not even born before the Second World War, and so are unable to contrast the anxieties and deprivations of prewar years with the increased supplies of goods and services of all kinds that have accompanied economic growth.

But the general disappointment at the failure of increased prosperity, as conventionally measured, to lead to a commensurate increase in wellbeing or to resolve the numerous serious problems facing society is not simply a matter of vague, general nostalgia for a past age that was never so good as it seems in retrospect, or of the absence of any recollection of earlier times by an increasing proportion of the existing population. There have been tangible changes in the quality of life that, in many cases, are for the worse, or that will often *appear* to be for the worse even if they really are not.

One of the most obvious changes in the quality of life in the first decade after the war was due to the increased awareness of environmental pollution, including pollution of the air from smoke, sulphur dioxide and carbon monoxide (mainly from motorcars). Water pollution also rose sharply – and often visibly – in many places, and although there was no likelihood of a return to the insanitary conditions in which most town-dwellers lived in the nineteenth century, when typhoid, typhus and cholera were relatively frequent in western Europe, many leisure activities and holiday resorts had become affected by pollution of the rivers and the beaches. Noise – particularly traffic noise near airports or motorways – also seem to be on the increase. At the same time, crimes of violence were increasing in many cities of the world, as were other manifestations of social disorder in general or of urban deterioration and urban blight in particular.

These developments naturally led many people to question the extent to which the conventional measures of national income provided a good indicator of how much we were really 'better off'. They also led to a demand for some better measure that would make allowance for those other elements in the general 'quality of life' that were thought – often quite rightly – to be deteriorating, particularly if there was reason to believe that some of the deterioration was caused by the very increase in national product that the conventional measures seemed to indicate. Calls to dethrone the 'god of GNP' were widely heard and economists were often accused of being misled by their alleged subservience to the GNP concept.

But, in fact, economists have always known that national product was not a good measure of 'welfare' in the wider sense of the word. At best national product as measured – and even the general subject matter of economic science, irrespective of how much of it can be represented in some number such as the size of national product – has always been recognised as being

39

concerned only with *economic welfare*. And this again has always been recognised as constituting only one part of total welfare. One of the greatest economists of the twentieth century, Pigou, stated the position clearly in his famous book *The Economics of Welfare*, which was first published in 1920, i.e. about fifty years before the non-economists began to point out that national product was not identical to total welfare. He said that:

> 'Welfare, however, is a thing of very wide range. . . . A general investigation of the groups of causes by which welfare thus conceived may be affected would constitute a task so enormous and complicated as to be quite impracticable. It is, therefore, necessary to limit our subject matter. The one obvious instrument of measurement available in social life is money. Hence, the range of our inquiry becomes restricted to that part of social welfare that can be brought directly or indirectly into relation with the measuring-rod of money. This part of welfare may be called economic welfare.[1]

Pigou also went on to make precisely the point that economists are lately accused of having ignored, namely that:

> . . . there is no guarantee that the effects produced on the part of welfare that can be brought into relation with the measuring-rod of money may not be cancelled by effects of a contrary kind brought about in other parts, or aspects, of welfare. . . . The real objection then is, not that economic welfare is a bad index of total welfare, but that an economic cause may affect non-economic welfare in ways that cancel its effect on economic welfare.[2]

Pigou then gave many examples of the way that this might happen, such as urbanisation or the effects of industrialisation on working conditions, and other examples that have not even crossed the minds of those who presumptuously suggest that they alone have seen through the veil of money that obscured the vision of materialistic-minded economists. But he made it perfectly clear that national income, or what he called the

[1] A. C. Pigou *The Economics of Welfare*, 4th edn, Macmillan, London, 1932, pages 10–11.
[2] Pigou, op. cit., page 12.

national dividend, was simply 'that part of the objective income of the community . . . which can be measured in money. . . .' and that 'the national dividend is composed in the last resort of a number of objective services, some of which are embodied in commodities, while others are rendered direct'.[1]

Much more recently an eminent American economist, Arthur Okun, has put the issue very clearly in writing:

> It is hard to understand how anyone could seriously believe that GNP could be converted into a meaningful indicator of total social welfare. Obviously, any number of things could make the Nation better off without raising its real GNP as measured today: we might start the list with peace, equality of opportunity, the elimination of injustice and violence, greater brotherhood among Americans of different racial and ethnic backgrounds, better under-standing between parents and children and between hus-bands and wives, and we could go on endlessly. To suggest that GNP could become *the* indicator of social welfare is to imply that an appropriate price tag could be put on changes in all of these social factors from one year to the next . . . it is . . . asking the national income statistician to play the role of a philospher–king, quantifying and evaluating all changes in the human scene. And it is absurd to suggest that, if the national income statistician can't do that job, the figure for GNP is not interesting.[2]

Quite apart from elements of total welfare, such as those mentioned by Okun above, economists have also recognised numerous reasons why measured national product does not even provide a very good indicator of what it is supposed to measure – i.e. economic welfare. There are many reasons for this, most of them falling under one or other of the following.

First, many items that might be generally agreed to form part of economic welfare have been excluded from the estimates on account of practical estimation difficulties. For example, it might be accepted that GNP should include housewives' services and the services obtained, by owners, from consumer

[1] Pigou, op. cit., page 31.
[2] Arthur Okun 'Social Welfare Has No Price Tag', *Survey of Current Business*, 51, July 1971 (special anniversary issue).

durables. But at the same time, it would probably be agreed that objective estimates of these items are difficult to find. For they do not usually relate to market transactions, and so their prices and values are not reflected in any objective market transactions.

Secondly, there are numerous features of the market economy that drive a wedge between the value of market transactions and their contribution to economic welfare, ranging from imperfect competition, imperfect knowledge, externalities (of which pollution is only one example, and one that was also explicitly recognised by Pigou), to aspects of income distribution that would enter into most people's notions of welfare (see Chapter 7 below for more details of this problem). In addition, there are special difficulties that are well known to economists in making comparisons between economic welfare at different points of time (or between different countries), notably those arising out of changes in the relative prices of the goods and services, changes in the pattern of output, and changes in tastes (see Chapters 10 and 11 below for fuller discussion of these difficulties).

Thirdly, as we have seen in the previous chapter, one of the major decisions to be taken in defining GNP is the decision concerning the boundary line between those productive activities that give rise directly to *final* output and those that produce *intermediate* output – i.e. goods and services that are not wanted for their own sake but in order to be 'used up' in the course of some subsequent stage in the productive process. Thus, for example, nobody wants steel for its own sake; it is hence always an 'intermediate' product. It is wanted only in order to be embodied in automobiles, investment goods, dishwashers and so on. Hence, as explained in the previous chapter, we would not count steel in our total national product if we have already counted the final products that embody steel, since we do not want to count the steel twice.

This distinction between intermediate products and final products is vital in connection with the welfare significance of the GNP measure. First of all, it has some minor implications of a relatively non-controversial character such as the fact that we are interested in national product after deducting the investment that is 'used up' in the course of producing it. Whilst the precise concept of what investment is 'used up' is a complex one on which there is no complete agreement, by and large it is agreed that, in order to measure *sustainable* economic welfare, we are usually interested in *net* national product, not gross national product before deduction of depreciation.

But apart from the exclusion of depreciation there is far less agreement concerning how much of the total productive activity of the economy should be treated as intermediate output in order to arrive at a measure of national product that corresponded more closely to economic welfare. In particular, many economists would subscribe to the view that a large part of public expenditures, such as general administration, law and order and so on, are really 'inputs' into the productive system, since without them the whole productive system could not function as it does. Hence, it is argued, to treat these government expenditures as final products instead of as inputs into the productive sector is double-counting like counting both the steel and the automobiles. The measure of national product is thereby exaggerated. If, for example, the services of law and order were not provided by the government the private sector would probably finish up by purchasing the same sort of service on the free market. Private enterprise would fill the gap, as it has done in the past and as it still does today in many respects (e.g. private security officials employed by companies, security delivery services and so on). Where such a service is supplied through the market, GNP is lower than if the same service is supplied by the government, for the reasons explained in the previous chapter.

One difficulty of this approach, and one that has already been touched on in the previous chapter, is that, as Nancy Ruggles and Richard Ruggles recently put it:

> ... the problem of what is an intermediate good or service is not restricted to general government expenditure. A considerable portion of the expenditures of households could also be considered to be intermediate. An individual, for example, must commute to his job, and this expense can be considered an intermediate cost related to earning a living. ... Many household expenditures are essentially of the nature of regrettable necessities, and are part of the cost of living. Thus, an individual may live in a colder

climate rather than in a warmer climate because of his job; the cost of heavier clothing and of heating his home might then be considered part of the cost of living in the colder climate.[1]

The term 'regrettable necessities' used here by Professor and Mrs. Ruggles has recently been more widely adopted in some of the work carried out to obtain a measure of economic welfare that is thought to be a better approximation to economic welfare and which will be briefly surveyed below. Since this concept of regrettable necessities has played an important part in such estimates it is necessary to consider it carefully. At first sight it might appear that the issue of how far to exclude regrettable necessities is quite distinct from the issue of how far to exclude those activities of the government, such as law and order, that might be considered intermediate rather than final products. For example, national defence would be regarded as a regrettable necessity, but not as an intermediate product. It would not usually be maintained that the services of national defence are already counted once in the value of the productive sector's activity, or that, if the government did not provide the defence forces, they would be provided by the private sector (in the shape of Lt Minderbinder of *Catch 22*, presumably).

Instead it would be argued that national defence should be excluded because it does not really add to welfare. For example, Nordhaus and Tobin, who have made one of the most systematic attempts to adjust the conventional GNP measure in order to arrive at a better measure of economic welfare, write that: ' . . . we see no direct effect of defence expenditures on household economic welfare. No reasonable country (or household) buys "national defence" for its own sake. If there were no war or risk of war, there would be no need for defence expenditures and no one would be the worse without them.'[2]

But the same sort of reasoning applies to almost any com-

[1] Nancy Ruggles and Richard Ruggles *The Design of Economic Accounts*, National Bureau of Economic Research, New York, 1970, p. 46.

[2] William Nordhaus and James Tobin 'Is Growth Obsolete', in *Economic Growth*, National Bureau of Economic Research, New York, 1972 (proceedings of a colloquium in December 1970). Even as it stands this argument gives the game away; for insofar as there is believed to be a risk of war, the statement quoted implies that people *would* be worse off without the defence expenditures, and hence they must be better off with them than without them.

ponent of GNP. Nobody would want hospital accident wards, or even home first-aid kits, for their own sake. They are only required because of the risk of accidents. Motorcar seat-belts are required not for their own sake, but to prevent injury in accidents. It is not possible to draw logical distinctions of the Nordhaus–Tobin kind between the purposes served by various goods. If they are wanted they are wanted, and that is the end of the matter. If there were no winters, there would be no need for winter woollies or heating expenditure; if one never had toothache there would be no need to visit the dentist. For very poor people, even food, after all, is merely required in order to offset the pain of being hungry and dying of starvation. Surely it is not to be argued that in such cases the food in question (or other similar basic essentials) should *not* be included in GNP and that we should include only the more frivolous inessentials. If so, this runs quite counter to another popular view to the effect that much of the growth of GNP as measured is misleading because it includes so many of the items that are not really necessary. In other words, some people argue that we should exclude from a welfare-oriented measure of GNP the goods that we do not really need. And others – including, apparently, Nordhaus and Tobin – argue that we should exclude the goods that we *do* really need since these are just regrettable necessities.

In fact, Nordhaus and Tobin recognise the logical difficulties to which their procedure leads when they write: 'Maybe all our wants are just regrettable necessities; maybe productive activity does no better than satisfy the wants which it generates; maybe our net welfare is tautologically zero.' Unfortunately, they then proceed to suggest that this objection is not a serious one; but it is, and it applies as much to the inclusion in GNP of ordinary consumers' expenditure on consumer durables and clothes or more exotic foods and so on as to the 'regrettable necessities' that they wish to deduct from GNP in order to move towards a yardstick for measuring welfare.

But the 'regrettable necessities' issue is not entirely separate from the issue of where to draw the dividing line between intermediate and final output. If there were no crime, for example, there would be no need for law and order services to be supplied by anybody – government or the productive sector.

In that case 'sales of law and order' should not be included at all, let alone double-counted. If it is thought that they are already counted once as part of the output of the private sector then they should be deducted from the private sector's output as well as excluded from government output. It cannot be argued that there is any logically significant distinction between the loss of welfare that is caused by the imagined (or real) villainy of foreigners that exposes us to the hazard of foreign aggression and the certainly real villainy of our compatriots that exposes us to aggression on the streets or theft everywhere. In both cases the corresponding antidote expenditures – the 'goods' that are really fulfilling the role of 'anti-bads' – are only required in order partially or wholly to offset the loss of welfare that would be caused by the 'bads'.

And the same reasoning applies to the instances given above concerning the regrettable necessities purchased by consumers. Why only exclude their extra commuting costs, for example, on the grounds that these are really intermediate inputs into their total productive activity, like their purchases of special clothing for work purposes? Why not exclude their expenditures on clothing that are required merely to offset their villainous vanity, which may not be quite so anti-social as their criminal tendencies, but which constitutes a 'need' that has to be partly met by the input of fancy clothing? And many food expenditures are merely inputs to meet the 'needs' of gluttony, so such food is just an input into the output of gluttonous satisfaction.

In fact important developments in the theory of consumer's behaviour present the theory in terms of a consumer who uses the conventional goods and services as inputs into a production process by which he obtains final output in terms of various ultimate satisfactions that could be expressed in units of, say, warmth, comfort, nutrition, amusement and so on. Information provided by advertising, for example, would help him improve on his production 'technology'. With such an approach, it would be natural to regard consumers as productive units and there would be no distinction between inputs of, say, transport costs incurred in going to work and inputs of food or clothing. Final output of consumer goods would no longer comprise the goods and services treated as final output in the national accounts but would comprise the final utilities derived from

46

them. In other words, the present conventional distinction between intermediate and final output does not represent any sharp logical distinction but is adopted solely on account of the practical statistical impossibility of measuring the final output of the consumers' productive activity in terms of his ultimate satisfactions.

Of course it is always open to everybody to make value judgements to the effect that some 'needs' or 'wants' are morally good and others are bad, but there is no scientific, objective, basis for such ethical distinctions. Hence, insofar as all output is used only to satisfy some need or other, there is no clear basis for distinguishing those that provide regrettable necessities to combat 'bad' needs and those that constitute desirable inputs into the satisfaction of good 'needs'. Steel is not counted in final product insofar as we include the automobiles and the like, in which it is used. But why count the automobiles? After all many people regard automobiles as regrettable necessities; they are a 'bad' need that reflects human laziness and disinclination to walk.

One particular 'regrettable necessity' that has attracted much attention lately has been the rise in anti-pollution expenditures. For environmental pollution is a clear case of a failure of GNP to measure economic welfare adequately. If a rise in output is accompanied by a rise in pollution, welfare is reduced by the extra pollution but this is not deducted from the increase in GNP. Conversely, if anti-pollution laws result in more resources being devoted to the prevention of pollution, and hence diverted from other final output, GNP as measured will probably be cut (other things being equal), but welfare will rise. Hence it is argued that the increasing need for environmental protection constitutes a rise in some 'bad' need so that a rise in expenditures to protect the environment is not an unambiguous measure of the contribution to welfare that we have obtained, under the environmental heading, from these expenditures.

Of course, the issue is really the same as that concerning the expenditures on law and order, which may have increased on account of increasing lawlessness. In both cases, given the state of villainy of the population or the state of environmental pollution, we would be worse off without the corresponding anti-bad expenditures than with them (other things being

47

equal, including expenditures on other items). No accounting rules will tell us how 'well-off' we are if we net out our needs against the expenditures incurred in satisfying them. Hence, we must accept the impossibility of finding a measure of welfare that takes precise account of changes in needs as well as of changes in the extent to which they are satisfied.

So we must accept GNP as an indicator of how far the productive system provides output that can be used to meet needs of all kinds, good or bad, and changing over time. It is reasonable to assume that, at least in the short-run, the more output is available to meet needs the better off we tend to be, subject to the qualifications already mentioned. However, this does not imply that, in general, welfare is necessarily equal to the gap between needs and satisfaction. Such a proposition would be highly debatable. For some needs may add to welfare, not subtract from it. In other words, some needs may be judged to be 'good', not 'bad', either because they may be thought to be morally good or because they are believed to make people 'happier' whether they are morally good or not. For example, one of the reasons why we spend more on the environment is that, with rising incomes (as well as increases in some forms of pollution), we are more concerned with the environment and hence feel more need for a clean environment. This might be considered morally good, like a 'need' for education or religious activity or an increase in social awareness of the need to provide adequate housing for people. It is incorrect to regard all needs as 'bad' so that welfare would consist only of the gap between them and their satisfactions.[1] Either all needs are regrettable, in which case, as a measure of 'net' welfare, GNP is zero, or some are desirable, in which case it is wrong to regard welfare as consisting of the extent to which they are eliminated.

The rough and ready assumption that, although GNP and welfare are not commensurate at any point of time, changes in GNP are usually associated with changes in economic welfare provided needs have not changed much is, of course, increasingly weak the longer the time period in question. The previous examples of needs that rise over time or according to circumstances (such as the activities of environmental protection

[1] For a fuller discussion of this point see my *In Defence of Economic Growth*, Jonathan Cape, London, 1974, pages 89–92.

pressure groups) are illustrations of the more general fact that there is no limit to the possible expansion of needs. What are regarded as luxuries at one point of time (and hence only 'needs' for the very rich) become conventional necessities at other points of time.

This would explain, for example, the recent interesting survey by Richard Easterlin which found that, between nineteen countries at very different levels of *per capita* income, the proportions of the population that considered themselves to be 'very happy' or 'happy' and so on were remarkably similar.[1] In other words, although at any point of time in any one country, higher incomes were associated with a more subjective feeling of being happy, a general rise in income over time did not lead to any corresponding rise in the proportion of people who regarded themselves as 'happy'. Of course, an alternative explanation could be in terms of the so-called famous 'relative income hypothesis', according to which one's welfare depended on one's income relative to that of other people in the same community. But unless this hypothesis is taken to the extreme and welfare is assumed to be entirely a matter of one's position relative to other people, it would have to be assumed that it was also a matter of one's command over goods and services relative to one's subjective 'wants' for them – i.e. of some concept of 'needs' – and that these, too, rise over time.

In addition to these philosophical reasons why it is difficult to take account of needs in any measure of economic welfare, it is also impossible to measure them. For example, how would one measure society's 'needs' for health expenditures? As pointed out in a recent article in connection with the issue of the social need for health expenditures, ' . . . if it is said that "society needs" . . . it is not clear whether what is meant implies that the speaker himself needs it, whether Society *ought* to have it in his opinion, whether a majority of members of Society want it, or all of them want it. Moreover, it is not clear whether it is "needed" regardless of the social and humanitarian cost to Society'.[2]

[1] R. A. Easterlin 'Does Economic Growth Improve the Human Lot? Some Empirical Evidence', in P. David (ed.), *Nations and Households in Economic Growth: Essays in Honor of Moses Abramovitz*, Stanford University Press, California, 1974.

[2] A. J. Culyer, R. J. Lavers and Alan Williams 'Social Indicators: Health' in *Social Trends No. 2*, HMSO, London, 1971, page 35.

Innumerable, and often vague, medical, social and psychological factors would have to enter into the determination of what health needs really were. And they would change all the time, of course. If everybody gave up smoking many health needs would vanish. But we would not want to say that GNP had risen as a result (though it probably would on account of increased production resulting from the loss of working time caused by illness).

In view of these limitations on the welfare significance of conventional GNP measures, it might be asked what is the point of measuring GNP at all. The answer is twofold. First, as long as GNP covers roughly one part of welfare, namely economic welfare, it is the only component of welfare that has a wide coverage and that can be measured at all in a way that bears any clear theoretical relationship to some coherent theory of individual welfare. Hence, even those who are under the illusion that total welfare is something that one should try to measure should welcome this measure of one of its ingredients and should not reject it simply because nobody has yet solved the problem of measuring all the others. Even the possibility that increases in economic welfare may lead to decreases in some of the other non-measurable components of welfare is not a serious objection, since the same may apply to any of the other components of welfare. For example, there is little doubt that, in the interests of protecting the environment or reducing crime, certain limitations may have to be put on freedom, which is also an ingredient of welfare. If we were limited to measuring those components of welfare that could not possibly conflict with each other in any way not many items could be included!

Secondly, even if GNP cannot measure 'welfare' it is still a useful measure of what the economy produces. Changes in output as measured by GNP, at least in the short and medium run, have important implications for the state of the economy in general and for certain aspects of it in particular, such as the level of employment, or the proportion of it devoted to alternative uses, or the way it is distributed among various groups of individuals or families, or how it compares with the GNP of other countries having roughly similar tastes and hence 'needs'.

2. Alternative measures

(i) General

Because of the uses to which the GNP concept may be put there is no question of abandoning it in favour of some other concept that might be a better measure of welfare. The only serious issue is whether the conventional GNP concept can be supplemented by other measures which, whilst not possessing the properties of the GNP measure, might come closer to a measure of economic welfare.

There are basically two kinds of supplementary measures. First, there are amended versions of the conventional GNP measure – i.e. measures that start from the conventional concepts but adjust them in certain detailed respects, such as the treatment of government expenditures and so on. Secondly, there is the so-called 'social indicator' approach. Although there is some slight connection between the two it is preferable to consider them separately.

(ii) Measurable economic welfare

This is the term used by Nordhaus and Tobin in the previously quoted study in which they attempted, by means of adjustments to the conventional national accounts and certain other calculations, to obtain a measure of economic welfare that would be superior to the usual measure.[1] Other economists had earlier analysed the scope for similar measures, and in some cases had proceeded to make the corresponding estimates. In fact, the whole idea of making special adjustments in order to obtain a variant of GNP that corresponds more closely to economic welfare goes back a long way in the literature, and is associated chiefly with the name of the Nobel Prize winner, Simon Kuznets.

Until recently, the kind of adjustments that were widely accepted as legitimate, up to a point, were the addition of the services of government capital (e.g. roads, public buildings, and so on which are excluded from GNP), or of the services of consumers' capital assets, such as the services provided by consumer durables. A more debatable item has been an allowance for the change over time in the amount of leisure enjoyed by individuals. For example, working hours have greatly fallen over the last century and this component of welfare is not reflected in GNP. More recently, partly on account of the

[1] William Nordhaus and James Tobin 'Is Growth Obsolete?'

51

growing concern with the environment or the expansion of government 'defensive expenditures' on law and order, military defence and so on, there have been attempts to construct a more comprehensive estimate of 'measurable economic welfare', of which the Nordhaus and Tobin estimates are the most sophisticated.

These estimates made adjustments of a positive and negative kind to the conventional GNP figures in order to arrive at a measure of economic welfare. The positive adjustments included notably the rise in leisure, which has been extremely important, and also the increase in various non-marketed services, principally those domestic activities such as looking after the house, that are carried out in 'leisure' time and that often involve the use of consumer durables such as cooking equipment or garden implements. The positive items also included the services of public capital. On the other hand, adjustments were made to exclude regrettable necessities, such as defence expenditures, as well as the estimated monetary equivalent of certain disamenities, such as those arising out of environmental damage or urbanisation and congestion.

Table 3.1

Nordhaus and Tobin estimates of Measure of Economic Welfare for the USA: summary table (billions of dollars, 1958 prices, and indices)

	1929	1965	1965 as index 1929
Net National Product			
(conventional definitions)	183·6	563·1	306·5
of which: 'regrettable necessities'	− 17·0	− 94·1	
leisure	339·5	626·9	
non-market activities	85·7	295·4	
disamenities	− 12·5	− 34·6	
services of public and private capital	29·7	78·9	
other adjustments	− 65·4	−194·5	
measure of 'economic welfare'	543·6	1241·1	228·5

Source: Nordhaus and Tobin, op. cit. (Table 2 of mimeographed edition, page 21).

The outcome of these calculations for the USA are summarised in Table 3.1 and Figure 3.1. As can be seen from these figures, the conventional measure of net national product in 1929 was only $183·6 billion[1] (at 1958 prices) whereas the value

[1] '000 million.

of leisure (\$340 billion) plus the value of non-market activities (\$85·7 billion) amounted to about \$425 billion, which is very much greater than the negative adjustments that had to be made of \$30 billion for the regrettable necessities and disamenities such as defence or the costs of urbanisation. Hence, the total initial measure of economic welfare in 1929, after making both

Figure 3.1

Changes in National Product and 'measurable economic welfare', USA, 1929 to 1965 (\$ billion at 1958 prices)

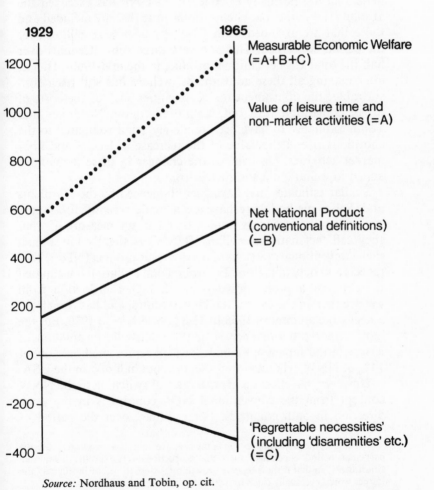

Source: Nordhaus and Tobin, op. cit.

53

kinds of adjustment, was $543·6 billion. As a result, even though the absolute increase in the favourable items, notably leisure and non-market activities, has been very much larger than the absolute increase in the unfavourable items since 1929, the proportionate rise in what was initially a much larger total has been less. Figure 3.1 summarises these relationships. In other words, it is true that the growth rate of 'measured economic welfare', according to these estimates, is slower than the growth of GNP as conventionally measured, but the absolute rise in the 'good' items that are normally excluded from GNP has exceeded the absolute rise in the 'bad' items (both those that are included and those that are excluded from GNP) by over $318 billion over the period concerned. This is a very large sum; it equals over half the total US net national product in the mid-1960s. Hence, after making all these adjustments, welfare has still risen considerably; the adjustment for disamenities such as the costs of urban congestion turn out, according to the Nordhaus and Tobin estimates, to have been relatively small compared to the enormous rise in the value of the increase in leisure and non-market activities. On balance the changes in these items have added to welfare, not subtracted from it.[1]

Similar estimates that have been influenced by the Nordhaus and Tobin methodology have been made recently for Japan, but with rather different results. In Japan the measure of what they call 'net national welfare' (NNW) is slightly lower than their conventional measures of net domestic product (NDP). This reflects a variety of factors. Environmental pollution is estimated to represent a proportionately much higher deduction from welfare than in the case of the United States, and has risen from a negligible amount in 1955 to 13·8% of NNW in 1970. But the most important difference is in the relative low valuation of leisure in the Japanese estimates, which represented only about 14% of NNW, whereas it represents about half of it in the USA.

However, the effect on growth rates of switching to the NNW concept from the conventional NDP concept is in the same direction in both countries. For example, over the period of

---

[1] Of course, the *proportionate* rise in the negative items has been faster, over the particular period concerned, than the proportionate rise in the favourable adjustments, so that if these relative growth rates were to persist indefinitely the former would eventually catch up with and then overtake the latter.

1955 to 1970, conventional NDP rose by 322% in Japan whereas over the same period Japanese net national welfare rose by 257%. Nevertheless, this is an astonishingly fast growth rate by any standard, so that even though Japan is also an outstanding example of the way that the environment has been sacrificed in the course of economic growth, a measure of welfare that takes account of it still shows an extraordinary increase.

(iii) Social Indicators
Another offshoot of the growing dissatisfaction with the conventional measure of GNP has been the development of interest in what are known as 'social indicators'. Broadly speaking, these are direct measures of specific features of a society that will be accepted as indicators of wellbeing such as the level of protein consumption or the number of doctors per head of population or housing conditions, rather than measures of expenditures on these items or the monetary value of the flow of services from certain kinds of social or private capital, as in the case of the housing stock.

A wide variety of specific items can be, and have been, included in different lists of relevant 'social indicators', such as the number of hospital beds, infant mortality rates, suicides, road accidents, telephones, student enrolment ratios, frequency of work accidents, exposure to harmful pollutants, degree of social equality and so on. Some of these items are really 'inputs' into welfare, such as nutritional standards, or the number of hospital beds or doctors per head of population, whereas others may be the 'outputs' corresponding to these inputs such as the health of the population in terms of various sickness rates, infant mortality rates and so on.

There is no doubt that the provision of such indicators has a very useful role to play in policy discussion and decision-making. Policy makers are inevitably concerned with finding quantitative indicators of the impact of alternative policy measures, particularly those designed to affect social conditions. Even from a cost–benefit point of view it is important to be able to quantify the effect of, say, increased maternity homes on the infant mortality rate or the effect of increased law and order expenditures on the incidence of violence in the streets. It is also useful, in this connection, to be able to make quantitative predictions

55

of future trends in 'needs' for certain inputs, such as those of a health or educational character, in relation to trends in the supplies of these inputs, even if, in the end, the alternative policies have to be converted into a monetary form. Quite apart from the scope for using such indicators or combinations of them as substitutes for GNP as a measure of welfare, therefore, the development of social indicators will add both directly to the information needed by policy makers and, indirectly, by providing background information concerning the success of certain policies in meeting social goals.

As a result of the growing recognition of the value of social indicators many countries have started producing regular statistical surveys of such indicators and the United Nations is now obliged to provide regular reports on them to the General Assembly. The increased interest in social indicators has also been accompanied by some discussion concerning the principles that should govern the choice of indicators, such as: (i) the extent to which they should always be of a normative character, i.e. that a movement up or down in a social indicator should be unambiguously interpreted as 'good' or 'bad'; (ii) whether they should always be related to 'outputs', such as improvements in health rather than increased supply of doctors (particularly since it is very debatable how far more doctors leads to better health); (iii) how far indicators should be combined into sub-aggregates instead of being presented in terms of basic components, and so on. But these issues are best left to specialists and the main issue here is whether social indicators, presumably combined together in some way or other, can provide any measure of welfare that will be better than the GNP measure. Unfortunately, the answer is 'no'.

There are various reasons for this. The most important is the impossibility of attaching any meaningful weights to all the various indicators that could be devised in order that they should each represent their respective proportional contributions to total welfare. With GNP the weights attached to the various component flows of goods and services entering into the total GNP figure can at least be considered to reflect the (marginal) value attached to the goods by consumers, for these weights are the prices of the goods and services concerned. Although in practice, as mentioned above, there are numerous qualifications to this assumption, by and large the use of price weights prevents, for example, the same weight being given to one unit of television set as to one bar of soap. Hence, unless there is an extraordinary difference in the relative prices of television sets and soap in two countries – we can be sure that a country that produces two television sets and one bar of soap will, other things being equal, show up as having a higher GNP than a country producing one television set and two bars of soap. But how are we to weight together a rise in the daily protein intake per head from 60 to 65 grams with a rise in the suicide rate?

It is not possible to avoid this weighting problem by the procedure that some prople have adopted, namely to experiment with various statistical correlations in order to find which method of combining different indicators (including which weights attached to them) gives the closest correlation between the individual indicators and some aggregate of them all. For in the end a value judgement has to be made as to whether the aggregate represents what one regards as welfare, and no amount of statistical correlations can be a substitute for one's value judgements. That is to say, the decision as to whether economic welfare or development is a matter of the size of the national product, or the crime rate, or the beauty of the architecture, or the purity of the environment, or some suitably weighted combination of these and many other factors is a pure value judgement. If one person says that welfare is only a matter of GNP and another says it is a matter of the stock of human and capital resources, they are not making positive statements about the real world; they are making statements about their value judgements. Hence, there is no conceivable empirical test that can enable us to discriminate between their rival propositions. For these are questions of definition, not of fact; no amount of statistical manipulation will tell us whether the number of doctors per head is a better guide to welfare than the number of motorcars per head. The search for some statistical correlations to make our value judgements for us is the search for a chimera.

If it is accepted that the degree of correlation between individual indicators and some combination of themselves cannot provide a firm conceptual basis for allocating weights to them, how else is one to proceed to decide whether welfare has improved when, say, the infant mortality rate has risen but the level of environmental pollution has fallen? Some weights have to be attached to these different indicators. If it is thought that some rough arbitrary weights will be selected that reflect direct value judgements then we will still be faced with insuperable problems in finding statistical measures of the items in question to which sensible weights can be attached. For there is no way to avoid the fact that we want the weights to reflect, roughly speaking, the relative net addition to welfare made by an addition of one unit of the item in question (and vice versa). So let us consider, as an exercise, the practical problems that would arise in trying to attach weights to indicators of environmental pollution.

First, we would want to take account of the number of people affected by the pollution. For example, welfare would not be reduced to the same extent by the emission of some smoke in the middle of a desert as by the emission of the same amount of smoke in the middle of London or Manhattan. Hence, the usual national aggregates of pollution, such as the total national emissions of smoke, are useless since the number of people affected will depend heavily on the locality in which the smoke is emitted. It should be noted that, on account of the 'public bad' character of pollution, one must not convert pollution to a *per capita* basis, as would be the case with, say, an aggregate figure of total meat supplies, where the greater the population the less meat is available per head. The fact that one person breathes smoky air in a city does not reduce the amount by which another person will also breathe equally foul air. The more people are affected by the pollution the greater is the sum of the loss of welfare incurred by all the victims. But it would be exceedingly difficult to obtain anything like reasonably accurate data on the number of people affected by pollution in units that were comparable. Some people may work in the centre of a city with polluted air and others may merely pass through it for a few minutes. Others may be there only at night when the pollution level may be relatively low, and others may be in peak-hour traffic jams when the carbon monoxide levels in the streets rise to a maximum.

A second difficulty, which is related to the first one, is that,

ideally, pollution indicators should not be in terms of discharges – such as of the amount of mercury entering the sea –
but in terms of 'ambient standards', such as the ground-level
urban concentration of sulphur dioxide. It follows from what has
been said above concerning the effect on human beings that the
latter would be more relevant. But accurate data on ambient
standards are very difficult to obtain. Ground-level con-
centrations of smoke, for example, can vary greatly according
to wind conditions, time of day, precise point of measurement,
proximity to tall buildings and so on. Similarly, it may be
relatively easy to obtain data from a factory concerning the
amount of pollutant that it discharges into a river, but it will be
incomparably more difficult to obtain reliable data on the state
of the water in the river that mean anything in terms of its
state when people are in contact with it directly or indirectly.
For example, the level of dissolved oxygen in the river, which is
one indicator of its purity (since bacteria consume oxygen),
rises sharply as one goes downstream from the point of dis-
charge of the bacterial pollution, and at a rate that varies
greatly with wind speed, water speed and temperature, air
temperature, inflow of other streams and so on.

A third insuperable difficulty from the point of view of
attaching weights that represent any precise value judgements
concerning the disamenity impact of pollution arises from the
fact that the disamenity effect of a given degree of pollution in,
say, a river or a stretch of coastline depends on the extent to
which alternative water resources are available. In terms of
conventional economic theory this would correspond to the
law of diminishing marginal utility, according to which the
marginal utility of almost any good declines as more of that
good is consumed. In the same way, the loss of utility through
the pollution of some water resource will be less for those
people who have easy access to alternative sources. Pollution
of a water-hole in the desert will be far more serious than an
equal amount of pollution of a small, remote, and unfrequented
beach on the Atlantic seashore. A further complication is that
the disamenity impact of some pollutant – such as noise – will
depend on the ease (and cost) of recourse to some anti-pollutant,
which in this case would be soundproofing.

Apart from these basic conceptual and practical difficulties

59

of finding suitable weights with which to combine individual social indicators into some overall index of 'wellbeing', there are other obvious difficulties, such as the fact that, in the end, social indicators are only partial indicators of welfare. They are invariably limited to a small selection of the innumerable thousands of factors that go to make up the quality of life in general. GNP may not be everything in life, but it covers a lot.

And in a sense, social indicators really tell one only how different societies happen to prefer to allocate their total output (which is measured, if imperfectly, by their national products) among alternative uses. Some countries may prefer to spend relatively more on hospitals and less on education or law and order or the protection of the environment. How they choose will depend on their private and social values and the relative costs of the alternatives. GNP attempts to combine these choices in a way that indicates roughly the outcome of these various considerations, since the monetary valuations attached to the various items reflects, if imperfectly, each society's preferences and relative costs. It is far from clear, therefore, that a selection of individual quantitative indicators of particular choices can add much, if anything, to our knowledge of the overall scope for choice that each society has, although it may throw interesting light on the way that this choice is exercised.

3. GNP, welfare and choice

This brings us to the final point that needs to be made about the relation between GNP and welfare. It has been argued above that GNP has never been regarded by economists as an indicator of welfare as a whole. Welfare obviously includes innumerable factors, such as peace, tolerance, love of one's neighbour, family life, satisfaction in one's job or surroundings, justice and many other items that cannot be brought into relation with the measuring rod of money.

Furthermore, for reasons which have been well known in the economic profession, GNP is far from being a perfect measure of *economic* welfare. Nor would it be possible to establish a measure of economic welfare that avoided the problems of making basic value judgements upon which everybody could agree. But it does provide a total measure, up to a point, in a meaningful way, of very many of the items that do contribute to welfare and without which most people would consider themselves worse off. There is, no doubt, always room for improvement, both from the point of view of the statistical coverage and accuracy with which the conventional components are measured and also from the point of view of taking some account of certain ingredients of welfare that have hitherto been regarded as unmeasurable in monetary terms. Quantitative estimates of some of these, such as leisure hours or environmental change, add to our knowledge of the condition of society, as do social indicators. Work on the development of these is therefore to be welcomed as a supplement to the conventional GNP estimates, but they do not make GNP estimates redundant or even misleading to those who know what these estimates really mean and what the real limitations on them are.

But there is no great new approach to be adopted that will provide a single measure of welfare or even of economic welfare. The concept of welfare is basically a subjective concept relating to how people feel, and this cannot be measurable in a meaningful way. GNP provides an indicator of what society has available to promote certain aspects of welfare. It can choose to use it wisely or badly. One can make the value judgement that choice in itself is desirable. But whether, in fact, increased choice succeeds in making people happier or not is another question that cannot be answered by any amount of measurement.

Chapter 4

The components of
final output

1. The two main uses of final product

In Chapter 2 it was seen that the crux of the definition of
national product was the decision as to what goods and services
were defined as crossing the production boundary and hence as
constituting 'final output' or sales to 'final demand'. Final
output, or 'final demand', is what the economy, in the end, gets
out of all its activity. The rest of output, namely intermediate
product, is simply a means to the end because it is used up in
order to produce the end product. Final product thus represents
what the economy wanted for its own sake. In this chapter we
shall examine the main ways in which an economy may use the
final product obtained. A classification of final product along
these lines is, in fact, often shown in statistical tables under the
heading 'the use of resources'. In such tables, the resources to
which reference is made are not the machines, raw materials,
labour time and so on that are used up in the productive process
but the final output of the economy.

Unlikely though it may sound, it happens to be possible to
proceed some way with the classification of the uses to which
final output may be put simply by deduction from the initial
concept of the production boundary presented above (plus one
or two additional, and equally arbitrary, decisions). For all
output is either used up in the production of other goods and
services or it is not. And output that is not used up in the
production of goods and services must be either (i) used up for
its own sake – such as the food we eat or (ii) not used up at all –
i.e. it is part of output that is simply put aside for purposes of
adding to the nation's wealth.

The former of these two classes of final output, namely that
part of final output which is used up for its own sake, is known as

consumption. It will include current expenditure on goods and services by consumers, such as the food, drink and clothing bought by private individuals, or the current expenditure by governments, such as current expenditures on education or on law and order, since these expenditures are not incurred primarily in order to use the goods and services obtained for purposes of producing other goods and services.[1] In other words, the part of final product known as 'consumption' includes all sales of goods and services which are regarded as 'consumed' – i.e. used up, but not in the course of further production.[2]

Since, by definition, final output must also include goods that are not used up at all, it must clearly comprise goods (and services) that are devoted to increasing the nation's wealth, or its stock of capital. This is known as *investment*. As a matter of convention, investment is taken to include the output of all goods that have a length of life of more than a year, as well as additions to stocks (of any goods) and accumulation of overseas assets of any kind (including financial claims on other countries).[3]

---

[1] Some of these goods or services, such as education, may also add to the nation's productive capacity, which is why it is often suggested that education should be classified partly as consumption and partly as investment. This would, of course, mean including human resources in a measure of the nation's capital stock – an unattractive and hardly practicable procedure.

[2] In what sense they are really 'used up' is another matter, as will be seen below in discussing consumer durables.

[3] This classification of final output into consumption and investment implies that foreign trade appears in final output as the net excess of exports over imports. It would have been equally reasonable to define final output so that the whole of exports is included but in that case national product would be equal to final output minus imports, as will be shown more fully below. The significance of this point here is that total exports do not fall neatly into the category of goods that are required either for their own sake to be used up or for the sake of adding to wealth, since they may be regarded as being required in order to buy imports which may be partly consumption goods and partly investment goods, apart from the excess of exports over these total imports, which would constitute net investment overseas. It is frequently useful, for analytical purposes, to show the total of exports in a table of the final use of resources, in which case the simplified distinction adopted here, between goods that are either used up for consumption or not so used up, would not apply to this part of final output. For, out of total exports, it would not be possible to say which particular exports were desired to buy the imported consumption goods, for example, which ones for buying investment goods and which ones for net investment overseas.

That is to say, sales to final demand can be classified as being used in two ways:

(i) for *consumption*; in principle this comprises the purchases (and hence sales) of goods and services that are 'used up' or consumed, in the period concerned, but which are not used up in the production of other goods and so which are part of what the economy, in the end, is getting out of all its productive activities;[1] and

(ii) for *investment*; this comprises the purchases (and hence sales) of all goods and services that are not used up in the period concerned (a year) and which must therefore constitute additions to the nation's wealth.

The reader might note that this involves a form of double counting, since we would be including in final output (and therefore in national product) both a capital good (e.g. a machine) and also the goods produced by it during the course of its life. This is true in the long run, and for certain purposes the measure of final output in any year is adjusted by deducting an amount corresponding to that fraction of the capital stock that is, in fact, 'used up' during the year. The amount of this adjustment, which is known as 'capital consumption' or, more loosely, as *depreciation*, will be discussed in more detail below.

If, for the sake of brevity, we use the symbols Y, C and I to represent national product (equals income or output), consumption and investment, respectively, then we may write:

$$Y \equiv C + I$$

It should be noted that this is not an *equation*, but an *identity*, which is indicated by using the sign $\equiv$. In other words, it states that C and I have been *defined* so that they exhaust the whole of national product.

This two-part classification of all final demand into consumption and investment is fundamental to the discussion in later chapters of the process by which the level of income is determined, which is one of the main analytical purposes for which national income data are required. For a full analysis of the process of income determination, however, as well as for many other problems of economic policy, this classification is too

[1] In practice, of course, the distinction between the consumption part of final demand and certain 'intermediate' transactions is not easy to apply. Entertainment expenditures allowed to business men are an example.

simplified and aggregative. It lumps together in large aggregates different types of consumption and investment that, for most important problems, need to be separately distinguished. Hence, both of these two classes of transactions need to be split up into further sub-categories of transactions.

2. Consumption: Introduction
Consumption expenditure can be sub-divided into

(i) *Private consumption*
This comprises mainly the consumption of *households* – i.e. the private consumption expenditure of individuals, such as their purchases of food or domestic heating and lighting,[1] and

(ii) *Public consumption*
This is, as the name suggests, the consumption expenditure of the public authorities, such as expenditures by central or local government on health, education, defence, law and order, and so on.

The main reason for separating these two components of the wider category of total consumption is that their size and composition are determined by very different forces. And the object of the classification system used in national accounts is to arrange transactions in a manner that will enable the economist to understand the forces at work in the economy. The consumption of the private individuals who constitute the 'household' sector of the economy will be determined largely by their tastes, their incomes, and the relative prices of the goods and services that private individuals buy. But the consumption levels and patterns of the public authorities will be determined by more political and social considerations, such as how much education it is thought desirable to supply and how much defence expenditure to incur, as well as by how much taxation can be raised or by how much the government thinks that it needs to stimulate or dampen the level of private activity in the economy.

3. Consumption: Private consumption
The two main characteristics of private consumption are that (i) it covers the expenditure of persons in their private capacities – i.e. as members of the household sector – and (ii) like the wider

[1] As shown below, it also includes expenditures by 'non-profit making' bodies.

category of total consumption, these expenditures are for goods and services for current use.

(i) Non-profit making bodies

These characteristics give rise to two qualifications. First, what is meant by 'persons' in national accounting is not the same as what is meant by this term in common parlance. For in the national accounts we also include as 'persons' certain types of organisation known as 'non-profit making' organisations, such as charities, labour unions, certain educational establishments, and so on. These are not regarded as productive bodies, but as types of mutual benefit society entered into by private individuals.

The expenditures of these bodies on goods and services, such as the salaries of their employees or the stationery they use, are treated as part of consumers' expenditures on final product, whereas if the non-profit making organisations had been treated as part of the productive sector of the economy, their salary payments would have been part of value added in the productive sector and the goods they purchased would have been regarded as intermediate products. To counterbalance the inclusion of the expenditures of non-profit making bodies under the heading of private consumption, the payments by individuals to such bodies – for example, labour unions' membership subscriptions or the fees paid to certain educational institutions – have to be excluded from consumers' expenditure on final product. For they are not regarded as expenditures by the household sector on the output of the productive sector, and hence they do not generate factor incomes. They are merely transfer payments from some members of the household sector to others – they do not cross the production boundary.

Only when the non-profit making organisations use their receipts from fees, subscriptions, donations and so on to purchase goods and services are the payments regarded as crossing the production boundary and hence as constituting consumers' expenditure on the final output of the productive sector. Similarly, only the income that such bodies may receive from outside the household sector – such as dividends on investments – will be included as additions to personal income. In the case of the labour union dues, for example, what is happening in the end is that the union members are transferring some of their income to the union which then proceeds to spend it on final product, on their behalf, under the heading of consumers' expenditure, in the form of payments to union employees and purchases of stationery, heating of office premises and so on. The union members' fees do not enter private consumption at all, being merely a transfer payment.

(ii) The treatment of consumer durables

The second important aspect of the definition of private consumption that gives rise to special problems is the treatment of consumer durables, such as television sets or washing machines, when bought by private individuals.[1] For it might be argued that such goods should be classified as investment goods, according to the 'using-up' rule, since they are clearly not 'used up' in a year. But if consumer durables were to be treated as investment rather than as part of consumption this implies that they are an addition to national wealth and hence add to the future stream of output. This, in turn, would logically imply that the services produced by them during their life should be added to national output. In other words, the production boundary would have been implicitly drawn so that it was not only, say, a television set itself that became part of final output by virtue of its crossing the production boundary, but also the subsequent services 'produced' by the television set. This illustrates, once more, how crucial is the definition of the production boundary as a starting point for settling the conceptual problems in national accounting. If, in fact, it is defined so that the services produced by television sets cross the production boundary, then the activity of producing these services would, in the interests of consistency, have to be regarded as taking place within the boundary.

In the case of consumer durables, this would give rise to all sorts of practical complications. For example, an estimate would have to be made of the value of the services that the owner of a T V set derives from it, in order to add these services both to final expenditure and to the output of an imaginary productive sector, namely the domestic television service sector – though, in order to compute only the *value added* by the private householder in

[1] The purchase of durables, such as passenger cars or washing machines, by firms does not come under the heading of consumption, of course, but is regarded as investment.

providing himself with the services of the television set, one would also have to deduct any other costs he incurred, such as repair and electricity.

For these, and other, reasons, it is generally accepted that it is simply not worth while making so many estimates for which hardly any objective basis for valuation exists, and it is conventionally accepted that consumer durables should be treated *as if they were used up when they are bought*. That is, the production frontier is defined so that it is only the set which crosses it, not the subsequent watching of the programmes as well. This means that all consumer durables are classified under the heading of 'private consumption', and not under the heading of 'investment'. However, this convention sometimes leads to difficulties of analysis, such as the analysis of consumers' behaviour as regards savings.

(iii) Purchases of dwellings

One important exception to this treatment of durables bought by private individuals concerns their purchases of new dwellings. These are excluded from private consumption altogether and are counted as part of the investment of the economy together with all other new dwellings, such as those purchased by real estate companies or by public authorities. Of course, as with any other second-hand asset, purchases of dwellings other than those built during the accounting period concerned are not part of the investment and output of the economy as a whole in that period, since for these 'old' dwellings somebody must have been reducing his capital assets in the form of dwellings by the amount that somebody else is increasing his. But *new* dwellings bought by the occupiers usually form a large part of total capital formation, and the services provided by owner-occupied dwellings are a substantial part of national product. If all new dwellings purchased by individuals were treated as consumption instead of investment and hence excluded from national capital one would obtain a grossly misleading picture of the economic wealth of the country.[1] For this and other reasons purchases of *all* new dwellings are regarded as part of investment – i.e. as adding to productive capital – irrespective of whether they are bought by

---

[1] The corresponding rents would also have to be excluded from national product.

their occupiers or not. But it is necessary to be quite clear what this implies.

First, if owner-occupied houses are part of the economy's productive capital, then an output has to be attributed to them. But since, by definition, owner-occupied dwellings are not rented out this has to be done by the process of *imputing* a rent to such dwellings. As explained on page 9 the word imputation is used in national accounts to denote an estimate of the value of a good or service when no payment is actually made for the good or service.

Secondly, this imputed transaction has to appear whichever of the three possible ways of valuing national product one adopts. That is, it must appear as part of the value added of the productive sector, as part of the incomes of the owners, and as part of expenditures on final demand. Of course, from the point of view of the owners of the dwellings, all these three aspects cancel out – the householder who obtains the value added from the renting of the dwelling to himself also pays it all out to himself in the form of incomes, but at the same time, he is paying the consumers' expenditure on the final product, rent, that gives rise to the value added. In other words no transactions at all really take place, but if national product from the expenditure point of view is to be raised by the amount of the imputed rent expenditure, then for the sake of consistency, the estimate of national product from the income and the value added points. of view have to be adjusted upwards accordingly.

It must be emphasised that the distinction adopted between owner-occupied dwellings and the other household durables mentioned earlier, such as washing machines and television sets, is essentially arbitrary. For example, the services of washing machines can also be bought in various self-service and clothes-washing shops, so that it would not be impossible to make an estimate of the imputed value of the services of the private washing machines used in the home. The most important border-line item that is included in private consumption rather than investment (so that its services are excluded from national product along with the other household durables) is, of course, privately-owned passenger cars. Again it would not be difficult to find comparable prices for the services of hired cars, if one preferred to classify privately-owned automobiles as investment and hence to include their services in national product. One could use the price of car-hire by commercial enterprises. The fact that such comparable services exist means that institutional changes in the extent, say, to which people buy their own television sets or automobiles, rather than hire them, will affect the level of national product. For example, the practice of using car-hire services instead of buying cars is apparently becoming very widespread in New York. This trend raises national product, since the incomes from such services add to it when the automobiles are hired out but not when they are privately owned and driven.[1] By contrast, a switch from owner-occupied dwellings to commercially-rented dwellings would not affect national product, since commercial rents and imputed rents as owner-occupied dwellings are both included in national product anyway.

Thus the difference between the treatment of owner-occupied dwellings and of other consumer durables is, in the last resort, based on an arbitrary distinction between those items that lie inside the production boundary and those that do not. The housing services provided by owner-occupied dwellings are defined as crossing the production boundary. The services that individuals get out of their television sets or automobiles are defined as lying outside the production boundary although if the same type of goods are hired out by a business firm the services provided by them are defined as crossing it.

4. Consumption: Public consumption

The first point to be noted about the definition of public consumption, as a category of final expenditure on national product, is that, like private consumption, it includes only *current expenditures on goods and services*. That is, it excludes (a) public investment and (b) transfer payments made by the public authorities.

As regards the former, all capital formation carried out by the government, such as the building of roads or schools or hospitals, is included under investment. As regards the latter, we have to exclude from public consumption of *goods and services –*

[1] For reasons which will be more apparent after the discussion of the concept of depreciation, however, in the long-run such a change only raises *gross* national product, not 'net' national product.

i.e. that part of public expenditure which enters final product – the many transfer payments that the government makes, such as interest on the national debt, current grants to persons or local authorities, and subsidies, as well as all capital grants, of course. The distinction between transfer payments and other payments is of great importance. Since the former are not payments for goods and services produced they do not directly divert any goods and services from other uses.

Hence, if one wanted to assess the direct burden on the economy of total public expenditures it would be misleading to lump all the transfer payments together with purchases of goods and services by the government, since it is only the latter that are directly diverting the goods and services concerned from other uses, such as exports or investment. Statements such as 'government expenditure amounts to 40% of national product' can be very misleading if transfer payments are included in the government expenditures. If transfer payments are included it is perfectly possible for government expenditures to amount to, say, 500% (or any other percentage) of national product. For example, if the government decided that old-age pensioners should receive pensions of £100,000 per annum but that the tax rates on people who did not work at all would be so high that the old-age pensioners found themselves paying out about £99,000 per annum in taxes, total public expenditures would be several times as large as total national product. Every time the government transfers purchasing power through the tax system from some people to some others, government expenditure will increase without there necessarily being any change in the government's direct claim on the output of goods and services.[1]

How the public expenditure on final product is distributed among different categories of goods and services depends, of course, on the particular social and political objectives of the given country. As far as the internationally accepted national accounting concepts and conventions are concerned, however, one important item to note is that *all* defence expenditures (except residential accommodation for the armed forces) are included as *current* expenditures, even though the items concerned may be expected to last much longer than the conven-

---

[1] Nevertheless changes in income distribution resulting from transfer payments have an *indirect* effect on the real demand for the output of the economy.

tional accounting period of one year.[1] For example, the purchase of an aircraft-carrier is part of the *current* consumption of government, along with the payments of the wages of the sailors serving on it.[2] In most Western countries, the other major items of public consumption are health and education, general administration, and expenditures on what passes for law and order.

So far, we have been discussing government expenditure from the point of view of its contribution to final demand or final output. There is, however, another aspect of the place of government in the national accounts. The government is also part of the productive sector. Although the government's role as a producer does not, strictly speaking, concern us in this chapter, where we are only enumerating the components of final demand and hence are mainly concerned with the government as a consumer, this is, perhaps, the best place to deal with it.

As has been seen, any expenditure on final output creates some value added in some producing industry or industries. For example, consumers' purchases of food will correspond to some output and value added in a whole chain of industries, notably, retail distribution (such as in the supermarkets or other food shops concerned), in the food processing industry, in the industries supplying the packaging material and the transport, and in agriculture. Government expenditure on final output therefore must also correspond to some production and value added in the productive sector of the economy. But in the case of government expenditure, one of the most important 'industries' producing the final output that the government buys is the government itself. For it is the government which 'produces' the State education, the services of law and order, the defence and the foreign policy and so on which it then proceeds to buy, as it were, on behalf of the public.

In producing these services the government is acting as part of the productive sector of the economy, and the value added that it creates in the course of this production is part of value added by industry of origin. In purchasing these services, the government is acting as part of the final demand that is being

[1] Individual countries do not follow these internationally accepted conventions for their own purposes, of course. For example, the USA includes substantial government investment under public consumption.

[2] This will include payments 'in kind' to the sailors, such as food and clothing, which must therefore be added as an 'imputed' part of the sailors' wages.

examined in this chapter. Thus, the government has a dual role of producer and consumer. On the one hand, it acts as a productive entity which produces State education, defence, and so on for which purpose it employs manpower and buys goods and services as intermediate inputs from other parts of the productive sector. On the other hand, it buys, on behalf of the public, all the output of State education, defence and so on, because it is the government which pays the wages and salaries of the civil servants, soldiers, etc., as well as paying for the files, school-books and rifles used by them. It is not the private individuals who directly pay the bills, as would be the case if these services were part of private consumption instead of public consumption, though in the end it is the individual who pays, of course, through the tax system. In order to produce the amount of education, defence, law and order, foreign policy, etc., that the community requires, the government, in its capacity as a productive enterprise within the productive sector of the economy, has to employ people, like any other productive enterprise, and also to buy intermediate goods, such as school stationery, hospital drugs, administrative files, fuel and lighting, ammunition and tanks, and so on. The only difference is that the government, unlike other productive enterprises, cannot receive a profit since the only valuation of its output of education, defence and so on, is that obtained by simply adding up the various cost items that it pays itself, namely the wages and salaries paid out to government employees and the intermediate products purchased. For, as the government is the sole purchaser as well as the producer, there is no real market in those services that could permit the price paid for them to exceed (or fall short of) the cost of the employees and the intermediate goods used to produce them. As with any other productive enterprise, the 'value added' in government is simply equal to the factor incomes it pays out, but in the case of the government this comprises only wages and salaries of government employees; there cannot be any residual profit. But looked at from the point of view of its contribution to final demand, the total expenditure of government on goods and services (to be distinguished from its transfer payments) is, of course, equal to the wages and salaries of government employees plus the intermediate goods and services that the government had to buy in

73

order to carry out its functions of educating, defending and so on.

The question might now be put 'Why adopt this double way of treating the government?' The answer to this is that it is essential for analytical purposes. If the government were shown in the accounts *only* in its capacity as a productive entity, then one would be obliged to show its output as being bought by households instead of by government. But it is clear that, apart from their opportunities to signify general approval or disapproval of the authorities at election times, it is not the individuals who decide how much is to be spent on defence or public street lighting or road repairs. Hence, since this very large category of consumption expenditures are not decided by ordinary persons in their private capacity, their inclusion with private consumption would obscure and confuse the picture of the way that the main groups of transactions in the economy are determined. Furthermore, it would not be possible for most of the services concerned to be allocated among identifiable groups of consumers. Which individuals buy the foreign policy?

Similar arguments in favour of the procedure adopted arise in connection with the receipts of governments. A large part of these receipts, which comprise mainly taxes, come from private individuals. If the government, as a consumer, were to be classified together with private individuals then much important information would be lost. In fact, the whole structure of the impact of government on the economic life of the country is of great importance. Hence, it is desirable that its accounts should be presented in the way that most facilitates the analysis of this impact.

5. Investment: Introduction

We have seen that final output is defined so that it is not, in fact, restricted to the output of goods (and services) that are 'used up' in the accounting period concerned (which is a year) but also includes output of goods and services which may be used up over the course of the years. This use of final output, which is known as 'investment', is desired as a means of adding to the economy's wealth – i.e. to its capacity to produce future incomes or satisfactions. In ordinary parlance, the notion of wealth may be used more vaguely to mean either an individual's income or his capital wealth; for example, one may speak of a 'wealthy' man as one who has a large income rather than one who is the owner of a large amount of capital. But in economics it is desirable to distinguish between *income*, on the one hand, which is a *current flow* of goods and services, and *wealth*, on the other hand, which refers to the *stock* of capital that permits or creates this flow of income. The distinction between flow concepts and stock concepts is, in fact, one of the most important distinctions in economic analysis and enters into numerous economic problems. For present purposes, the point is that 'investment' is that part of the current output of goods and services which is devoted to adding to the stock of capital and hence to raising the future potential income flow of the community.

In this respect the term 'investment' has the same meaning as in ordinary parlance, where it also means an increase in the capacity to provide an income stream in the future, whether of an individual or of a nation. Although it must not be pressed too far, the analogy between what constitutes investment for an individual and for a nation can also help in understanding the distinction that has to be made between two sub-classes of investment.

In the first place, it is possible for both an individual and a nation to experience an increase in wealth without any sacrifice of present consumption at all, namely as a result of some 'windfall', such as a legacy in the case of an individual, or the discovery of natural gas in the case of a nation. But such windfall increases in wealth are not necessarily related to – let alone equal to – the amount put aside out of current income (equals output) for purposes of adding to wealth – except in the sense that the individual may have regularly sent birthday presents to some rich aunt, or the nation may have used up resources in prospecting for natural gas. Such windfall increases in wealth must be ignored when defining that part of total current output that is devoted to investment – i.e. that part of output that is not consumed.

In this sense an individual can add to his stock of wealth in one of two ways, namely (i) by devoting some of his activity to the *direct* creation of capital goods; for example, building an extension to his house, or (ii) by consuming less than his income. This enables him *indirectly* to accumulate assets, by using his surplus income to buy, say, fixed assets, such as a house, or financial assets (such as bank deposits or bonds) that constitute a claim on other resources.

The same distinction applies to the ways that a nation can add to its wealth – again ignoring windfalls. That is, a nation can invest either by (i) devoting some of its own productive activity to the direct creation of tangible physical capital – whether in fixed assets such as machines or in stocks of finished goods or raw materials, or by (ii) buying less from other countries than it is selling to other countries – i.e. exporting more than it is importing.[1]

In either case the nation is consuming less than it is producing. The former, direct, means of adding to its capital is known as *domestic* investment, since the resulting increase in its wealth takes place inside the domestic territory of the country concerned. By contrast the latter, and indirect, means of adding to its wealth, namely an excess of exports over imports, permits the country concerned to carry out what is known as *net investment abroad*, which may take the form of an increase in its holding of financial assets (such as foreign currencies or bonds) or of ownership of foreign physical assets (gold mines or plantations or railroads, etc.), in the same way that an individual who spends less than his income can either accumulate financial claims on others or buy physical assets. Of course, exports are not always greater than imports; indeed, where exports of one country exceed its imports, the imports of some other country must exceed its exports. If a country produces less than the total resources it uses in the form of consumption and domestic investment its exports will be less than its imports. In that case it will experience a fall in its holdings of overseas assets (unless this is offset by other transactions such as aid or gifts or loans), so that its net investment overseas will be negative. This is the same as saying that it is spending more than its income and to do so it is borrowing.

Finally, *domestic* investment can be conveniently sub-divided into (a) the production of fixed assets, such as machines or power stations or trucks or factories, and (b) a change in the stock of

---

[1] There are minor qualifications to the analogy between the private individual and the whole economy, such as the fact that the former may build assets in his leisure time.

raw materials or of finished or semi-finished inventories in the productive pipeline. These two sub-categories of domestic investment are known as *domestic fixed capital formation* and *changes in stocks* respectively.

Thus the total use of resources for investment can be divided into the following sub-classes of transaction, each of which will be examined below in more detail:

(i) Domestic fixed capital formation;
(ii) Changes in stocks; and
(iii) Exports minus imports.

6. Investment: Domestic fixed capital formation

The above general discussion of the components of 'investment' will have already given some idea of the main characteristics of fixed domestic capital formation and of the ways in which it differs from other items of investment. In the first place it comprises investment at home; that is, within the domestic territory of the country concerned. Secondly, it comprises the flow of capital goods, such as machinery and factories, rather than of working capital such as stocks of raw materials or of finished goods of any kind that have been produced but not yet sold to their final buyers.

On the borderline between fixed capital formation and changes in stocks the most important item is changes in *work in progress* such as the progress made during the year on building a machine or a road. Changes in the amount of work in progress are classified as 'fixed' capital formation rather than as 'changes in stocks' if the items concerned are items of heavy construction or equipment, for which progress payments are made. For example, if progress is made during the year with the construction of a bridge, this will usually be matched by progress payments to the contractors in which case the value of the payments will be regarded as part of fixed capital formation in that year.

The main reason for distinguishing between fixed capital formation and changes in stocks is that they are, by and large, determined by different motives and considerations and will also have different impacts on the rest of the economy. In general, firms carry out fixed capital formation in the light of relatively long-term views of the prospective demands for the particular

77

products produced by the items of equipment concerned. Although a firm's expenditure on machinery for producing automobiles at any moment of time may also be influenced by short-term factors, such as the immediate funds available to the business enterprise concerned, or by the prevailing general climate of business optimism and pessimism, one of the main factors will be the firm's estimates of the future demand for automobiles and the extent to which the machine concerned is expected to make a profit *over the whole of its length of life*. These considerations are very different from those that determine changes in stocks, as will be seen from the discussion of this category of investment in the next section of this chapter.

A final aspect of fixed capital formation that should be mentioned is the treatment of *depreciation*. We have already seen that, in the long-run, the inclusion of capital goods in final product together with the goods and services produced by them would involve a form of double counting. For this reason, as well as for other related reasons, it is sometimes important to take account of 'depreciation'. Roughly speaking, depreciation is the amount by which the capital *stock* has been used up during any given period – as a result of wear and tear, obsolescence, and the normal incidence of fires and earthquakes, and so on. If, every year, we deduct from capital formation (and hence from national product) the amount by which the capital stock has been used up during the year, then over the whole length of life of any capital asset we shall have deducted from national product the whole value of the asset. In this way we shall have avoided counting in national product both the asset and the goods produced by it, and so shall have avoided double counting.

The significance of 'depreciation' can be looked at from a completely different, though logically related, point of view, namely from the point of view of the distinction between 'income' and 'capital'. If an individual employs his capital in some productive venture, he would obviously gauge how well he was doing not merely by looking at his total receipts, but by reckoning also how much he has to put aside from these total receipts, after meeting current costs such as labour and raw materials, *to keep his capital intact*. Anybody can live off capital for a while by simply 'eating it up'. To make sure that one is making an *income* out of it, as distinct from living on the capital, one must put aside from the earnings enough to 'maintain capital intact'. Now the problem of how exactly one should measure what is required to 'keep capital intact' is one of the most intricate problems in the whole of national accounting, and is a major problem in economics in general. It is made more difficult by the fact that capital theory is one of the most difficult branches of economic theory. However, we are not concerned with these deep conceptual issues in this book, and only those features of the problem that are important for our main purposes need to be mentioned here.

From what has been said above the reader will already appreciate that, for some purposes, one wants to know how much the national economy is producing *after* allowing for the gradual using up of its capital stock – i.e. after deducting an estimate of 'depreciation'. Consequently, a distinction is made between two separate concepts of capital formation (i.e. investment), namely *gross* capital formation, which simply consists of the machines and factories and so on produced in the period concerned, and *net* capital formation, which equals gross capital formation minus 'depreciation' on the whole capital stock in existence in the period concerned. According to which of these two concepts of capital formation is employed, the resulting total of national product is known as either 'gross' national product or 'net' national product. That is, when the measure of final output comprises only consumption plus *net* capital formation (i.e. net investment), the resulting measure of national product must be *net* national product – i.e. what the nation has produced *after allowing for that part of its capital stock used up to produce it*. If final product is measured as comprising consumption plus *gross* capital formation, the resulting measure of national product is *gross* national product.

It might be asked why one ever bothers to show the figure of gross capital formation instead of net capital formation. There are several reasons for this, of which the most important is that for many purposes one is interested in the total gross flow of goods and services produced by the economy, irrespective of how much of this would have to be set aside in any year in order to maintain capital intact. For in certain situations, such as in war-time, it might be thought worthwhile allowing the capital stock to run down and make up the back-log later.[1] Further-more, even if the concept of depreciation were clear in theory, estimates of it would still never represent an objective valuation of a transaction that actually takes place on the market. It is an 'imputed' transaction – a purely internal book-keeping entry by the firms. And conventions for recording depreciation are variable at the best of times; during periods when the general price level is changing they become even more subject to the arbitrary judgement of the accountants and those responsible for drawing up the accounts of a company.

As we have seen, any change in the definition of final demand implies a corresponding change in value added. In this case, when one switches from *gross* to *net* capital formation, and hence from gross to net national product, a corresponding adjustment has to be made on the value added or income side. This involves estimating *net* national income, by deducting depreciation from total value added. In practice, it has become conventional simply to use the term 'national income' to refer to *net* national income. From this it follows that we have the following relationships:

Gross national product *minus* depreciation
= net national product
Net national product = national income

Gross national product is commonly referred to as 'GNP'.

7. Investment: Changes in stocks

This item includes changes in the economy's stocks (i.e. inventories) of raw materials, or of semi-finished goods (excluding work in progress on major items of capital equipment) or of finished goods. Consequently, it differs from fixed capital formation in many ways.

First, whereas fixed capital formation comprises mainly 'multiple use' objects – such as a machine which will be used over and over again – the goods comprised in the stocks to which the changes refer will generally be single use goods, such

---

[1] The best exposition of this view is in the classic article by Milton Gilbert and George Jaszi 'National Product as an aid in Economic Problems', in *Readings in the Theory of Income Distribution*, published for the American Economic Association, Blakiston Co., Philadelphia, 1946.

as raw cotton or semi-finished steel products or children's toys that have accumulated in the shops and that, given the definition of private consumption, will be regarded as being 'used up' as soon as they are sold.

Secondly, whereas 'domestic fixed capital formation' generally refers to more or less the same sort of goods – namely the lathes, the machine tools, the jigs, the roads and factories and so on, the item 'changes in stocks' may in any one year refer to completely different goods from those to which it applies in another year. If, one year, the weather is warmer than usual, the whole of any net increase in stocks in that year may comprise an increase in inventories of fuel that would normally have been used for heating purposes, but which have, instead, piled up at the pit-head or in the dealers' stocks. In the next year, on the other hand, the expectation of a prolonged steel strike may have led to a deliberate accumulation of stocks of steel by steel users. This means that, whereas changes in fixed capital formation will affect more or less the same type of heavy industries – such as the engineering or construction industries – it is not possible to generalise so easily as to which particular industries will be affected by changes in stocks.

The third, and most important, difference between the two forms of domestic capital formation is that, whereas fixed capital formation is usually carried out by the deliberate decision of the firms concerned, changes in stocks are often the outcome of quite unintentional short-run deviations between supply and demand (which will be partly beyond the control of the firm). This feature of stock changes plays a crucial role in the analysis of the process of income determination presented in later chapters. For example, if, for some reason or another, the demand for bicycles suddenly doubles, it is unlikely that the production of them will also be able to double overnight. Consequently, the first effect of the increase in demand relative to supply will be a fall in stocks of bicycles normally held in the economy (both by retailers and wholesalers or producers) in their attempt to satisfy the sudden increase in demand. Conversely a sudden fall in demand would lead to a rise in stocks which would only be eliminated when production had adjusted itself to the lower level of demand.

For all these reasons, therefore, it is essential to distinguish

81

between these two quite distinct classes of domestic investment, both in analysing the causes of changes in the economy and in predicting their effects, whether by industry or in terms of the subsequent equilibrium and productive capacity of the economy in the short run and the long run.

The valuation of changes in stocks also gives rise to special problems. First, there are no actual sales of the items concerned; for example, a firm may simply find that its stocks of fuel oil have risen or its stocks of bicycles have fallen. This means that, like some other items that we have encountered already (e.g. depreciation) the stock change transaction is an internal book-keeping entry.[1]

Secondly, a change in the prices of the items, in the economy's total stocks, gives rise to a change in the *value* of these stocks without there necessarily having been any physical change in the quantities of goods held in these total stocks. On the income side this means, for example, that if the prices of the stocks held by a firm rose during the year, that firm would have made a capital gain, which it might well wish to include in its profits for that year. But this part of its profits will not correspond to any *output*; it is simply a capital gain caused by a price rise. Since national product and income are supposed to measure the value only of what the national economy has *produced*, and the corresponding incomes, it is necessary to deduct from the change in the value of stocks (on the expenditure side) and from profits (on the income side) that part of the change that may be attributed to this price rise or capital gain element. Basically, this adjustment, which is known in the national accounts as 'stock appreciation', equals the difference between the extent to which the value of the stocks over the accounting period has changed as a result of the physical increase in the stocks (which is what one is really interested in) and the actual change in the value of the stocks. Needless to say, this part of the national income cannot be estimated very accurately, for various reasons, one of which being the above-mentioned absence of any actual transactions in the items concerned. The firms' internal book estimates of the

---

[1] However, there is, in principle, a clearly defined concept of the physical change in stocks, which is not the case with depreciation. In the national accounts the changes in stocks are valued at cost, not at the price they are expected to fetch when finally sold.

changes in their stocks between the beginning and the end of the year do not refer to transactions that have taken place on the market, in which case there would have been an objective valuation and also two 'transactors' concerned with the transaction, namely the buyer and the seller.[1]

8. Investment: Exports less imports

In addition to what has already been said about this category of final output only two further points need to be made here. First, why is it important to distinguish between, on the one hand, an export (or import) surplus, which permits net investment overseas and, on the other hand, the two ways in which domestic investment may be carried out (the production of fixed capital or the increase in stocks)? The main reason is that, of the two ways in which the nation's wealth may be increased, the former is so much more dependent on forces outside the economy concerned. For example, suppose there is inflation in Country Y with the result that it finds that Country X's goods are relatively cheaper, so that it increases its imports from Country X. Other things being equal, this might lead to X's developing an export surplus, thereby being able to carry out net investment overseas, as a result purely of changes initiated in Country Y.

The second point concerns the manner in which one arrives at the conclusion that the difference between exports and imports must be included in the definition of final product. So far this conclusion has been deduced logically from the definition of final product. From this definition, it followed that national product necessarily included resources used for purposes of adding to wealth. As a country may add to its wealth by accumulating claims on other countries, and as it will do this by means of an export surplus, it follows that national product must include exports less imports. The same conclusion could, however, have been reached by a slightly different chain of reasoning.

For example, if national product is estimated by the expenditure method, one would – as has been seen already – include all the goods sold to, say, private consumption or domestic invest-

[1] The term 'objective' is used here to indicate that where an actual transaction does take place on the market the valuation of the good or service sold is not somebody's subjective view of what it *would* fetch or what its *true* value is, but is simply an aspect of an actual event about which, in principle, there should be no dispute.

ment. These clearly include, say, the passenger cars bought by private individuals. But some of these automobiles may have been imported from other countries. Thus, if these, and other, imports were not deducted from the total of the ways the economy, in the end, used the resources available to it – i.e. the sum of private consumption, public consumption, gross domestic capital formation, etc. – the total would exaggerate what had been produced by the nation concerned, which is what 'national product' is supposed to be measuring.

The converse applies to exports. These are clearly part of what the nation produced, and they enable the nation either to buy imports from overseas or to add to its overseas wealth, as well as giving rise to incomes for the people who produce the exports. But, by their very nature, the exports will not be included in any list of the ways that the nationals of the given country have spent their incomes, such as on consumption or domestic investment. Hence, if exports are to be included in national product as estimated by the sum of final demands, these final demands must include the exports along with the other final purchases by the nationals of the country concerned. That is, although exports are not part of the expenditure *by* the nationals of the country concerned, they are part of expenditure on national product.

In other words, national product, being what the nation produces, does not have to be equal to the expenditures *by* nationals of the given country, for some of the product of the nation may have been bought by nationals of other countries. This would be the case with exports. Conversely, the expenditure of nationals of a given country will not give rise to any national product of the same country if it is spent on the products of another country. This would be the case with imports. Thus the expenditure total to which national product is equal is not expenditure *by* nationals, but expenditure *on* national product. This will obviously be equal to expenditure by nationals *plus* expenditure on national product by foreign nationals (exports) *minus* that part of expenditure by nationals that was spent on foreign products (imports). Thus by an apparently different route we arrive at the same conclusion, namely that national product is equal to expenditure by nationals (consumption and domestic investment) plus exports minus imports.

Since national product as estimated from the sum of final expenditures on national product must, in principle if not in practice, be identically equal to national product as estimated from the total of value added by the productive sectors or from the total of incomes, it follows that the last result could have been reached also in terms of the estimation of national product from the production or income end. For example, if national product is conceived from the value added (i.e. the production) point of view, it is obvious that value added in any firm will equal the value of its sales less its inputs irrespective of to whom it sold its output. Thus value added for some firms will include, as a credit item on the sales side, sales to foreigners – i.e. exports. Since the sum of all value added must equal the sum of final output, the latter must also include these export sales. Conversely, in deducting its inputs in order to arrive at the value added for any firm, inputs purchased from abroad must be deducted as well as any other inputs. If the inputs were purchased from another firm in the same economy, of course, the deduction from the value added of the firm buying the inputs would be offset by the fact that the input concerned will be part of the output – and hence contribute to value added – of the other firm. But inputs that are purchased from abroad are deducted from the value added of the importing firm and cannot re-appear as part of the value added of some other firm in the same economy. Hence all imports have to be deducted from final demand if the sum of final outputs is to equal the sum of value added in all the productive units.

It will be obvious that similar reasoning applies to the treatment of foreign trade in the context of national product looked at from the point of view of the incomes generated. For clearly sales of exports to foreigners generate incomes to the producers, whereas purchases of imports from foreigners only generate, at least directly, income for the foreign producers of the goods and services concerned.

9. The components of final demand: Summary and symbolic representation

The various components of final demand, and hence of national product looked at from the expenditure end, may now be brought together as follows:

Total expenditure on gross national product equals:

Private consumption
Public consumption } total consumption

Gross domestic fixed capital formation
Change in stocks
Exports
less Imports } total investment

For purposes of the subsequent analysis in this book of the way that changes in the income level are induced it will be useful to adopt a symbolic short-hand for these items. We have already seen (Chapter 4, page 64) that $Y \equiv C + I$. However, C and I have since been sub-divided into various components. C has been divided into 'private consumption' and 'public consumption', which may be denoted by C_h and C_g respectively. The subscripts h and g are appropriate because private consumption is mainly the consumption of 'households' and public consumption is the consumption of government. Given these symbols we have that

$$C \equiv C_h + C_g$$

Investment has been sub-divided into three classes, the first two of which are domestic – i.e. domestic fixed capital formation and changes in stocks – and the third of which is net investment overseas. The first two may be combined together as domestic capital formation and indicated by the symbol $GDCF$, if gross, or $NDCF$, if net. The investment overseas arising from the excess of exports over imports, may be represented symbolically as $X - M$ with X representing exports and M representing imports.

Thus total investment (gross) is constituted as follows:

$$I \equiv GDCF + X - M$$

Hence we can write total gross national product as follows:

$$Y \equiv C_g + C_h + GDCF + X - M$$

10. Eight alternative concepts of total product

In addition to the distinction between gross and net national product according to whether investment is counted gross or net, a distinction has been drawn between *domestic* and *national* product, according to whether we are measuring the output produced by nationals of the country concerned (including the net return on assets they may own abroad) or whether we are measuring what is produced within the domestic territory of the country. Furthermore, a distinction has been drawn between national product at market prices and national product at factor cost, according to whether or not indirect taxes (net of subsidies) have been included. This means that there are eight possible combinations of product concepts, as follows:

$$\text{Gross domestic product} \begin{cases} \text{at market prices} \\ \text{at factor cost} \end{cases}$$

$$\text{Gross national product} \begin{cases} \text{at market prices} \\ \text{at factor cost} \end{cases}$$

$$\text{Net domestic product} \begin{cases} \text{at market prices} \\ \text{at factor cost} \end{cases}$$

$$\text{Net national product} \begin{cases} \text{at market prices} \\ \text{at factor cost} \end{cases}$$

The way that these concepts are connected to each other can be seen schematically in the diagram overleaf.[1]

Some of the variants of national product are hardly ever used, and of those that are more frequently met there are, of course, various ways of ordering them or linking them. One of these is as follows:

(i) Gross domestic product at market prices
 plus net property income from abroad
equals
(ii) Gross national product at market prices
 less indirect taxes (net of subsidies)
equals
(iii) Gross national product at factor cost
 less depreciation
equals
(iv) Net national product at factor cost, which is known as *national income*.

In the next chapter we shall examine the way the major transactions fit together in an interlocking set of accounts. The first of these accounts will be seen to be merely one way of writing out the relationships between the different concepts of national product that are enumerated above.

[1] I am indebted to one of my first-year students at Balliol, Mr A.G. Foster-Carter, for this diagram and for helpful suggestions for Figure 5.3.

Figure 4.1
Relationships between eight national product concepts

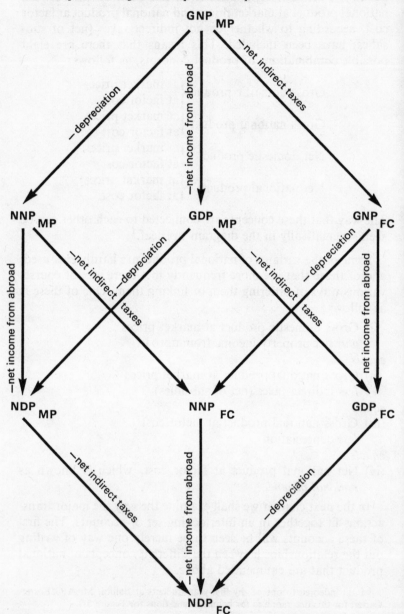

EXERCISES 4

1   Initially the following, and only the following, transactions take place in the economy:

    A sells to B for £50;

    B sells to C for £80;

    C sells to private consumption for £120.

(i) What is GNP by industry of origin?

(ii) What is GNP by industry of origin if, now, A imports for £20?

(iii) What is GNP by industry of origin if A imports for £10, B imports for £10?

(iv) What is GNP by industry of origin, and by category of final demand if A imports for £20 and C sells, in addition to his sales to private consumption indicated above, £30 to exports?

2   Mr A, who is a dealer in watches, goes on holiday abroad during the course of which he spends £200 on hotel expenses, etc., but he also buys 100 new watches for £50 each. He pays 20% import duty on them and re-sells them for £80 each.

(i) What is the direct effect of *all* these transactions on total GNP at market prices?

(ii) What would have been the effect if, instead of selling all the watches, he was left with 20 of them in stock at the end of the accounting period?

3   In the economies described below what is GNP (a) by category of final demand at market prices and (b) by industry of origin at factor cost?

example:

    A sells to B for £50 and to C for £30;

    B sells to private consumption for £40 and to export for £80;

    C sells to capital formation for £50.

answer:

(a) GNP by category of final demand equals:

Private consumption	£40
Capital formation	£50
Exports	£80
Total	£170

(b) GNP by industry of origin equals:
Value added in Industry A = £50 + £30 = £80
Value added in Industry B = £120 − £50 = £70
Value added in Industry C = £50 − £30 = £20

Total   = £170

(i) A sells to B for £20;
B sells to private consumption for £40;
C buys imports for £30 and sells to private consumption for £60.

(ii) A sells to private consumption for £60;
B sells to C for £30 and to exports for £50;
C, who also imports for £30, sells to capital formation for £70.

(iii) A imports for £50 and sells to exports for £20 and to B for £40;
B sells to private consumption for £60;
C sells to D for £40 and to capital formation for £10;
D sells to exports for £50 and to public consumption for £20.

(iv) Same as exercise (ii) but an indirect tax of 20% is imposed on A's sales; an indirect tax of 50% on B's sales to C, and a customs duty of $33\frac{1}{3}\%$ is imposed on imports. All these taxes and duties are 'passed on' in price increases on the goods concerned.

(v) Same as exercise (i) but a subsidy of $33\frac{1}{3}\%$ is granted on C's sales to private consumption.

(vi) In exercise (iii) above an indirect tax of 50% is imposed on C's sales to D, but D is unable to raise his export prices.
(a) What would GNP at market prices by category of final demand have to be if, nevertheless, D were to keep his value added unchanged by passing on the price increase?
(b) How would this differ from the pattern of GNP by category of final demand if he had been able to keep his value added constant by raising export prices as much (in per cent terms) as domestic prices? (c) What would happen if he could not raise any prices at all? In each case what is total GNP at factor cost?

4   Gross national product at market prices is £200; net property

income from abroad is £20, and indirect taxes are £20 and subsidies are £10. What is gross domestic product (a) at market prices and (b) at factor cost?

5 Gross national product at market prices is £120; the capital stock of the economy is worth £200 and it depreciates at a rate of 10% per annum. Indirect taxes amount to £30; subsidies amount to £15. What is 'national income'?

6 Show the steps linking net national product at market prices with gross national product at factor cost.

7 In how many ways can one link gross domestic product at market prices with gross national product at factor cost, without unnecessary steps or passing through the same stage more than once?

Chapter 5

The system of accounts

1. Nature of double-entry accounting

As has been said at the outset of this book, national accounting is simply a systematic way of classifying the multitude of economic activities that take place in the economy in different groups or classes that are regarded as being important for understanding how the economy works. We have then distinguished between classes of activities that contribute to national product and those that do not, and we have also considered, in more detail, the different classes of activities that do enter into national product. In this chapter we show how these various classes of activities – or the transactions which represent them – are linked together in an interlocking system of accounts.

To do this we must first consider what is meant by an account, or, more particularly, what we will mean here by a 'double-entry system of accounts'. The first point to note is that any transaction requires two 'transactors', the one who pays and the one who receives (though as has been seen in some cases, for example imputed rents on owner-occupied dwellings, the two 'transactors' may really be one and the same person). Each transactor can be allocated an account, in which his receipts are recorded on the credit side and his payments on the debit side. But since a receipt by one transactor is a payment by another, a credit item for one must be a debit item for another. Thus any transaction must appear in the accounts of both transactors – on the debit side of one's account and on the credit side of the other's. A double-entry accounting system is simply one in which both aspects of each transaction appear, once as a receipt in one account and again as a payment in another account.

More precisely, an account will show *debits* on one side and *credits* on the other, rather than *payments* and *receipts*. The reason for this apparently pedantic nuance of terminology is that, strictly speaking, it is not actual receipts and payments that should be recorded but the *liability* to pay and the *right* to receive. In technical terms, the national accounts are, in principle, valued in terms of 'receivables' and 'payables'. For example, if A sells a good to B, then, from the national accounts point of view, this transaction took place *at the moment of the change in ownership*. At that moment B incurs a liability to pay A, and A has acquired a credit for the amount concerned, irrespective of the date on which it has to be paid. Since the terms 'credits' and 'debits' do not imply that the money flows have actually taken place, they are used in national accounting in preference to the terms 'payments' and 'receipts'.

A further feature of the double-entry accounting system is that all the accounts are made to balance, in the following manner. If, say, an account has an excess of credits over debits, then it has 'saved' in the same way that an individual who receives more than he spends will have saved. By adding the savings of this account to the debit side, the two sides of the account will then balance, since the savings are simply the excess of the credits over the other debits. Similarly, if an account has an excess of debits over credits, an item representing borrowing could be added to the credit side of the account in order to preserve equality of the two sides, or 'savings' could be kept on the debit side, but they would have a negative value – i.e. they would be deducted from the other debit items in order to reach the total of debits.

Given this convention of preserving equality between the two sides of every account, a second way of representing an account would be in the form of an equation, using symbols to indicate the various items appearing on both sides of the account. A third way of representing an account is in the form of a box, like those shown in Figure 2.2 (page 22) with arrows entering the box to indicate credits and arrows leaving the box to indicate debits. The sum of the values of the arrows entering the box must then be made equal to the sum of the arrows leaving it, if necessary by means of the addition of an arrow representing the savings or borrowing (equals negative savings) of that account.

There are many classes of accounts that can be set up for any transactor. Three important classes of accounts are 'production' (or 'operating') accounts which show only the payments and receipts associated with that transactor's productive activities; 'appropriation' accounts which show all current receipts and payments including those – such as transfer payments – which may not arise out of productive activities; and 'capital' accounts which show transactions of a capital nature that affect the transactor's balance sheet of assets and liabilities. Accounts may be consolidated in various ways. For example, any sector of the economy, such as the productive sector or the household sector, will embrace a vast number of transactors, and the accounts of them all may be combined into one account for the whole sector. Transactions between members of the same sector would thus appear on both sides of such an account. If all such items are deleted the resulting 'consolidated' account shows only that sector's transactions with other sectors. Another form of 'consolidation' is the combination of different kinds of account for any transactor or sector.

In short, the classification of the economy into different sectors and the classification of accounts into different kinds of account are two different types of classification. In what follows we shall show only one account for each of the sectors of the economy that we identify. But, as shall be shown below, we do not necessarily use exactly the same kind of account for each sector. For the productive sector we use what is basically a production (or 'operating') account; for the household sector we use an appropriation account, the same as is used for another sector that is introduced, namely the government sector. A further sector that is introduced is the 'rest of the world' sector, for which we shall use an all-embracing consolidated account showing capital as well as current transactions. Finally an account is introduced that corresponds to the economy as a whole and not to any one sector; this is the capital account for the whole economy. These five accounts provide the nucleus of an interlocking social accounting framework that is needed in order to show, in an analytically convenient form, the way that the different major categories of final output enter into the transactions of the rest of the economy.

2. The production account[1]

(i) The production account as a double-entry account

The production account is the account that shows the value of what the productive sector finally produces and what are the claims on this product. As we have seen, the value of what the nation produces, at market prices, can be obtained by adding the following items:

Private consumption;

Public consumption;

Gross domestic capital formation; and

Exports *less* imports.

The sum of these items is equal to gross national product – or GNP – at market prices.

GNP at market prices has also been seen to be related to national income in the following manner:

GNP at market prices

less depreciation

less net indirect taxes

equals national income (or net national product at factor cost).

The production account is simply a way of writing out these two aspects of the composition of GNP at market prices. On the credit side of the account are listed, naturally, what the economy finally produced – the goods and services absorbed by private consumption, etc. And on the debit side are listed the claims on the product in the form of the depreciation required to maintain capital intact and the net indirect taxes that have to be deducted before arriving at the figure of the income that can be allocated to the primary factors of production – i.e. national income. This national income can then be divided up into wages, distributed and undistributed profits, and direct taxes paid by the productive sector (e.g. corporate taxes).[2] Thus, written out in these terms, the production account will appear as follows:

---

[1] Some readers may recognise this account as the 'consolidation' of what are known as the 'national product and expenditure' and 'national income' accounts.

[2] The reader may well ask why direct taxes paid by firms are shown separately but not the direct taxes paid by individuals on, say, the wages and salary incomes distributed to them. Furthermore in many countries direct taxes on wages and salaries are deducted at source and paid direct by the employers to the government. These tax payments could be shown as being paid by the firms instead of by the household sector after they have received, theoretically, the whole of their wages and salaries. Which procedure one adopts for profits taxes paid

95

Production account

Debit		Credit	
1	National income	1	Private consumption
	Wages	2	Public consumption
	Distributed profits	3	Gross domestic capital formation
	Undistributed profits	4	Exports
	Direct taxes paid by firms	5	(*minus*) Imports
2	Depreciation		
3	Net indirect taxes		
Gross national product at market prices		Expenditure on gross national product at market prices	

Thus another way of looking at the value of expenditure on gross national product is that it is simply the sum of the items on the credit side of an account set up for the productive sector. And the debit side of this account, as set out above, may be recognised as being simply a way of linking two of the eight possible variants of the national product concept that have been identified, namely (i) net national product at factor cost (equals national income) and (ii) gross national product at market prices.

The production account also, perhaps, helps to illustrate the manner in which some items can be quite reasonably moved from one side of the account to the other *provided their algebraic sign is changed* – i.e. provided that, if they appear as positive items on one side of the account, they have to be entered as negative items on the other in order to preserve the balance of the account. In the above production account this applies to the

---

direct by firms should depend, in principle, on whether (i) one regards the 'enterprise' as receiving the factor income 'profit' and paying some taxes on this before making a *transfer payment* of profits to the shareholders, or whether (ii) one regards the enterprise as merely paying the taxes on behalf of the shareholders, as in the case of the payments by firms of the taxes on wages and salaries due by their employees. The shareholders would then be recipients of real factor incomes, rather than of transfer payments. The procedure followed here conforms to the former view. The latter view would require the direct taxes paid by firms to appear only as a payment by the household sector to the government, and in the production account profits would be shown before payment of tax as if the whole of profits before tax were distributed to the household sector. But while the treatment adopted here (as in internationally accepted conventions) is consistent with the view that it is the enterprise that receives the factor income 'profit', it is adopted here chiefly because it represents more realistically the actual route that these tax payments take (direct from firms to the government, and not passing through the household sector), irrespective of the conceptual issue involved.

item imports, which has been entered as a negative item – i.e. as a deduction – on the credit side. It could equally well have been shown as a positive item – i.e. an addition – on the debit side of this account. In this case the account could have been read as saying, in effect, that, on the one hand, the productive sector produces a series of positive final outputs – private consumption, and so on down to exports – and on the other hand has to make payments such as wages, profits, indirect taxes and so on, *and* imports. The two sides of the account would still have balanced, of course, but the totals would now be greater than gross national product at market prices. As has been shown in the last chapter, only if the imports are subtracted from the sum of all the other sales to final demand do we obtain a total equal to gross national product. Hence, since it is convenient to have an account which does add up to gross national product, it is convenient to show imports as a deduction from the credit side of the above account rather than as a positive item on – i.e. an addition to – the debit side.

(ii) The production account as an equation

If symbols are used to represent the various items on the two sides of the account an 'equation' can be obtained, but before doing so it is convenient to re-group some of the items on the debit side. In particular, it is convenient to combine the undistributed profits part of national income together with the depreciation item to arrive at a single item called 'savings by firms', in the manner shown below.[1]

Debit items		Credit items	
Items	*Symbols*	*Items*	*Symbols*
Wages and distributed		Private consumption	C_h
profits	Y_h	Public consumption	C_g
Direct taxes paid by		Gross domestic capital	
firms	T_f	formation	GDCF
Depreciation and un-		Exports	X
distributed profits		(*less*) Imports	$-M$
(equals savings by			
firms)	S_f		
Net indirect taxes (i.e.			
indirect taxes less			
subsidies)	T_i		
Total = Gross national		Total = Expenditure on	
product at market		gross national product	
prices	GNP(MP)	at market prices	GNP(MP)

[1] More technically, savings by firms are generally known as 'corporate savings'.

Using the symbols indicated, the above account can be written out simply as an equation, namely:

$$Y_h + T_f + S_f + T_i = C_h + C_g + GDCF + X - M$$

(iii) The production account as a flow diagram

Finally, the type of flow diagram used in Figure 2.2 above can now be expanded to show some more details of the entries into, and out of, the box representing the productive sector of the economy.

Figure 5.1

Flow diagram for the production account

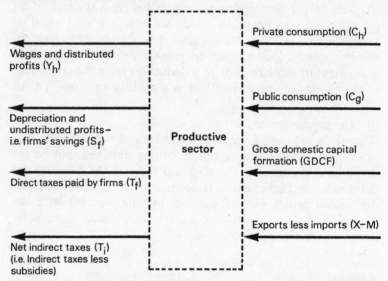

As before, credit items are shown by arrows entering the box, and debit items by arrows leaving it.

It will be seen that one single arrow has been used for exports and imports, instead of one arrow entering the box to represent the positive addition of exports and one arrow leaving the box to represent the deduction that has to be made for imports in order to arrive at GNP. This is because, by netting out the imports against the exports and representing *net* exports as a single arrow entering the box, GNP can always be seen as the total of the value of all the arrows entering the box, in the same way that, by treating imports as a negative item on the credit side of the production account, GNP is simply the sum of all the credit items in this account.

3. The counterpart entries to the items in the production account

The diagrammatic method of presenting the account emphasises clearly the need to show where the counterpart entries for all the items can be found, since there is clearly a problem of where the different arrows go to or come from. Each of the four arrows shown entering the production account must originate in an account in which the counterpart entry is found. The correspondence is as follows:

Credit item in production account	Account to which item shown is debited
1 Private consumption	Household account
2 Public consumption	Government account
3 Gross domestic capital formation	Capital account
4 Exports *less* imports	Rest of world account

The above relationships between the four main categories of credit item distinguished in the production account and their counterparts as debit items in other accounts may be represented diagrammatically in the following incomplete 'flow' diagram. In this diagram, as in the preceding ones, the arrows show the direction of the 'payments' (not the real goods and services to which they correspond). Thus the entry of an arrow into a box in such a diagram indicates that the account to which that box refers is to be credited with the transaction concerned, whereas the transaction is a debit item in the account from which the arrow has originated.[1]

The double-entry accounting principle also requires the existence of counterpart credit items for the various items shown on the debit side of the production account. The accounts that will be credited with most of these items are, in general, fairly obvious. For example, it is clear that it will be the government that 'receives' the net indirect taxes paid by the firms in the productive sector, so that this item, which is a debit item in the production account, will appear as a credit item in the government account. It will be equally obvious that the wages paid by firms, and therefore appearing on the debit side of the produc-

---

[1] As has been pointed out in Chapter 2, the real goods and services (including work) corresponding to these payments will flow in the opposite direction.

Figure 5.2

Flow diagram showing link between production account and other accounts for the four major categories of final expenditure

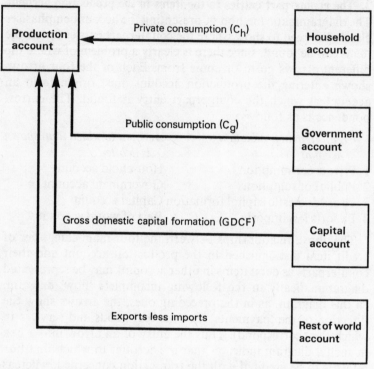

tion account, will be received by the account of the household sector. But for some of the payments by the productive sector the destination will not be quite so obvious and the full flow diagram can only be built up after some other accounts are discussed. In particular, the debit item indicated as the savings of firms (S_f) finds its counterpart in the capital account, an account that raises special problems.

4. The capital account

(i) The equality of savings and investment: A digression
One of the points made by Lord Keynes, in his analysis of the process of income determination, which led to great controversy for a time, was that, on certain reasonable definitions, *actual*

savings in an economy must always be identically equal to *actual* investment. The word 'actual' in this proposition is extremely important. The proposition is not that the total of the investment – such as construction of factories, installation of machines, etc. – that all members of the economy who carry out such activities would have *liked* to have made is always equal to the total of the savings that all those members of the economy who save would have *liked* to have made. The proposition that *actual* savings is necessarily equal to *actual* investment is not the same as the proposition that *desired*, or *planned*, saving is necessarily equal to *desired*, or *planned*, investment. Indeed, as is shown in Chapter 8 below, the disparity between desired saving and desired investment plays an important part in explaining fluctuations in the level of income. But in this chapter, where we are still only concerned with accounting relationships, it is the equality – in fact, the identity – of *actual* savings and investment that concerns us.

This necessary identity of actual savings and investment is, in fact, derived logically from a certain set of definitions. We have seen at the outset of Chapter 4 that all the output of the economy can be defined as falling into one or other of two exhaustive classes, namely consumption and investment. Thus we can write the verbal (i.e. non-mathematical) equation:

Output has been defined as (i.e. is identically equal to)
consumption plus investment

We may also proceed to define the ways that the incomes generated in the economy are disposed of as falling into two categories, namely, consumption and savings. Of course, many other classifications are possible, such as a classification into food, drink, tobacco, household durables, purchase of government bonds and all other forms of saving. But again, all that we are doing here is to group together all these ways that income may be used into only two classes which we define as consumption or saving. Thus we can write another verbal equation, namely:

Income has been defined as (i.e. is identically equal to)
consumption plus savings

But it has been seen in Chapter 2 that output and income in the economy are identically equal, and that they are, in fact, two alternative methods of measuring what is produced in the economy. Hence, if output is defined as being composed of consumption plus investment (first equation), and income is defined as being disposed of as consumption plus savings (second equation), then since output equals income it follows that consumption plus investment equals consumption plus savings. From this it is obvious that savings must be equal to investment.

The argument may, perhaps, be clearer in terms of symbols. As before, let Y, C and I represent output (or income), consumption and investment respectively, and let S represent savings. Then using these symbols to replace the words, the first definition can be written as:

$$Y \equiv C + I \text{ (as in Chapter 4, page 64)}$$

and the second definition can be written as:

$$Y \equiv C + S$$

from which is obvious that

$$C + I \equiv C + S$$

from which it is, in turn, obvious that

$$I \equiv S$$

To go back to words, if (a) income has been defined as equal to output and (b) output has been defined as comprising investment and consumption, and (c) income has been defined as having been disposed of in the form of savings or consumption, then implicitly, investment has been defined as equal to savings. An alternative way of putting the whole argument in one sentence is as follows. Since output is equal to income, and since the part of output that is composed of consumption must be equal to that part of incomes that is spent on consumption, the rest of output, which we have defined as investment, must be equal to the rest of incomes, which has been defined as savings.

No difference is made to the above conclusion if the definitions had allowed for different sub-classes of investment or savings; it would still be true that *all output that was non-consumption must be equal to that part of income that was not spent on consumption.* For example, if output were to be defined as being equal to consumption plus two kinds of investments, I_1 and I_2, and if income was defined as being used in the form of consumption or saved in three different forms of savings, S_1, S_2 and S_3, and if these two definitions were written out as:

$$Y = C + I_1 + I_2$$

(output equals consumption plus investment types 1 and 2)
and
$$Y = C + S_1 + S_2 + S_3$$

(incomes are disposed of as consumption or as savings 1, 2 or 3), then, again, since income is identically equal to output, it follows that $I_1 + I_2 = S_1 + S_2 + S_3$; that is, output of non-consumption goods (namely investment as defined here) is equal to that part of income that is not spent on consumption (that is, savings as defined here).

For many purposes total investment and total savings are, in fact, split up into sub-items. As has already been seen, it is useful to divide total investment into at least two categories, namely gross domestic investment (fixed plus change in stocks) and net investment overseas, which have been denoted by the symbols $GDFC$ and $(X - M)$ respectively. On the savings side, it is usual to distinguish between (i) household savings, (ii) government savings, and (iii) firms' savings – i.e. the savings of corporations in the productive sector. These three categories of savings may be indicated by the symbols S_h, S_g and S_f respectively.

Thus the last equation can be re-written as
$$GDCF + (X - M) = S_h + S_g + S_f$$

(ii) The accounting representation of S = I

We have seen that any account can be expressed in the form of an equation, and vice versa. The last equation is in fact the one that represents the capital account of an economy. This account brings together in a convenient manner the two aspects of the way that an economy adds to its wealth, for it shows, on one side, the assets that it acquired – namely, gross domestic capital formation or net investment abroad – and, on the other side, the sources of savings to match this investment, namely savings by households, firms and government. These are the various items represented symbolically in the last equation, and in an accounting presentation they would appear as follows:

Capital account

Debits	Credits
Gross domestic capital formation ($GDCF$)	Savings by households (S_h)
Net investment overseas ($X - M$)	Savings by government S_g)
	Savings by firms (S_f)
Total investment	Total savings

Two of the items listed above have already been encountered in the production account. Gross domestic capital formation has appeared as a credit item in the production account, savings by firms have appeared as a debit item in the production account, but was shown there in the form of their two major components, namely as 'undistributed profits' and 'depreciation'. To identify the counterpart entries for the remaining items in the capital account, namely savings by households, government and net investment overseas, three other accounts need to be examined.

5. The household account

The household sector has already been briefly introduced in Chapter 2 as the sector that groups individuals in their private capacities as recipients of income and as purchasers of ordinary individual goods and services, payers of personal income taxes and as private savers. The household account used here is a consolidated appropriation account for this household sector, showing all its current receipts and payments. It will be obvious that the wages and other factor incomes paid by the productive sector to the household sector should appear as a credit item on such an account. It should be equally obvious that the household sector's purchases of consumer goods and services from the productive sector, together with its payments of taxes, must appear as a debit item in the account of the household sector. As usual, an excess of credits over debits would be represented by adding an item for household savings to the debit items. But before striking the balance between its credits and debits for purposes of arriving at its savings, it is necessary to allow for an important source of household income on the credit side in addition to the wages and factor incomes paid out from the production sector. This is, of course, the incomes received by households in the form of transfer payments from the government, such as old-age pensions, grants to students, sickness or unemployment benefits, and the like. Households may also receive transfer payments from abroad, such as emigrants' remittances back home. This is not very important in Britain or the USA and we will ignore it here, though it will be a major item in some countries such as Ireland, Greece or Botswana.

Hence a basic household account would appear as follows:

Household account

Debits	Credits
Private consumption (C_h)	Wages and distributed profits (Y_h)
Direct taxes on households (T_h)	Transfer payments from government
Savings by households (S_h)	(TP_g)
Expenditure and savings of households	Income of households

Again, the origin or destination of some of the items listed above will have already been covered when the transactions concerned were met for the first time. For example, the private consumption and the savings of households, which appear, of course, as debit items above, have already been encountered in their other capacities, namely as credit items in the production and capital accounts respectively. The household income from wages and distributed profits on the credit side of the above account has also appeared already as a debit item on the production account. The origins or destinations of the remaining payments from government are fairly obvious; they are both linked to the government account, which will be examined next.

6. The government account

Like the account for the household sector this is a consolidated appropriation account showing all the current receipts and payments at the sector concerned which, in this case, is the government sector. All the transactions that need to be shown on the government account have, in fact, already been met. On the credit side it receives:

(i) direct taxes paid by firms, such as corporation taxes or taxes on undistributed profits;

(ii) net indirect taxes, many of which will be collected by firms on the goods that they sell (in the same way that the shop collects the sales (or 'excise') tax on a packet of cigarettes) but which they have to hand over to the government;[1] and

(iii) direct taxes paid by households, notably personal income taxes.

The first two of these items have been met already in the

---

[1] Some indirect taxes, such as customs duties, are collected by the government *before* being charged to consumers by the firms that paid the duties.

105

account of the productive sector and the third item has been met in the household account.

On the debit side, the government account will record:

(i) its expenditure on public consumption, which has appeared on the credit side of the production account;

(ii) its transfer payments, such as old-age pensions, which have appeared on the credit side of the household account; and

(iii) the balancing item between its credits and expenditures, namely the savings of government, which have appeared on the credit side of the capital account. It should be noted that government savings are not necessarily positive. The government may run a deficit on its current account in which case its savings will be negative. In that case these savings will appear as a subtraction from, rather than as an addition to, the other items on the credit side of the capital account.

All these items would be presented in an accounting form as follows:

The government account

Debits	Credits
Public consumption (C_g)	Net indirect taxes (T_i)
Transfer payments (TP_g)	Direct taxes by firms (T_f)
Savings by government (S_g)	Direct taxes by households (T_h)
Total current expenditure and savings of government	Total current revenue of government

7. The rest of the world account

The last account in the simplified system of accounts shown here is often rather a confusing one. This is for two reasons. First, it is not the account of a sector – such as 'the foreign trade sector' – of the same economy as that for which all the other accounts have been drawn up. The household account of an economy refers to persons in that economy, and the government account of an economy refers to the government of that economy. But in any economy's system of accounts, the rest of the world account refers to all the other economies – i.e. it is the account *of the rest of the world* taken together. That is, a set of accounts for the United States, say, would require, for purposes of completion, an account showing its transactions with Japan, Germany and so on. In the interest of consistency, these would have to be drawn up from the point of view of these other countries. For example, an account showing United States' trade with Japan would have to show Japanese imports from USA as a debit item, since they have already been shown as exports on the credit side of the production account of the USA. A rest of the world account, therefore, is simply a consolidated account for all the countries with which the given country trades.

Hence the exports of the given country, which are a credit item in the accounts of the given country, appear as a debit item in the rest of the world account in the same way that private and public consumption are shown as debit items in the household and government accounts respectively. For all final users' accounts are treated, in this presentation, as 'buying' from the production account of the economy concerned. Similarly, if the imports had been shown as a debit item on the production account of the given economy they would have to appear as a credit item on the account of the rest of the world. But instead of being shown as a debit item in the production account of the given economy, they have been shown as a deduction from exports on the credit side of this account. Hence, for consistency and symmetry, they have to be netted out against exports on the debit side of the rest of the world account.

The second reason why the rest of the world account may appear confusing is that, ignoring minor sub-categories of transaction, it has basically the same entry on both sides, though it is a different aspect of the amount shown which is emphasised on each side.[1] It has been seen that an excess of exports over imports is one way by which the given country may add to its stock of wealth, namely by carrying out net investment overseas. Conversely, it is by borrowing from the given country in some form or other (whether long-term loans or simply being allowed to run down its holdings of the given country's currency) that the rest of the world is able to buy more from the given country than it sells (i.e. to run an import surplus). Hence, if the rest of the world's account shows, on the debit side, an excess of the

[1] The minor items ignored here include, notably, current transfers, both between persons and governments (or inter-governmental organisations) which enter the balance of payments but which do not necessarily enter into the production account of the economy and hence do not enter national product. We have also followed the procedure here of including net property income from abroad in the net excess of exports over imports of goods and services.

given country's exports over its imports, indicating that the rest of the world has a deficit on foreign trade, it must also show, on the credit side, the borrowing from the given country that corresponds to its deficit. Thus the rest of the world will show, on the credit side of the account, the net investment abroad by the given country. This, as has been seen already, appears on the debit side of the given country's capital account. The $X - M$ on the debit side of this account refers to the actual trade taking place and is hence the counterpart entry to the $X - M$ on the credit side of the production account. The $X - M$ on the credit side of the rest of the world account refers to the corresponding change in assets or liabilities and is hence the counterpart of the debit item on the capital account.

Rest of world account

Debits	Credits
Exports *less* imports $(X - M)$	Net investment abroad $(X - M)$

8. The complete flow diagram

This completes the identification of the origin and destination of all the flows that are of interest here, so that a complete flow diagram for these transactions can now be shown, as opposite. In terms of equations the whole set of transactions shown above can be expressed as follows, with much less use of space:

Production account: $\quad Y_h + T_f + T_i + S_f = C_h + C_g + GDCF + X - M$

Capital account: $\quad GDCF + (X - M) = S_h + S_g + S_f$

Household account: $\quad C_h + S_h + T_h = Y_h + TP_g$

Government account: $\quad C_g + TP_g + S_g = T_i + T_f + T_h$

Rest of world account: $\quad X - M = (X - M)$

EXERCISES 5

1 An economy has the following set of accounts. Fill in the missing items (marked X) – both the names of the items and the figures, as appropriate – and draw the corresponding flow diagram.

Figure 5.3

Complete flow diagram of accounting framework

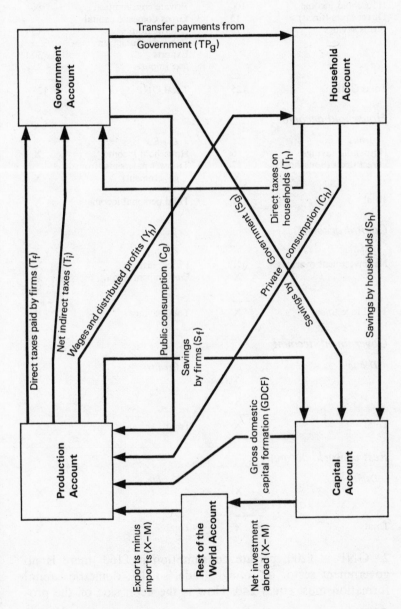

109

Production account

Debits		Credits	
Household income	100	Private consumption	80
Direct taxes (firms)	15	Gross domestic capital	
Firms savings	10	formation	15
		Public consumption	25
		Exports	30
		less Imports	−25
Total GNP	125	Total GNP	125

Household account

Debits		Credits	
Household savings	6	Household income	X
Direct taxes (households)	17	Transfer payments (from	
	X	government)	X
Total	X	Total personal income	X

Capital account

Debits		Credits	
Net investment overseas	X	Firms' savings	X
	X	Government savings	X
			X
Total investment	X	Total savings	X

Government account

Debits		Credits	
	X		X
	X		X
	X		
Total	X	Total	X

Rest of world account

Debits		Credits	
	X		X
	X		
Total	X	Total	X

2 GNP is £200, private consumption is £160, there is no government sector or foreign trade, so that domestic capital formation must equal £40. How is the debit side of the pro-

duction account distributed between firms' savings and household income if

  (i) households and firms' share equally the total savings of the economy;

 (ii) households save three times as much as firms;

(iii) households spend 80% of their income?

3   GNP is £200, private consumption is £160, public consumption is £10, there is no foreign trade or household savings, and the government's consumption is matched by its net tax receipts from households.

(a) What is the households' income?

(b) What items (if any) appear on the credit side of the capital account?

(c) If the households' consumption, at £160, absorbed the whole of their incomes (so that they paid no taxes or saved), and if the government still covered all its consumption by tax receipts, where could these taxes come from, and what would be the composition of the debit side of the production account?

In the following five questions, in which no government sector is involved, the symbols used will be:

   I = Total investment,

   C_h = Private consumption,

   S_h = Households' savings,

   S_f = Firms' savings,

   Y_h = Households' income (wages and profit).

example: GNP = 100; Y_h = 90; S_h = 10. What is I?

answer: either (a) S_f = GNP − Y_h = 100 − 90 = 10

                so total savings = $S_f + S_h$ = 10 + 10 = 20

                so I = 20

      or (b) C_h = $Y_h − S_h$ = 90 − 10 = 80

                so I equals GNP − C_h = 100 − 80 = 20.

4   I = 15; S_h = 10; Y_h = 85. What are GNP and private consumption (C_h)?

5   C_h = 85; S_h = 5; S_f = 10. What are I and GNP?

6   GNP = 100; S_f = 20; S_h = 25% of Y_h. What is I?

7 $S_f = 20\%$ of GNP; $S_h = 10\%$ of Y_h; $C_h = 90$. What are GNP and I?

8 $S_h = 20\%$ of Y_h; $I = 30$; $S_f = S_h$. What is GNP?

The following additional symbols will be used:
C_g = Public consumption,
T_h = Household taxes,
T_f = Firms' taxes,
S_g = Government surplus (or deficit if negative).

9 $S_h = 10$; $T_h = 15$; $C_h = 85$; firms make no savings or tax payments; the governments' current surplus = 5. What are GNP and public consumption?

10 Firms make no savings or tax payments; $C_g = 25$. After spending on private consumption, households distribute their income as follows:
$S_h = 5$; $T_h = 35$. What is I?

11 GNP = 100; $C_h = 60$; $S_f = 0$; $T_f = 15$; $T_h = 10$; $S_g = 5$. What are I and C_g?

12 $T_f = 10$; $T_h = 5$; $C_g = 20$; $S_h = 10$; $Y_h = 80$; $S_f = 15$. What is I?

Chapter 6

The system of accounts and economic theory

1. Matrix presentation of accounting system

So far three alternative methods of presenting the accounts have been considered, namely (i) the conventional accounting presentation with debits on one side and credits on the other; (ii) the symbolic presentation in the form of equations; and (iii) the flow diagram. The last presentation is the most economical in a sense, in that one arrow does the job of representing both a credit and a debit at the same time, as well as indicating both of the accounts involved in any transaction – i.e. who pays to whom.

There is yet another method of presentation which also fulfils this function. This is the presentation of the transactions between the different accounts or sectors in the form of a 'matrix'. A 'matrix', for present purposes, is simply the presentation of transactions in a set of rows and columns, with all the sales or credits of any transactor in its rows and the debits in its columns. Since a credit by one transactor is a debit for another, any transaction will appear in one transactor's row and in another transactor's column. For example, the set of transactions set out in the flow diagram or in the set of five equations at the end of the last chapter can be shown in a very simple matrix (p. 90).

In the following matrix all the arrows contained in the flow diagram at the end of the last chapter are presented with a relatively economical and less confusing use of space. All the credits of the production account, which are represented by arrows flowing out of the production account in the flow diagram presentation, are shown here as entries in the *row* of the production account. As there is both a row and a column for each account, every credit of the production account in its row can be placed in a corresponding column. For example, the credit to the pro-

Figure 6.1

Matrix presentation of accounting system (a) In symbols

Debits of ▶ Credits of ▼	Production account	Household account	Capital account	Government account	Rest of world account
Production account		C_h	GDCF	C_g	X–M
Household account	Y_h			TP_g	
Capital account	S_f	S_h		S_g	
Government account	T_i T_f	T_h			
Rest of world account			X–M		

(b) In numbers

Debits of ▶ Credits of ▼	Production account	Household account	Capital account	Government account	Rest of world account	Total
Production account		90	40	35	85	245
Household account	115			5		120
Capital account	40	10		25		75
Government account	45	20				65
Rest of world account	50		35			85
Total	245	120	75	65	85	

duction account arising out of sales to private consumption which is represented by the symbol C_h, can be inserted in the production account's row at the point where it intersects the column of the household sector. Thus, looking down the debit items of the household sector contained in the *column* of the household sector, the first item encountered will be its purchases of consumer goods – i.e. private consumption. In other words, the matrix system of presentation enables one entry to do two jobs – both contributing to the list of credit items of one sector and, at the same time, contributing to the list of debit items for other sectors.

The correspondence between the matrix presentation and the set of five equations is, of course, that the rows correspond to the entries on the right-hand side and the columns correspond to the entries on the left-hand side of the equation for any sector. For example, the equation for the household account can be read off from the matrix as

$$C_h + S_h + T_h = Y_h + TP_g$$

the left-hand side being the debit items in the household sector's column and the right-hand side of the equation being the credit items in the row.

Corresponding to the fact that transactions *within* any sector have not been shown in the flow diagram, so in the matrix as shown above there are no entries in the 'cells' at the intersections of the column for any sector with the row of the same sector. These cells are all in what is known as the 'leading diagonal' – i.e. the diagonal running down from the top left-hand corner of the matrix to the bottom right-hand corner. An entry in a cell in the leading diagonal would indicate a payment by some sector to itself. An entry in this diagonal would thus represent a transaction *within* a sector, since it did not affect any other sector. For example, an entry in the leading diagonal at the intersection of the row and column for the household sector would represent a payment by one member of the household sector to another. But the absence of any entries in the leading diagonal in the above matrix does not indicate that no such transactions within sectors exist. It is simply that such transactions have not been important, so far, for our purposes.

One form of intra-sectoral transactions that is very important, however, for some purposes are the intra-sectoral transactions for the productive sector – i.e. 'inter-industry transactions'. All payments by firms in the productive sector to other firms in the sector, except payments for capital goods (or increases in stocks) are, as has been seen already, intermediate transactions. The total of these transactions can be, and sometimes is, shown in the leading diagonal at the intersection of the row and column for the productive sector. We have seen that this total is meaningless by itself, since it depends largely on the degree to which we have sub-divided the various industries and firms included in the production sector. It may also depend on the degree of 'vertical integration' in any industry. For example, if a steel mill firm also owns the iron ore and coal mines supplying its main inputs, and, in addition, owns the shipyards and automobile and machinery factories that 'buy' its steel, then there will be fewer transactions shown than if there are separate firms at each stage of the process.

But if the productive sector is broken down into individual industries and if the 'transactions' are recorded to indicate that goods (or services) pass from one productive stage to another, irrespective of whether this takes place in the same firm, then valuable information about the technical links within the productive sector will emerge. This information indicates the structure of production in an economy from the point of view of the dependence of any industry on other industries – either as suppliers of its inputs or as purchasers of its output.

2. The 'input–output' table

In the same way that the transactions between the different *sectors* can be represented by a matrix, so can the transactions between different industries. That is to say, a matrix can be drawn up in which each industry within the productive sector is allocated both a row and a column. Such a matrix is known as an 'input–output' table. Analogously to the social accounting matrix shown above, the row for any industry will indicate its credits and the column will show its debits. Thus, looking down the column for any industry one can see, first, the different suppliers from whom that industry bought its intermediate goods and services. Looking along the row for any industry one can see how its sales are distributed among different purchasers. These will include, first, the sales to other industries – i.e. the intermediate sales within the productive sector, that were not shown in the more aggregative social accounting matrix above as this did not contain any breakdown of the productive sector and merely showed the sales between whole sectors. Following the sales of the given industry to other industries the row for the given industry will show its sales outside the productive sector – i.e. to households or to government or any of the other sectors of final demand whose purchases from the productive sector are shown on the credit side of the productive sector's account.

The way in which such an 'input–output table' (or table of 'inter-industry transactions' as it is often called) fits into the aggregative social accounting matrix shown above can be seen by imagining that a magnifying glass is put over the top left-hand cell of the latter (i.e. the element in the leading diagonal where the row of the productive sector crosses its column). If this cell is suitably magnified, the detail that will become apparent is the matrix of transactions within the productive sector. With some distortion of reality and some stretching of the imagination this might be expected to look as follows:

Figure 6.2

Debit of ▶ Credit of ▼	Intermediate sales (first three rows only)			Sales to final demand (first three rows only)				Total
	Agric.	Indust.	Servs.	House-hold	Cap.	Gov.	Rest of world	
Agriculture		40	10	20		10	40	120
Industry	20		30	40	35	15	15	155
Services	10	15		30	5	10	30	100
Household	30	55	30			(5)		120
Capital	15	15	10	(10)		(25)		75
Government	20	20	5	(20)				65
Rest of world	25	10	15		(35)			85
Total	120	155	100	120	75	65	85	

In this table (the figures in which match those on page 114 above) the row belonging to, say, agriculture, shows its sales, and the column for agriculture shows, first, its purchases from other 'industries' – i.e. intermediate transactions. The difference between its total credits and its debits to other industries is then shown in the remaining elements in its column, namely in the form of payments to households of wages and profits, in taxes paid to the government, in savings of agriculture and finally in imports into agriculture, such as imported feedstuffs. The row and column for any part of the productive sector in such a presentation can, in other words, be regarded as merely the two sides of an account, with the difference that one side of the account, namely its receipts side, is written out horizontally in a row, rather than vertically with all the items one below the other as in the more familiar accounting presentation. Taking the figures in the above matrix of transaction, for example, the account for agriculture, in its usual presentation, would be set out as follows:

Simplified operating account for agriculture

Debits			Credits		
(a)	Intermediate		(a)	Intermediate sales	
	From industry	£20		To industry	£40
	From services	£10		To services	£10
(b)	Imports	£25	(b)	Remainder (equals sales to final demand)	
				To government	£10
				To exports	£60
(c)	Remainder (equals value added)				
	Wages and profits paid to households	£30			
	Taxes	£20			
	Savings	£15			
	TOTAL DEBITS	£120		TOTAL CREDITS	£120

Several properties of this method of presenting the network of accounts of the economy can be noted. First, apart from the payments for imports to the rest of the world, all the rows below the double line represent payments out of value added. Hence, if instead of showing imports as a separate row they are netted out against exports in the column for exports, all the rows below the double line that marks the boundary of the productive sector would constitute value added. In other words, the rest of world column would be changed to represent *net* exports – i.e. exports less imports. Such a procedure would be the counterpart of that used already in showing imports as a deduction from the credit side of the production account instead of an addition to the debit side, or in showing one line representing net exports in the flow diagram instead of one line for exports and another, flowing in the opposite direction, for imports. For some purposes, however, it might be preferable to retain the separate import figures, irrespective of whether they are shown as positive entries in a row or as negative entries in a column.

Figure 6.3

A (INTERMEDIATE TRANSACTIONS)

Intermediate sales to:

agriculture	industry	services
	40	10
20		30
10	15	

B (SALES TO FINAL DEMAND)

Sales to final demand category:

household	capital	government	exports *less* imports	total final demand
20		10	15	45
40	35	15	5	95
30	5	10	15	60

C (VALUE ADDED)

Disposal of value added to:	household	30	55	30
	capital	15	15	10
	government	20	20	5
Total value added		65	90	45

In the above presentation, the four 'corners' of the matrix in Figure 6.2 have been separated; the bottom right-hand corner has been discarded completely since the transactions it contained did not concern the productive sector, and so were transfer payments of one kind or another. The top left-hand corner (A) contains only intermediate transactions. The top right-hand corner (B) shows the sales of the various parts of the productive sector to final demand, so that the sum of the sales appearing in the box equals GNP. The bottom left-hand corner (C) contains the elements in value added, such as taxes paid out of the value added by firms, the factor incomes paid out by firms to the household sector, and, as a residual, the savings of firms, which are 'paid' to the capital account. Since the sum of value added in each industry must equal final output, the sum of the entries in box C should equal the sum of the entries in box B, and, indeed, it can be seen that this is the case, for the sum of value added in each industry is shown by the row at the foot of box C to be $65+90+45=200$, and the total sales to final demand of each industry is shown in the column at the right-hand side of box B as $45+95+60=200$. Of course it is not necessary for the sales to final demand of any or each industry to equal value added in the same industry. Some industries do not sell anything to final demand, since they sell only intermediate products used by other industries. But, as has been seen in the simple arithmetical examples of earlier chapters (such as on page 90), these industries still give rise to value added and the total of the value added in each industry is still equal to the sum of final outputs. The way that this equality is preserved in the more complicated cases can, perhaps, be seen easily in the following highly-simplified presentation of the next diagram, as follows:

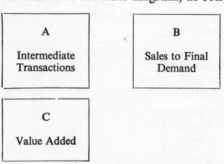

Since the sum of the column for any industry had been made equal, in the original arithmetic, to the sum of all the entries in its row, as profits and savings are residuals after the firms have paid for intermediate purchases, wages and taxes, it follows that the sum of all the rows taken together must be equal to the sum of all the columns. Now the sum of all the rows is, in the last diagram, equal to boxes A plus B. And the sum of all the columns in the same diagram is equal to boxes A plus C. This is therefore another way of demonstrating the identity of B and C, i.e. the fact that, irrespective of the degree of disaggregation, final demand is always identically equal to value added. For if $A + B = A + C$, then $B = C$.

Before the reader cheerfully adds up the rows below the intermediate transaction in any such matrix presentation, it is necessary to exclude the items in the lower right-hand quadrant of the table (as has been done here) before assuming that the result is equal to GNP. For example, a government transfer payment of £5 to households appears as a payment from the government account to the household account and so appears in the matrix representation as an entry at the intersection of the government column with the household row, which is in the lower right-hand quadrant of Figure 6.2.

The production sector can, of course, be broken down into many more 'industries' than the three shown above, and, up to a point, a breakdown into only three industries is not of very great use in developed economies. On the other hand too fine a breakdown can sometimes be a handicap, because the relationships between the inputs and outputs may become unstable past a certain level of disaggregation.

3. Application of input–output table

In the above example shown in Figure 6.2, *assuming that the relationship between its total output and its inputs remained constant*, a 29% rise in industrial output, from £155 to £200, would involve a rise in its inputs from agriculture of 29% of £40 – i.e. of £11·60. As total agricultural output is £120, this represents a proportionate rise in agricultural output of 11·6/120 – i.e. of about 9·7%. If agricultural imports rise in the same proportion as agricultural output then imports into agriculture would have to increase by 9·7% of £25, or about £2·50. If, however, imports into agriculture had been only £5 instead of £25, or if industry's inputs from agriculture had been only £10, instead of £40, the indirect impact of the expansion of industrial output on imports would be very much less. This is an example of the way that the 'input–output' table can enable the analyst to make much more precise and detailed calculations of the total effect on the rest of the economy of many of the changes in which he may be interested. In this particular example, it will be noted that use has been made of the Figure 6.2 presentation, in which imports have been shown separately instead of being netted out against exports. Such fairly aggregative analysis may often be quite useful in fairly simple economies.

In more complex developed countries, similar uses are found for input–output tables, usually on the basis of much more detailed tables of the inter-industry transactions. For example, it might be important to estimate what the effect on imports will be if the government reduces personal income taxes. This can be estimated by taking into account the pattern of consumer expenditures among different industries – provided the household sector column is divided into the corresponding number of industries – and the secondary effects of the changes in the outputs of these industries on each other and on imports. It is not even necessary to go round and round in ever decreasing circles to find out the final sum of all the successive indirect effects since this can be short-circuited by means of mathematical techniques for solving a set of simultaneous equations with which we are not concerned here. But it should be observed that all such manipulations depend on certain strong assumptions being made about the extent to which the relationship between any industry's inputs and its total output does, in fact, remain constant.

4. The accounting framework and economic theory

One advantage of the matrix presentation of the accounts as in Figure 6.2 above is that it is a convenient diagrammatic way of showing how the main areas of economic theory are related. The column headed 'households', which shows how households spend their incomes, after paying taxes, among the different industries, or as savings, is the subject of the theory of consumers' behaviour. The rows and columns showing the distribution of the government's receipts and expenditures relate to the theory of public finance. The rows and columns that show the distribution, among different industries, of exports and imports is the subject matter of the part of the theory of international trade that is concerned with comparative advantage. The rows and columns for the capital account are related both to the theory of the role of capital in production and to the theory of the way that the forces acting on savings and investment influence the level of income in the economy and its rate of growth. Finally, the part of the matrix that shows the pattern of inter-industry transactions is concerned with the whole theory of production and the way that inputs into the productive process are related to outputs.

In other words, the matrix presentation of the system of accounts enables one to see at a glance the way that the different areas of economic theory are linked to each other. This is no accident, of course; it emerges from the point that has been emphasised throughout this book, namely that the classification system used in national account has been built up in the interests of economic analysis. Hence transactions, or sectors, have been classified according to some model of how they operate. This classification has tended to group together transactions that are determined by factors that, on the whole, do not determine the transactions of another group. It is not surprising, therefore, that there is a different theory about the way that each of the major groups behave.[1] Thus the accounting relationships that have been illustrated are subordinate to the *behavioural relationships* – i.e. the relationships that specify the way one group will behave in response to a change in the variables that are supposed to determine its behaviour.

5. Accounting equations and behavioural equations
This brings us to a very important aspect of the accounting network set out above, namely the distinction between satisfying the need for accounting consistency between the different transactions shown, and satisfying their behavioural consistency. For example, there are innumerable patterns of transactions that, in Figure 6.2 (page 117) are consistent with the numbers shown in

---

[1] This does not mean that there are no underlying principles common to each of the particular parts of the theory that have been mentioned.

Figure 6.1 (page 114). But only a few, if any, will be consistent with the relationships determining the way the different sectors behave. For example, we know from Figure 6.2 that household income is £120 and that it spends £90 of this on consumption (itself an assumption about one of the key behavioural relationships for the household sector, namely its 'propensity to consume'), but it might not necessarily distribute its consumption in quite the way set out in Figure 6.2. And the way it does so will affect the total sales of the three different productive branches shown, which, in turn, will affect the savings (amongst other things) of the different branches. It may well be that the particular way we have allocated consumers' expenditure among different industries in Figure 6.2 is such that firms' savings could not, in fact, be as shown in the same figure, given the particular behavioural relationship linking the total receipts of the individual industries to the amount they are each willing to save. The set of transactions shown in Figure 6.2, therefore is consistent and feasible from the accounting point of view but may not be feasible from the point of view of the implied behavioural relationships.

The whole art of economic management, therefore, is to find a set of transactions that is (i) consistent from an accounting point of view – otherwise it is not an internally feasible set of transactions; (ii) consistent with the real relationships governing the behaviour of the various groups of the economy; and (iii) consistent with the objectives of the policy makers.

The matrix presentation is merely one way of illustrating the type of sequence of considerations that have to be satisfied. For example, suppose that the government wishes to spend more on the national highway network, but does not want this to lead to any increase in the total pressure of demand on the economy. It might then aim at offsetting the increase in capital formation that such an increase in the road programme would entail by increasing government savings. And suppose that it wishes to increase its savings by raising its tax receipts rather than by reducing its own current consumption. Various choices immediately arise. For example, it can raise business taxes or taxes on households, and according to which it does, the effect on the consumption of households and on the investment of firms will be different. It might, for example, decide that if it raised business taxes investment would fall, and that it is averse to this happening because it would conflict with some other objective of policy, such as maintaining a fast rate of economic growth. Suppose then that it decides to raise taxes paid by households; it still has a choice between direct taxes on their incomes or indirect taxes on the goods they buy, and again, according to which combination is chosen, so the effect on, say, total consumption or the pattern of output by industry (and hence the pattern of imports) will be different and so have different implications for, say, objectives in the field of the foreign balance, or the level of employment. For example, if extra taxes are imposed on personal incomes, it will be important to know how much of the tax will be paid by reducing household consumption rather than household savings. Thus, in principle, in order to arrive at a final decision the government should know not only how the different sectors are related to each other in the accounting sense – i.e. whose payments are whose receipts – but also in the behavioural sense – i.e. how a change in the receipts of one group of transactors affects, in turn, its payments, both in total and in terms of its composition. For example, it is not enough to know that, if the government raises taxes on households, households will reduce their consumption and their savings; it is also important to know by how much and on what goods. Similarly, it is important to know by how much this, in turn, will affect firms' investment, and the balance of payments and so on.

It may be recognised that the problem of reconciling simultaneously (i) the objectives of the authorities, (ii) the accounting relationships and (iii) the behavioural relationships is by no means simple, even in the highly over-simplified economies such as those shown in Figure 6.2, since it appears that one can go on round and round in circles for a long time – each successive adjustment leading to the need to make another. In mathematical terms, finding a set of transactions that achieves consistency under the three headings listed above amounts to solving a set of equations. More accurately, it amounts to maximising certain functions – such as employment, or the growth rate or price stability or whatever are the objectives – subject to certain 'constraints', which are the 'structural' equations of the system. These equations either (i) represent the accounting relationships,

125

in which case they are identities, or (ii) they are behavioural equations.

For example, the equation

$$C_h + S_h + T_h = Y_h + TP_g$$

will be recognised as simply the equation for the household account, which merely states that households' disposal of their incomes in the three ways indicated on the left-hand side must equal total incomes, which must clearly be true by definition, since one of the ways that households have been shown to dispose of their incomes in the above equation is by savings (i.e. the balance of income over expenditure). This equation is clearly a different sort of equation from a *behavioural* equation, such as the following:

$$C_h = £5 + 0·8(Y_h + TP_g - T_h)$$

This equation says that

(a) if households have no income left after paying taxes (so that the items in brackets on the right-hand side of the equation add to zero), they will still spend £5 (so that, presumably, they have to borrow or dis-save); and

(b) for every £1 increase in their disposable income (i.e. their income after paying taxes) they will spend an extra £0·8 on consumption (and so, presumably, save the remaining £0·2).

Both these propositions are statements about the way that households behave and both are empirically verifiable (i.e. they may be found to be true or false). From the accounting matrix set out in Figure 6.1(a), five purely accounting, or balancing, equations can be constructed, one for each account, as shown at the end of the last chapter (page 108). But how many behavioural equations are used depends on one's particular theory about how the groups behave. For any large number of groups (unless the behavioural equations are particularly simple) a solution that reconciles all the objectives, the accounting equations and the behavioural equations can only be accurately worked out by means of a computer that will solve all the equations simultaneously.

6. Economic 'models'

A set of equations representing the accounting relationships and the behavioural relationships that have to be satisfied would constitute a mathematical 'model' of the economy. The theory of the relationships between the different parts of the economy represented by the equations is, of course, also a 'model' of the way the economy behaves, and it is not its presentation in mathematical form that converts it from a 'non-model' into a 'model'. The mathematical presentation simply converts it into a mathematical model. Some of these mathematical models are very complicated, particularly those designed to predict short-term fluctuations in the economy. For example, in addition to the basic balancing equations (the number of which depends on the number of groups of transactions identified) there will be equations, say, relating household consumption to household incomes net of their tax liability, or relating government receipts to total incomes, or relating firms' savings to their output, or relating imports to the level of industrial production, or relating stock changes to the rate of growth of output, or relating invest-ment levels to the rate of growth of output or past profits, and possibly several equations to allow for the effect of some variables on wages and prices and hence on the proportion of their incomes that households spend on consumption.

When using such models for purposes of maximising certain policy objectives – such as the growth rate or the level of em-ployment – the authorities might also want to adjust the balancing equations in order to incorporate certain other policy objectives. For example, the balancing equation for the rest of the world account might be adjusted to incorporate the objective of a surplus of given amount in the foreign payments. In this case the balance of payments objective is not treated like the objectives which are being *maximised*, such as the growth rate or the degree of price stability, but as a constraint on the various ways (i.e. the various solutions to the set of equations) by which these maxima may be achieved. Thus, one of the equations might read:

$$X - M = £100 \text{ million}$$

In practice, the models are rarely used to indicate how some objective can be *maximised*. Instead, the policy maker merely 'asks' the model to indicate the consequences of aiming at certain selected objectives over a range that he knows in advance to reach the limits of what is feasible. For example, he might use the model to see the implications of attempting to achieve a rate of economic growth of 3%, 5% and 7% per annum. Alterna-

127

tively the model might be used to show the consequences of raising the proportion of national product devoted to domestic investment (I/GNP) from, say, 16% to 20%. If no constraint on the foreign balance had been included in the set of equations solved it might then be found, for example, that the particular solution obtained implied too heavy an import bill, and the model might indicate that the only way, in the short period, that the required level of investment could be reconciled with the balance of payments objective would be by means of severe restrictions on consumer spending – e.g. by means of heavy taxation. The authorities would then have to decide how far they were prepared to insist on their investment objectives and the foreign balance objectives at the expense of other objectives, such as keeping down the rate of taxation. Of course the model might well indicate that the selected objectives could not be attained, given the set of structural equations used – i.e. there was no solution to the set of equations including those expressing the objectives. In the longer term the authorities might then try to change some of the behavioural relationships in the economy in such a way as to increase the chances of reconciling their objectives. For example, if it were thought that more expenditure on education and on research would add to the growth rate of the economy then the target ratio of investment of output could be relaxed – e.g. it could be altered to $I/GNP=12\%$ – which might make everything else a lot easier to reconcile.

Some economic models are very simple and involve only a handful of equations. Some models of long-term growth, for example, fall into this category. The Keynesian model is another such simple model in its basic form (and ignoring monetary effects such as effects on the rate of interest), though, like any other model, there is no limit to the amount of refinement that can be incorporated into it by means of more and more equations or ever more complex forms of equations.

In Chapter 8 we will examine the basic Keynesian model of the way that short-term variations in the level of income and employment are generated – i.e. what makes national product change.

Chapter 7

Equality and the distribution of income

1. Introduction

One of the topics that is most widely discussed these days in connection with the economic, political or social problems facing society is the problem of 'equality'. The concept of 'equality' is, of course, very vague and can be defined in innumerable ways. It has many dimensions, including political equality, legal equality and economic equality, not to mention an unlimited number of personal or social attributes that make for inequalities between individuals. If all men were equal in every respect life would be very boring and the world would be a very dull place. Inequalities in intellectual capacity, physical abilities, artistic sensibilities, perseverance, moral fibre, courage, compassion, and so on all contribute to the diversity of the human race.

But some of the inequalities between people are regarded as 'unjust', or at least as matters of social concern. What is 'just' is, of course, a major philosophical problem to which we cannot provide any definite answer. In fact, there is no possibility of providing any definite answer in the sense that it might be possible one day to provide a scientific objective demonstration that one particular concept of justice is 'correct'. It is not surprising, therefore, that society's notions of what sort of inequalities are important or ought to be reduced have changed over time, or that society has become increasingly concerned with equality in economic terms. For it is understandable that, at an earlier stage of society, what mattered most was that people should be equal before the law, for otherwise the minimum respect for the law which is the cement of civilised societies will not hold. This has been followed by the struggle for political equality in the sense of 'one man one vote', and later 'one woman one vote'. Once this was achieved it was inevitable that the political power in the hands of those who most suffer from economic inequalities has been used in trying to redress the latter. After all, what is the point of incurring incredible sacrifices and risks in the struggle for political representation if it is not to be used when it is attained?

But political power cannot be used to make ugly people beautiful, slow people fast, stupid people intelligent or dull people witty (though it is often used to induce intelligent people to concur with the views of the stupid, or to induce witty people to laugh at the feeble jokes of the dull). But what it can be used for, up to a point, and would seem to be most desired for anyway, is to redress some of the economic inequalities that are regarded as being socially unjust or economically or socially harmful in one way or another. Most of the issues that have a bearing on social notions of an equitable degree of economic equality are far beyond the scope of this book, however, and the main task in this chapter is to point to some of the purely statistical problems that arise when one wants merely to describe the degree of economic equality in any useful and relevant manner.

For the curious thing is that almost anybody today who is interested in the broad economic issues of our time – and this presumably includes the reader of this book; why else should he be reading it? – would have a view on whether the degree of economic equality that exists in present-day society is adequate. He may think we need more economic equality – as do most people – or that we need less, or that it is about right. Almost any student of economics will have a view on this question. But if one asks what would appear to be the obvious next question, namely 'Well, how much equality do we actually have?', hardly anybody can give an answer. Now this is very strange. How can one know that there is not enough equality if one does not know how much equality there is? And how can one know whether we have the right amount of equality if one cannot – as is usually also the case – define what this is in any measurable way. And how can one even know whether equality is getting better or worse if one does not know how to measure it – even roughly? And the sad fact is that hardly anybody knows the answers to any of these questions.

One of the reasons for this apparently strange state of affairs is that even the notion of economic equality is extremely difficult to define or measure in any useful way. But at the same time many figures are often bandied about concerning the degree of economic equality, so the best we can do is to try to understand what sort of meaning can be attached to these figures, and what sort of statistical or conceptual problems have to be taken into account in trying to relate them to any value judgements we may have concerning what aspects of economic equality are important.

2. Factor shares

One of the statistical concepts that is most commonly used in connection with economic equality, as well as in connection with other economic problems, is the share of *wages* in national income – as distinct from the share of *profits*. This corresponds closely to the traditional micro-economic analysis of the production process in terms of the main factors of production, which are often classified as land, labour and capital. According to one conventional presentation of micro-economic theory, these three distinct factors of production earn rents, wages (and salaries) and profits (including interest). Hence, a natural way of breaking up the total of national income is into these 'factor shares' or 'distributive shares' as they are often known – namely rent, wages and profits.

In what has been described in earlier chapters of this book as the 'household account' only two credit items were listed, namely 'wages and distributed profits' and 'transfer payments from government'. This lumping together of wages and profits precludes all analysis of the way national income is distributed to the different economic groups in society. In practice, of course, the national accounts published by countries contain far more detail than the two items given above. For example, even summary forms of the 'personal income and expenditure account' (British terminology) or the 'personal income and outlay account' (USA terminology) would contain the items shown in Tables 7.1 and 7.2, in which, as can be seen, wages and distributed profits have been broken down into various sub-components, such as wages, salaries, income from self-employment and so on.

Table 7.1

Personal income and outlay account; USA, 1966 (billions of dollars)

1	Personal tax and nontax payments	75·2	7	Wage and salary disbursements	394·6
2	Personal outlays:	479·0	8	Other labour income	20·8
3	Personal consumption expenditures	465·9	9	Proprietors' income	59·3
			10	Rental income of persons	19·4
4	Interest paid by consumers	12·4	11	Dividends	21·5
			12	Personal interest income:	42·4
5	Personal transfer payments to foreigners, net	·6	13	Net interest	20·2
			14	Net interest paid by government	9·9
6	Personal saving	29·8	15	Interest paid by consumers	12·4
			16	Transfer payments to persons:	43·9
			17	from business	2·7
			18	from government	41·2
			19	*Less:* personal contributions for social insurance	17·9

PERSONAL TAXES, OUTLAYS AND SAVING	584·0	PERSONAL INCOME	584·0

Source: Nancy and Richard Ruggles *The Design of Economic Accounts*, New York, 1970, page 13.

Whilst, in general, the more detailed the data the more useful, there are many exceptions to this rule and for several purposes it is necessary to simplify somewhat the classification of national income. For example, it may not be possible to obtain exactly the same classification for different countries or for the same country at different points of time, except on a rather less detailed basis. Also, too much detail may obscure the broad picture that is needed for purposes of analysing certain major economic developments over time or certain major economic differences between countries. Hence, for many analytical purposes, it has been customary to use a much more limited classification than that given for the USA and the UK above.

This is sometimes a classification according to the income accruing to the three factors of production mentioned above, land, labour and capital. However, there are some economists who take the view that the most useful classification of these distributive shares is into four classes in order to show interest payments separately from profits, on the grounds that the resulting four classes of income – rent, interest, profits and wages – reflect classes of payments that are determined in very different ways. Others take the view that only two classes are necessary, namely profits and wages – i.e. income to property and income to labour respectively – corresponding to the two

Table 7.2

Personal income and expenditure account, UK, 1966 (£ million)

Income before tax		Expenditure	
Wages	11,935	Consumers' expenditure	24,116
Salaries	8,185	Transfers abroad (net)	62
Pay in cash and kind of HM		Taxes paid abroad	8
Forces	513	United Kingdom taxes on	
Employers' contributions:		income:	
National insurance and		Payments	3,646
health	902	Additions to tax reserves	35
Other	902	National insurance and	
		health contributions	1,797
Total income from	22,437		
employment		Total current expenditure	29,664
Professional persons*	449	Balance: saving before	
Farmers*	595	providing for depreciation	
Other sole traders and		and stock appreciation	1,844
partnerships*	1,426		
Total income from self-			
employment*	2,470		
Rent, dividends and net			
interest:			
Receipts by life assurance			
and superannuation funds	870		
Other receipts	2,728		
Total	3,598		
Current transfers to charities			
from companies	30		
National insurance benefits			
and other current grants			
from public authorities	2,973		
TOTAL PERSONAL INCOME*	31,508	TOTAL	31,508

* Before providing for depreciation and stock appreciation.

Source: Central Statistical Office *National Accounts Statistics: Sources and Methods*, HMSO, London, 1968, page 102.

classes used in Chapter 2 above in connection with the distribution of value added and the estimation of GNP by the 'income method'. This twofold classification is usually defended on the grounds that rent and interest are really just transfer payments out of profits, and the question of how the surplus available after paying wages is shared out among the various groups in society that have appropriated that surplus is of little interest as far as the basic distribution is concerned. What matters, it is argued, is that the workers do not get it.

But to some extent the debate about the rights or wrongs of alternative classifications is irrelevant since the fact is that the income share data that are available in the national accounts do not really correspond to the conventional micro-economic concepts anyway! For example, the 'rent' figure shown in the national accounts of most countries does not even include all the net income from leased property, let alone other returns to factors in temporarily fixed supply. And the imputed rent on real estate owned by businesses – such as their own factories or shops – is included in their profits, not under 'rent'. In fact, rent as measured in the national accounts is limited basically to rent income accruing to private individuals in their personal capacity.

Similar qualifications apply to wages and other 'factor' incomes. For example, the income of self-employed persons or unincorporated enterprises is a mixture of (i) pure wage income – i.e. the standard rate of pay that, say, the professional man or the manager of his own family business would earn if he were employed by somebody else; (ii) some rent for the premises that he might be using (including his own house or shop) to carry out the business; (iii) some pure interest on the capital locked up in the business; and (iv) some pure profit as a reward to the risks he runs of not making any money in the end. One conclusion that can be drawn from the data limitations is, as Irving Kravis put it, 'Given this accounting framework, a three-fold division of income into employee compensation, entrepreneurial (unincorporated) income, and property income (rent, interest and corporate profit) is perhaps most relevant to the study of functional shares'.[1]

[1] Irving Kravis *The Structure of Income*, University of Pennsylvania, Philadelphia, 1962, page 123.

Of course, there are various estimates of the way such mixed items in the national accounts could be unscrambled in order to obtain a purer estimate of wages and profits, but there is an essentially arbitrary element about all such methods. Hence, another way of proceeding is to say that the data problems merely reinforce the view that the way the total surplus of income over wages is then shared out among rent, interests and dividends is unimportant and that one might as well simply use the twofold classification into wages and all the rest.

Whatever the merits of the different points of view it is this latter procedure that is reflected in the classification used to describe the distribution of national income in the internationally standardised tables. Although they also allow for some sub-classification, the two main classes used are 'compensation of employees' (i.e. wages and salaries) and 'property and entrepreneurial income net'. For the years 1961 and 1971, the relevant figures in the USA and the UK according to these

Table 7.3

Distribution of national income by factor shares; USA and UK, 1971 (current prices)*

	USA				UK			
	\$ billion		%		£ million		%	
	1961	1971	1961	1971	1961	1971	1961	1971
1. Compensation of employees	303·4	647·4	70·5	75·0	16,407	33,331	74·4	77·9
2. Property and entrepreneural income net	126·7	219·2	29·5	25·0	5,658	9,481	25·6	22·1
3. National income (excluding indirect taxes less subsidies)*	430·1	866·7	100·0	100·0	22·066	42,813	100·0	100·0

* The presentation here departs slightly from the internationally accepted standard presentation as used in the source in that, in the interests of consistency with the previous chapters of this book, national income has been defined here as excluding indirect taxes less subsidies. The source (OECD *National Accounts of OECD Countries, 1961–1972*, Paris, 1974) uses the concept of national income including indirect taxes net of subsidies. Exclusion of this item makes no difference, of course, to the ratio of items 1 to 2. The 'statistical discrepancy' that is given in the original source has also been omitted here, so that the total national income as given above is simply the sum of the two items 1 and 2 shown.

internationally standardised concepts are shown in Table 7.3. It can be seen that in both countries the share of national income accruing to labour – i.e. to employees – is now nearly 80%, though slightly lower in the USA than in the UK. Not much significance can be attached to the differences between the countries with respect to these shares, for reasons that will become more apparent later. But the two countries have one thing in common in the above table, namely that the share of labour income has risen over the decade shown. This is not a new phenomenon by any means, and some discussion of the longer-term trends in these 'factor shares' will also bring out some of the reasons why care is needed in drawing conclusions from any inter-country comparisons of the shares.

The rise in the share of labour income (wages plus salaries) implies, of course, a fall in the share of property income (defined widely to include profits, interest and rent). As pointed out above, one problem that arises with this two-way split of income is how to divide up the income accruing to the self-employed and entrepreneurs into that part of it that is pure profit rather than that part which constitutes a wage or salary for their work. If we leave this awkward category of income aside for the time being, income accruing to capital assets would comprise (i) the property income of households (namely dividends, interest and rent – both money income received and imputed rent on owner-occupied dwellings); (ii) net profits of corporations after depreciation and distribution of dividends but before payment of direct taxes; and (iii) property and trading income accruing to governments.[1] On this 'narrow' definition of property income the share of national income going to property has been falling for about a century – i.e. for about as long as reliable records exist.

Estimates for a few major countries on this definition are shown below. It will be seen that the share of national income going to income from assets as so defined has fallen from 36% to 21% in the UK over the century beginning in 1860, and from 22% to 12% in the USA from the end of the last century to the

---

[1] It should be noted that the imputed rents on owner-occupied trading property, such as a factory owned by the occupier, would be included under his profits instead of under rent, and so would not affect the total of income accruing to the concept of 'property income' as just defined.

latter half of the 1950s. A similar fall has taken place in France and Switzerland over the last half century, but not in Germany. However, if income from capital assets are measured in such a way as to allocate profits accruing to self-employed and entrepreneurs – by splitting it off from the wage and salary component of their total income – the fall in the profit share is more pronounced in the UK and the USA, and applies also, albeit only slightly, to Germany, as can be seen in the final column of Table 7.4. On this wider definition of 'property income', or 'income to assets' – or just plain 'profits' – the share in national income has fallen from 41% to 22% in the UK over the last century up to the late 1950s, and from 31% to 22% in the USA from the beginning of this century to the late 1950s.

Table 7.4

Share of profits in national income: selected countries; long-period changes (*percentages of national income at current prices*)

Country	Time period	Excluding profits of self-employed etc.	Including profits of self-employed etc.
United Kingdom	1860–69	36	41
	1954–60	21	22
France	1911	26	39
	1954–60	12	16
Germany	1913	18	23
	1954–60 (Fed. Rep.)	18	21
Switzerland	1913	34	na
	1954–60	22	27
USA	1899–1908	22	31
	1954–60	19	22

Source: Simon Kuznets *Modern Economic Growth*, Yale University Press, New Haven and London, 1966, Table 4.2, pages 168–9.

The corollary of this long-term downward trend in the share of profits in national income is, of course, that the share of labour income must have risen. This result, which has been well known to some commentators for some time, might come as a surprise to others who have relied on an earlier widely accepted assumption that the constancy of the labour share was one of the great, but nevertheless firmly established, mysteries of economic history. After all, even Keynes wrote, in 1939, that 'the stability of the proportion of the national dividend accruing to labour' was 'one of the most surprising, yet best-established, facts in the whole range of economic statistics, both for Great Britain and for the United States'.[1] Joseph Schumpeter and Joan Robinson have also referred to this apparent mystery. So how can this 'mystery' be reconciled with the figures just given?

One common reaction is to check how far the results would be changed by taking different statistical concepts, for example by taking the profit shares in gross – as distinct from *net* – national income (i.e. before, instead of after, allowing for depreciation, which has certainly been taking a rising proportion of GNP), or by excluding rental income of dwellings, and so on. But as one authority has put it, 'Whatever variant is considered there is an unmistakable upward trend in labour's share, but one which is almost entirely the result of the shifts which occur during or immediately after both the world wars. . . . Other variants which might be calculated . . . would alter the details but would not disturb the basic trends'.[2]

The main reason why it has often been thought that the *labour* share has been constant over the last century or so is that it is fairly constant when it is measured in such a way as to exclude from the definition of labour large numbers of people who are in administrative, technical, managerial and clerical occupations, as well as the self-employed. For it is true that if the share of labour is confined to wages – i.e. excludes salaries and so on – and leaves out of account also the wage element in the income of self-employed, the wage share has, indeed, remained fairly constant over very long periods. For example, in the UK it was 40% of national income in 1870–2 and 42% in 1948–50. Since the wage share has remained constant over this period in spite of a large decline in the proportion of wage earners in the total occupied population, the 'wage ratio' – i.e.

[1] J. M. Keynes 'Relative Movements of Real Wages and Output', *Economic Journal*, XLIX, 1939.

[2] C. H. Feinstein 'Changes in the Distribution of the National Income in the UK since 1860' in J. Marchal and B. Duclos (eds), *The Distribution of the National Income*, International Economic Association, 1968, pages 127–8.

the ratio of average wages to average income per total occupied person – must have risen.

The fall in the proportion of wage-earners, together with the rise in the wage ratio, has, however, been one important reason for the rise in the overall share of *all* labour income. For it has reflected a large increase in the proportion of salaried employees in technical, professional or managerial posts. In the UK, for example, the ratio of wage-earners to salary-earners has fallen from 3.2:1 in 1910–14 to 1.6:1 in 1960–3. But this could not be the only cause of the rise in the total labour share, for much of the extra employment in salaried grades of labour has been in low-paid clerical posts.

Another important reason has been the fall in the numbers of self-employed and independent entrepreneurs. The whole process of industrialisation, in fact, has meant that large numbers of hitherto self-employed, small traders and business-men, independent farmers and so on, have gradually been absorbed into the employed labour force, not to mention hitherto unpaid family labour that was characteristic of the smaller-scale enterprise and farms of the nineteenth and early twentieth centuries. In short, the rise in the share of total *employee* income, as distinct from just *wage* income, has been partly the result of a rise in the proportion of employees of all kinds in the total active population. For example, in the USA the share of employees in the total labour force has risen from 74·9% in 1900 to 93·0% in 1960.[1] This trend has been common to all advanced economies. As Kuznets points out,

> This trend in the distribution of the labour force – a drop in the share of entrepreneurs and self-employed from over 35 to less than 20 per cent, and an increase in the share of employees from less than 65 to over 80 per cent of the total labour force – was due, at least in the free market economies, partly to shifts in industrial structure and partly to changes in status within specific industrial sectors.[2]

To summarise, the rise in the labour share in national income has been the result of various forces, notably (i) changes in the economic structure of countries, leading to a decline in the

[1] Kuznets, op. cit., page 192.
[2] Kuznets, op. cit., page 187.

importance of agriculture and related industries which had been characterised by small-scale operations and unpaid family labour; (ii) a rise in the average size of firms in industry in general, leading to a fall in the numbers of entrepreneurs relative to paid employees; (iii) a fall in the proportion of employees who were unskilled and manual workers – i.e. a rise in the share of managerial, technical and professional employees, who are relatively highly paid. This last factor reflects, to some extent, the increasing education of the labour force in general. Many more people now are able to earn high incomes, not by being owners of conventional assets but by having become owners of what is known as 'human capital' – i.e. the skill and knowledge that they have acquired through investment in education. This, too, of course, has been partly the result of the rising demand for such skills that accompanied the increasing mechanisation and technical complexity of modern industry.

The rise in the quality of the labour force is no doubt one of the reasons why the rise in the numbers of employees has not led to a fall in their real wage relative to the return on capital – as would be the case in the context of a simple marginal productivity theory of wages, with a given quality of labour force. But another reason has no doubt been the general technological progress in industry which leads to increases in output per unit of total factor input – i.e. per unit of inputs of both labour and capital. How this increment of output is to be shared out is, of course, partly a matter of the relative bargaining strength of the various groups in society. But as long as output increases more than the increase in inputs of labour and capital multiplied by their marginal products, there is scope for a rise both in the real wage *and* in the rate of return on capital. Hence, there is no conflict between the observed rise in the labour share and the maintenance of the rate of return on capital.

In any case, as already noted, the rise in the labour share has been partly the result of a fall in the share accruing to self-employed etc. Furthermore, of the decline in total profits, a large element has been a fall in rents, particularly agricultural rent on account of the declining importance and prosperity of agriculture over the course of the century up to the late 1950s. These two factors mean that the rise in the labour share has not meant a particularly sharp fall in company (i.e. corporate) profits, at least not pre-tax profits. In fact, leaving aside the developments over the last ten years, which still cannot be placed in a longer-run historical context, the rate of return on capital has probably not shown any significant long-run decline over the previous half-century, in spite of the significant rise in the share of labour in national income.

This brings out one of the limitations on the whole concept of 'factor shares' as an object of analysis. For in the absence of data on the size of the capital stock, the share of profits in national income tells us nothing about the rate of return on capital. Hence it tells us very little about the variable that is important for assessing growth prospects, or even for explaining past growth trends. Nor does it tell us much about the relative income of employees, since, as we have seen, a change in the labour share may – and mainly does – reflect changes in the whole industrial structure leading to changes in the proportion of people who are paid employees, as much as changes in the real wage per employee. And even where this average real wage has risen – as it undoubtedly has over the course of the century – this still does not rule out the possibility that some of the people who may now enjoy high salaries in the employee category are 'worse off' than they were when they were independent entrepreneurs or self-employed.

Thus, for various reasons, factor shares also tell us nothing about whether the distribution of income has changed in the direction of more or less equality or what is happening to the rates of return to capital or labour. In other words, they tell us nothing of great interest either about economic objectives in terms of equality or about economic performance in terms of rates of return. They are simply the arithmetic results of a complex of changes taking place in the economy, some of which (such as the rise in the proportion of employees in the population) tend to raise the labour share, while others tend to reduce it, such as a rise in the ratio of labour to capital, for instance, which would tend to reduce the relative marginal product of labour. In addition there is an indeterminate struggle for the growth of incomes brought about by technical progress, not to mention the increasing element of labour income that is a return to 'human capital'. Data that represent a mixture of various

141

forces are of little analytical significance. In particular, one might well ask why, if we are interested in the whole problem of equality, do we not go straight to data on equality of the distribution of income between persons – such as what proportion of the population receive some given proportion of income, and so on. So we shall now proceed to do this.

3. The size distribution of income

We have arrived at the point where it would seem that the obvious way to see how equally income is distributed is to go direct to figures that indicate the distribution of income between individuals, rather than between certain types of income, such as wages of salaries, since the latter data will be affected by changes in the numbers of individuals who receive wages or salaries or other forms of income. Thus, for example, the ratio of profits to wages in an economy might remain stable over time, but the ratio of profit-receivers to wage-earners might go up or down, implying different effects on the relative incomes of wage-earners to profit-earners. Anyway, one is not necessarily interested in what *type* of income people receive but how big it is. And one is not interested only in, say, the average income from profit relative to the average wage income; there are also large differences between the incomes of unskilled workers, or the unemployed, and the wages of the highly skilled workers or the salaries of business executives and so on. Hence, it would appear that, insofar as one is interested in the overall degree of equality of incomes in a country, what is required is some data that tell us, roughly speaking, what proportion of the population receives low incomes as distinct from the proportion that receives high incomes or middle incomes and so on.

Slightly more precisely, one would want to know, for example, how much better off are, say, the richest 5% of the population, compared with, say, the poorest 5% or some such ratio. This is another way of saying how much of total national income goes to the top 5% of population as compared with the bottom 5%. For example, if the top 5% of the population were found to receive 50% of national income whilst the bottom 5% received only 1% of total national income, it would follow that the average member of the richest 5% of the population received fifty times as much income each as did the average person in the poorest 5% of the population. If, however, for the same top and bottom 5% of the population, the proportions of national income received were 20% and 2% respectively, we could see that the richest 5% of the population received, on average, only ten times as much per head as the poorest 5%. And this sort of comparison does seem to be closer to the vague notion of inequality that one has in mind in this context of income distribution.

Consequently, data have frequently been presented in this form – i.e. in the form of what are known as 'size distribution of income'. This shows the way the population is distributed among different income ranges. This corresponds to the statistical concept of a 'frequency distribution' – i.e. how many observations (in this case people) fall into a given class (in this case income). This information may be presented in a wide variety of ways, but before coming on to some of the problems involved in interpreting the data, it may be as well to look at one convenient comparison that has been made between the frequency distributions of income in the USA and the UK in Table 7.5. In this table, the details of which we shall ignore for the time being, it can be seen that in the USA the richest 10% of the population received 28% of total national income, as compared with the mere 1% of national income received by the

Table 7.5

Comparison of size distribution of income in the USA and the UK, 1952

Tenths of spending units after ranking by income after taxes	Per cent of total income after taxes taken by each tenth	
	USA	UK
Top tenth	28	26
2nd tenth	15	14
3rd tenth	13	13
4th tenth	11	11
5th tenth	9	10
6th tenth	8	8
7th tenth	7	7
8th tenth	5	5
9th tenth	3	4
Bottom tenth	1	2

Source: H. F. Lydall and J. B. Lansing 'A Comparison of the Distribution of Personal Income and Wealth in the United States and Great Britain', *American Economic Review*, 1959; reprinted in A. B. Atkinson (ed.) *Wealth, Income and Inequality*, Penguin, Harmondsworth, 1973, Table 2.

poorest tenth of the population. In the UK the disparity is much smaller – 26% against 2% – i.e. a ratio of 13 to 1 as compared with a ratio of 28 to 1 in the USA. But if the poorest tenth of the population is not taken into account, the distribution of income in the two countries was not much more unequal in the USA than in the UK.

But, as one could expect, it is not quite as simple as that. The notion of inequality of income distribution is far too complex to be able to capture all its aspects in one table, though one must avoid going to the other extreme and becoming so lost in technical detail and qualifications that one fails to see the wood for the trees. It is possible to know too much about statistics. There are always people who will say that, given their immense knowledge of the subtle technical limitations on income distribution statistics, it is not really possible to say, for example, that incomes are distributed more equally in Norway than in France; although anybody who knows nothing at all about statistics but who is simply not blind can see the difference if he visits the two countries.

On the other hand, it is necessary to be familiar with some of the main technical problems that arise in this field, particularly if one is interested in the statistics not so much from the technical point of view, but from the point of view of the welfare implications of different income distributions. One of the first problems that arises is illustrated already in Table 7.5, namely the choice of 'income unit'. Hitherto we had been talking blithely about what proportion of the population fell in different income brackets – e.g. what proportion of the population earned $5,000 per year, or £2,000 per year. But are we really interested in the *whole* population, children and all? Do we really want to know that millions of people earn *no* income, simply because they are still in their cradles? Figures that showed that a high proportion of the population were very poor simply because children were included would not be very helpful. It is partly for this reason that the size distribution of income is usually shown not in terms of individuals, but in terms of families. That is to say, instead of showing how many *individuals* receive different levels of income, the data usually shows how many *families*, or '*households*', or income-tax units, receive certain incomes.

For example, since data on income distribution are often taken from income tax data available to the authorities, they are often shown – as in Table 7.5 – in terms of the units used for income tax purposes. In these 'tax units' husband and wife are generally included in the same unit, and their incomes are combined even though they may each earn a separate income. But other adult members of the family who have separate incomes would normally be counted as separate units. Thus the tax unit is not the most suitable unit to use since it is probably preferable to work in terms of units that pool their resources, or at least form a coherent unit of decision regarding the degree to which their incomes are pooled and the way the total resources of the unit are to be spent. For this purpose, therefore, it is probably better to work in terms of family units.

Use of the family unit has another advantage, namely that for welfare purposes one may be interested not just in people's incomes but in the relation between their incomes and their needs. And most people would accept that a large family containing many children would have greater 'needs' than one with few or no children. Hence, it would seem preferable to analyse the distribution of incomes of family groups in relation to the size of the families.

Of course, the assumption that allowance for family size, and hence for the additional needs that these create, is necessary in order to make valid welfare comparisons is a value judgement that is not beyond dispute by reasonable men. After all, the size of one's family in modern times in advanced countries is largely a matter of free choice. So it can be assumed that married couples have usually chosen to have children quite freely, which implies that they expect the children to add to their welfare or happiness in one way or another. Hence, if it is *welfare* that one is interested in equalising, such people are already getting some more of it by virtue of having children, and it could be argued that there is no more reason to 'compensate' for the extra costs of this particular way they have chosen of adding to their welfare than for compensating people who do so by keeping pet dogs. On the other hand, although the parents may exercise free choice in deciding whether to have children or not, this does not apply to the children (or to the dogs, or their parents for that matter) and it is the children who will be deprived

145

insofar as their parents' resources are not correspondingly increased.

Of course, it is unlikely that everybody can agree as to what 'needs' should be taken into account in deciding how far incomes should be brought into equality with needs. For example, some people may have insatiable needs for wine, women and song, but it is unlikely that society would agree to give them wine or women allowances in the same way as most societies provide children's allowances in some form or other. Many less extreme examples can be found, however, such as needs for special health care or education, that society as a whole would regard as justifying special consideration. But the extra needs associated with children are almost universally accepted as relevant to the notion of equality, which, in addition to the point made above concerning the grouping of individuals in units that enjoy pooled resources or at least act as units of decision for the disposal of resources, constitutes a major reason for preferring the family unit to either tax units or the individual as a basis for analysing income distribution.

In this connection another closely related unit that is commonly used is the 'household', which would cover all people living together and more or less acting as a unit of decision concerning expenditures, even though they may not all be related by narrow family ties – e.g. they may include aunts and uncles, grandparents or others who share the family abode.

The importance of relating means to needs, which is recognised in practice by the use of family or household units, introduces another key concept, namely the distinction between what is known as '*vertical*' as distinct from '*horizontal*' inequality of incomes. Vertical equality of income distribution means that all households with the same composition (mainly in terms of numbers of children) would have the same income, whereas horizontal equality means that the average income of each household type was equal. It would be possible to have complete vertical equality, therefore, although the average incomes of each household type need not be proportional to the different size, and hence needs, of the different household type. For example, it could mean that every household in the country with, say, two adults and two children had the same income, and that each household with only one child had the same income. But if the former's was no greater than the latter's, this might not be regarded as a very equitable distribution of income.

Conversely, it would be possible to have horizontal equality in the sense that the *average* incomes of larger families were proportionately greater than the incomes of smaller families, but there might be big variations within each group, some large families, say, having much bigger incomes than other equally large families.

Income distribution data that made no allowance for household composition would be of little use. They would show a large number of people having apparently very low incomes, but who were simply young people at the beginning of the earnings scale and who were living at home with their parents, as well as many retired people who may be living with their children. They would also fail to make allowance for the fact that, to some extent, older workers who tend to have children also often tend to earn more, not to mention the additional children's allowances and other benefits that are often associated with larger families.

The use of a household unit (or family unit) raises fresh problems, however, in connection with the welfare implications of the data, particularly when one wants to consider the way that income distribution changes over time. For changes in family size on account of demographic or other factors will affect the degree of inequality in various ways. For example, there has been a general decline in average family size in the western world over the last century. To some extent this has greatly reduced income inequalities in terms of the relation between income and needs, for there have been fewer large families obliged to exist on the same sort of incomes as received by much smaller families. On the other hand, the general rise in income levels throughout the last few decades has enabled many people to choose to split off from the family unit and to set up home on their own, whether they be older people who no longer feel obliged to live with their children, or younger people whose earnings now permit them to live separately from their parents. This splitting up of family units will tend to add to the number of low-income household units, so that the statistics would show that an increase in the proportion of all families that have relatively low incomes. But since this splitting off will be the result of their free choice, their welfare has presumably

147

increased. In addition, the reduction in the numbers of children per family will, as already mentioned, mean a narrowing of the gap between needs and incomes in very many cases. Hence, for both reasons demographic changes that would imply an increase in welfare will be reflected, in aggregate figures of the distribution of income between all families, as an increase in inequality, which might be expected to imply a fall in welfare.

Other changes over time in demographic and social factors that affect household size have important effects on the measured inequality of income distribution. For example, it is probably true that, together with the decline in the number of children per family, the other major contribution to the greater equality of income distribution has been the increased proportion of married women who go to work. Since this has been, until recently, predominantly among the lower-paid income groups, it has tended to raise the combined incomes of the parents of such households as compared with the more affluent income groups where the wives do not so readily go to work. Whether this has led to a corresponding equalisation of *welfare*, however, is another matter. It depends partly on how one evaluates the disutility of the wives' work and their absence from home and family. In this connection it is interesting that the recent 'Women's Lib' movement, or at any rate the general secular trend towards greater participation of women of all income groups and social groups in the economic and productive processes of a country, will mean greater inequality of incomes between households; for it will mean that the proportion of richer wives who go to work and supplement their family incomes will tend to rise towards the level of that already found in the lower income groups. In other words, it will tend to eliminate the equalising effect of the previous greater employment rate among married women in lower-income groups.

Another important conceptual problem concerns the *time period* to which the recorded income relates. It is usually taken for granted that the data refer to income obtained in the course of a year, simply because data – particularly tax data – are usually on an annual basis. But many economists take the view that it would be more useful, from a welfare point of view, to have data on the distribution of *lifetime* incomes. There are various issues that arise here. For example, suppose that everybody began his working life with the same pay, and received the same annual increments throughout his working life, and retired at the same age with a pension that represented some low proportion of the average income he had received, say, during the whole of his life. If exactly the same rules were applied to everybody over their whole lives, so that everybody earned exactly the same income throughout his life as well as at any given age, there is a sense in which one could say that incomes are equal. But, if we look at the usual annual figures we will see that the distribution of income is far from equal simply because there will be many young people and retired people whose incomes in any one year will be below those of people nearer their final peak incomes from employment. The distribution of incomes, in other words, will reflect the age distribution of the population.

And this will be the case to some extent even if we abandon the strong assumption made in the last example; for it is true that in the real world younger people and retired people tend to receive lower incomes than those in the middle of their economically active lives. (Also, there tends to be more progression in annual rates of pay among salaried and managerial and professional occupations than in manual labour.) Hence, a rise in the proportion of young or retired people in the population will show up in the figures as increased inequality of income distribution in any one year. But again, it is not clear that this would correspond to a genuine reduction in welfare. Indeed, in some cases it might reflect a genuine increase in welfare. For example, the rise in income levels in general over the last century, together with the trend, during the last two decades, towards more generous retirement pension provisions, means that more people now retire earlier than had been financially possible in earlier times. In doing so they may take a cut in income, but insofar as they prefer to do this, rather than to continue working, their welfare is presumably increased.

If the data were expressed in terms of the distribution of lifetime incomes – i.e. what proportion of people were in different income brackets over their whole life – such changes in incomes throughout one's life on account of the relation between age and earnings would not affect the estimates. Another reason for concentrating on the distribution of lifetime incomes could be that one might take the view, simply as a matter of justice, that a person who is poor but who has dissipated a large income when he was younger, instead of putting some of it aside for a rainy day or his old age, is less deserving of help, in the form of charity or income maintenance benefits or other social aid, than somebody who has not had such a good time earlier on. In other words, it would be argued that justice and equity and all that require an attempt to equalise – at least as far as economic processes are concerned – the welfare that people have had throughout their lives. On this basis, the person who has had a fine time with lots of money for much of his life does not deserve the same consideration as the person who has not. Hence, it is equality in terms of lifetime incomes that would be needed. Such a view would, of course, reflect what is perhaps rather an extreme value judgement, and many people would say that one poor man deserves as much aid as another poor man, irrespective of his previous affluence. Indeed, one could go even further than that and argue that the richer a person has been before suffering a fall in income the more he will suffer from a given low income later, since his acquired 'needs' will be greater. If this view is adopted it would follow that a rich man who falls on hard times should receive more consideration than one who had always been poor.

But without pursuing further these philosophical aspects of the choice between annual income and lifetime income, there are still other ways in which the choice of the time period used affects the interpretation of the data. For, in addition to changes in the proportion of young or retired people in the population and so on, there will be other factors that will make the lifetime distribution of incomes behave differently from the usual annual income data. One of these is the degree of short-term fluctuations in the fortunes of individuals, on account of economic uncertainties and so on. Many people, for example, are often temporarily unemployed or temporarily unable to work at the level of pay to which they can normally aspire. During such periods they will appear, in the income distribution statistics, among the relatively low-income groups. But they may not necessarily experience any great hardship if their reduction of income is a short-lived matter, particularly if they have some savings of other disposable assets.

150

More generally, on account of fluctuating fortunes, some people who are in the low-income groups at some points in time will be in higher-income groups at other points of time, either on account of short-term fluctuations or on account of the longer-run changes in people's incomes at various stages in their lives. Hence, as Simon Kuznets has pointed out, ' . . . there is little meaning to the question whether the poor are getting poorer and the rich richer'.[1] All that one can say, on the basis of annual data, is that so many people are poor at a given time, and possibly the same number or a different number are poor at some other point in time. But they may not be the same people. Income distribution data in terms of lifetime incomes would clearly be more relevant to answering the question posed by Kuznets.

However, insofar as it is agreed that data in terms of household or family units would be more useful from a welfare point of view, this creates difficulties for the measurement of the distribution of lifetime earnings. For the composition of a household will change over time. Individuals are members of different households during the course of their lives. An individual remains the same person throughout his life, but a household does not. Hence, whilst it may make sense to talk about the lifetime income of an individual, it makes less sense to talk about the lifetime income of a family.

These various conceptual problems in the distribution of incomes by size immediately suggest some of the possible causes of changes over time in the inequality of incomes. It is useful to distinguish between two types of influences on the size distribution of income, though they are inter-related. First, there are the relatively economic factors that affect wages relative to profits and the relative earnings of different groups of employees – e.g. how unequal are the wages paid in different occupations or to different sexes or ages. Secondly, there are those factors of a largely demographic and social nature that determine, for example, average family size, the degree of female participation in the labour force, the age of retirement and so on.

For example, we have already seen how the trend towards smaller families has narrowed the earlier disparity between

[1] Simon Kuznets *Modern Economic Growth*, Yale University Press, New Haven and London, 1966, page 205.

earnings and needs in large families, or the way that the splitting up of households, or a tendency towards earlier retirement, will have added to the proportion of households in lower-income brackets. But we have said little so far about the purely economic factors affecting the dispersion of incomes among individuals. The only development mentioned so far under this heading has been the secular decline in the share of property income in total income and the corresponding rise in income from employment. Insofar as people enjoying property income were, on the whole, in the upper-income groups, this trend will have tended to reduce the inequality of income distribution by size of income.

But another important factor is the degree of inequality among earned incomes – i.e. the extent to which some wage- or salary-earners receive much more than others. Here one of the important longer-run changes – which is particularly important for developing countries – has been the emergence of 'modern' sectors, by comparison with traditional sectors, particularly agriculture. Insofar as average incomes per head are much higher in the new modern sectors, with much higher capital per head, the shift of population from the former to the latter could affect inequality either way. At first it might increase inequality insofar as nearly the whole population had hitherto existed on a rather low income per head, so that the rise in incomes in the new sectors was confined to a fortunate group in the total population. However, if the process continued a point might be reached beyond which relatively few people were left in the low-income sector, so that a further shift would reduce measured inequality. On the other hand, the effect of this inter-sectoral shift is also complicated by the fact that earnings might be more unequally distributed in the modern sector than in old-fashioned agriculture, so that the rising weight of the modern sector could increase overall inequality. Furthermore, the process of economic development and modernisation might mean the opening up of a large gap between the very productive and less productive units in the old sector – e.g. there might be dramatic changes in agricultural techniques, marketing, scale of operations and so on, such as those associated with the 'Green Revolution', which could add to inequality in the old sector and hence in the population as a whole.

Apart from inter-sectoral shifts, the factors affecting the degree of dispersion of earned incomes will also include the relative size of the unskilled labour force as against managerial, technical and professional grades, to which reference has been made in the first part of this chapter. They will also include the importance of part-time employment, or the relative pay of men to women, which is an example of the interaction between the purely economic factors and the social or quasi-economic factors. For insofar as women are generally paid less than men, an increased weight of women in the labour force will increase the inequality of *earned* income distribution in terms of individuals (though, as indicated above, it could reduce it in terms of families as long as it is mainly women in lower-income groups who take up employment).[1]

Thus it is extremely difficult to generalise about the manner in which economic development or economic growth in particular will affect the size distribution of income, although there is quite a lot of evidence to support the view that inter-sectoral shifts have tended to increase inequality in the early stages of development but to reduce it in later stages. For what are no doubt similar reasons, there is considerable evidence for the view that the inequality of income today is greater in the developing countries than in the advanced countries.[2]

It also appears that, although there was some reduction of inequality in the advanced countries from near the end of the last century (and even earlier in the UK) until shortly after the Second World War, this process has more or less come to a halt during the last decade or so, particularly if no allowance is made for the effect on the size distribution of income of government taxes and benefits. For example, in the USA in 1947 the poorest fifth of families received only 5·1% of total pre-tax incomes whereas the richest 5% of families received 43·3%. In 1972 the corresponding percentages were 5·4% and 41·4% respectively, a slight narrowing of the dispersion but nothing

[1] A very detailed list of the numerous factors that will affect the size distribution of income over time is given in J. L. Nicholson's 'The Distribution and Redistribution of Income in the United Kingdom' in D. Wedderburn (ed.) *Poverty, Inequality and Class Structure*, Cambridge, University Press, 1974.

[2] One of the best and most recent surveys is by Felix Paukert 'Income distribution at different levels of development: a survey of evidence' in *International Labour Review*, 108, Aug./Sept. 1973.

dramatic.[1] In the UK, too, it appears that there has been no statistically significant change in the inequality of income distribution during the last twenty years, or even since just before the Second World War, and if anything there may have been a slight increase in pre-tax inequality.

After allowances for all government taxes and benefits, of course, the inequality of the size distribution of income is much smaller than the inequality of income distribution before taxes and benefits are taken into account. Exactly how far the redistributive activities of the State affect the final inequality of income distribution raises three main types of question.

First, it depends how inequality is measured to begin with – i.e. what overall statistic is used to sum up the overall inequality of the income distribution. There are several alternatives on the market, such as the Gini coefficient, the variance in the natural logs of income, the ratio between the proportions of income going to the top and bottom tenths in the income distributions and so on. It would be beyond the scope of this book to go into the pros and cons of the alternative measures. The only point that needs to be made here is that in order to say by how much inequality has changes – over time or as a result of some policy measures – the best one can do is to say by how much some particular measure of inequality has changed.

Secondly, a major conceptual problem is the extent to which taxes and benefits, or any other government policies affecting income distribution, 'feed back' on the original distribution. For example, suppose the government imposes a payroll tax on labour that has to be paid by the employers (e.g. social insurance contributions) in order to finance benefits that will go mainly to employees. The outcome may merely be that wages will be less than would have been the case had the tax on labour not been imposed, so that, in the end, final wage-earners' income including benefits is no greater. Conversely, if the government gives generous family allowances to employees, they may accept lower wages in the course of wage negotiations than if such benefits had not been available. Of course, the precise distribution among individuals, or groups, of the feed back effects of government taxes and benefits will not always correspond to the

---

[1] Economic Report of the President and Annual Report of the Council of Economic Advisers, Washington, DC, 1974, Table 34, page 140.

154

distribution of the taxes and benefits, so that some people will still lose and others gain. But it is far from certain that, across the board, the final distribution of income will be any less un-equal after allowing for the manner in which taxes and benefits feed back on the original distribution of incomes. Hence, at best, measures of the difference between the distribution of final incomes and the distribution of original incomes, which might appear to represent measures of the equalising effect of the State's redistributive activities, probably exaggerate this effect insofar as the taxes and benefits used for this purpose merely make the distribution of original incomes more unequal.

Thirdly, much depends on precisely which taxes and benefits are taken into account in measuring the impact of the State on income distribution. For example, in the UK, where regular estimates are published, in *Economic Trends*, of the distribution of income before and after taxes and benefits, account is taken of direct taxes on personal income and employees' contributions to national insurance and health. Taxes on capital – such as death duties or capital gains taxes – are not included. But allow-ance is made for indirect taxes according to the pattern of expenditures of the various income groups and family types under consideration.

On the benefits side, account is taken of direct benefits in cash or in kind. The former include family allowances, pensions and national insurance benefits, and the latter include the use of the national health service, state education and certain other welfare services or special transfer payments (educational scholarships and grants). But no attempt is made to allocate to different income groups, or family types, their respective 'benefits' from public expenditures such as general administra-tion, defence, police, museums and so on. In fact, it is doubtful whether it is possible to find a satisfactory method of allocating this sort of public expenditures among different income groups in a meaningful manner. The British estimates, which do allocate public education and health services, go much further than those of almost any other country in distributing major public expenditures among the various income and family groups.

One of the important findings of the work carried out in

Britain on redistribution is that, for each type of family, total direct and indirect taxes 'form a remarkably stable proportion of income over a wide range of incomes. . .'.[1] A similar conclusion has been reached in a recent extremely sophisticated study of the USA.[2] In Britain the overall lack of progressivity of taxes appears to be because, although income tax is progressive (i.e., the higher the income the greater the share of it taken by the tax), national insurance and health contributions are regressive. This is not surprising given that they have tended to be on a flat rate basis in Britain and hence take a larger share of low incomes than of high incomes. The same applies to indirect taxes, most of which – but not all – are regressive. This is the case, for example, with indirect taxes on most alcoholic drink and tobacco, but not with excise taxes on motorcars, or cigars or wines or jewellery. But if we consider the effect of taxes on horizontal equality the story is slightly different and the proportion of income taken by taxes falls with size of family; largely on account of the tax allowances for children in Britain (relatively large in Britain and the USA by contrast with many European countries which rely much more on special cash payments to families with children).

Since all taxes taken together have a negligible effect on vertical equality and only a slight progressive effect on horizontal equality, the redistributive impact of the State depends largely on the impact of the benefits. Here it appears that the progressive effect is more pronounced, particularly because of the progressive effect on horizontal equality of all social service benefits, such as family allowances and education. Some benefits, notably pensions and the National Health Service, also reduce vertical inequality significantly.

Thus, the size of the State's egalitarian impact on income distribution will depend to some extent on the precise coverage of the taxes and benefits included and the assumptions made as to who *finally* pays the various taxes (e.g. whether some are passed on in higher prices or wages) and who finally receives the benefits, etc. Since measures of the inequality of income dis-

[1] J. L. Nicholson 'The Distribution and Redistribution of Income in the UK', op. cit.
[2] Joseph A. Pechman and Benjamin A. Okner *Who Bears the Tax Burden?* Brookings Institution, Washington, DC, 1974, especially pages 5–10.

tribution for any given country at any point of time differ considerably according to what particular taxes and benefits are included, it is important to ascertain their coverage before drawing conclusions as to the scope of the State's redistributive impact.

Also, we have not yet raised the question of how income is defined in the first place, and again there is scope for difference of opinion or differences in practical possibility concerning the concept of income used. For example, how far does family income include, for purposes of this sort of analysis, income in kind (e.g. from an owner-occupied house) and how far are capital gains included? This leads on to another whole area for discussion, namely the importance of the inequality in the distribution of wealth – i.e. of assets such as stocks and bonds, fixed assets such as houses and land, insurance policies and so on.

So far we have discussed only the distribution of income. But from a welfare point of view there is much to be said for the view that what matters is the inequality in people's total command over goods and services – i.e. differences in their purchasing power. And this is clearly not a matter of income only. Some people may maintain high standards of living by consuming their capital. Also, ownership of capital confers other advantages, such as security, possibilities of making capital gains (which are generally taxed at a relatively low rate) and the power and opportunity to invest in education for one's children (or oneself) and hence enhance their future income-earning potential. But while this is an extremely interesting topic, and has a major bearing on the causes of inequalities of income as well as on the welfare implications of such inequalities as exist, it is a topic that cannot be pursued here, since this is a book about national *income*, not about national *wealth*.

Chapter 8

What makes national product change? (I)

1. Introduction

The previous chapters explain the various concepts and categories used by economists for purposes of answering many of
the important questions about the economy in which they are
interested. One of these questions is 'What makes the level
of income (or national product) change?' The categories of
transactions described so far are generally agreed to be of
central importance for answering this question (as well as
others). But this agreement among economists about the determinants of changes in the level of income only applies to short-
run changes. The forces determining economic change in the
longer run – say over a period of three to five years and upward –
are still not very satisfactorily understood. This is, partly, no
doubt, because many of these forces lie outside the scope of
economics proper and are much more the concern of sociology,
politics and other social sciences. Thus, there is no 'model' of
long-run economic growth that is generally accepted in the
same way as the model of short-run variations in the level of
income or output.

What is meant by 'short-run' and 'long-run'? In economics,
one often distinguishes between the short and the long run
according to whether or not productive capacity can be significantly changed. In the theory of the way that a firm fixes its
level of output, for example, a distinction is made between its
short-run cost curve and its long-run cost curve. The former is
related to the change in the firm's costs as it changes output
without being able to vary all the factors of production it uses
(particularly plant and equipment). The long-run cost curve is
related to costs of production with different sizes of plant. In the
theory of income determination the distinction between the

short and the long run is between, on the one hand, fluctuations in income or output that are caused by disequilibria between demand and a more or less given potential output and, on the other hand, the forces that, over the longer run, determine the growth of potential output and capacity. The latter is the province of the theory of economic growth and is not dealt with at all in this book. In this book we shall be concerned only with the causes of fluctuations in the level of output in the short-run – i.e. taking the capacity of the economy (or its productive potential) as something that cannot vary significantly within the period concerned.

This is not a very precise distinction between the short and the long run, since what is a 'significant' change in the capacity of the economy is a matter of judgement. As will be seen in this chapter, one of the components of total demand on which we shall concentrate is investment, so that insofar as there is any net investment there must be some violation of the assumption that the capacity of the economy is given. This is the price one pays, however, for the simplification that is necessary in order to exclude from our analysis the forces responsible for the longer-run growth of the economy.

A related problem is the notion of 'equilibrium' which we shall be forced to use frequently in the course of the following chapters. The student will no doubt have encountered this concept already in elementary price theory, the 'equilibrium' price for a commodity being one where demand is equal to supply. The concept of equilibrium is not, however, quite as straightforward as might seem at first sight. It is frequently convenient to think of it as representing a situation in which there is a balance of forces, but this interpretation is not entirely satisfactory. In the context of the short period with which we are concerned here it is preferable to follow Professor Hicks' description of the state of equilibrium as prevailing 'when all the "individuals" in it are choosing those quantities, which, out of the alternatives available to them, they prefer to produce and to consume. *Individuals* is to be taken in a wide sense, to include any units, as for instance firms, to which we attribute some freedom of independent choice.'[1] For example, to anticipate

[1] Professor Sir John Hicks *Capital and Growth* (page 15), Oxford University Press, 1965.

159

again the essence of the following chapters, it will be seen that the level of national product will be in short-run 'equilibrium' when the amount of capital formation (investment) that 'individuals' wish to carry out is equal to the amount of savings that 'individuals' wish to make. As regards the investment, the 'individuals' will comprise mainly firms and the government, though as regards savings it might also comprise 'individuals' in the more normal sense of the word. The point is that, as far as their choice between investment and non-investment or between savings and non-savings is concerned, equilibrium will hold when all 'individuals' are choosing those combinations that they wish (given the alternatives available to them).

Finally, we shall be concerned, in the next two chapters, with the way that national output or income changes *on the assumption that prices are constant*. That is, we are concerned with 'real' changes in the volume of national product, not its nominal value. Since we have also excluded changes in capacity from our equilibrating mechanism, this implies that the changes in output which we are trying to explain must be taking place inside the capacity limitations set by existing factors of production and techniques and tastes (such as tastes for work rather than leisure). Changes in total demand for national product, therefore, will be matched by changes in output within our short period – though the immediate effect might be a change in stocks, as will be explained below. In the situations we shall be examining, for example, a rise in total demand in the economy will not produce any rise in prices and so will not lead to any adjustment of demand. Apart from a possible temporary change in stocks it will be met by a rise in output and most of this, and the next chapter is about the process by which this comes about.

2. 'Leakages' and 're-injections' in the circular flow of incomes

In Chapter 2, it was pointed out that one way of looking at the three alternative concepts of national product (namely, final output, value added or incomes), was in terms of the point in a circular flow of transactions at which the flow is measured. For the very simple economy of Figure 2.2, in which there are only two sectors, the income flow is composed of payments by the household sector to the productive sector, these payments then being converted into payments of wages and other factor incomes paid out by the productive sector to the household sector, thereby closing the circle. But if there is any leak in this circuit the volume of the flow will obviously gradually decline until the system is emptied, *unless* either (i) the leak is stopped up, or (ii) a countervailing re-injection takes place to compensate all the time for the losses through the leak.

What, in fact, could constitute a leak in the sort of two-sector economy illustrated in Figure 2.2? The answer is obviously that a leak in the circular flow of incomes would occur if either of the two sectors did not pay out to the other sector the whole of its own receipts. For example, firms might prefer not to distribute to households the whole of the value added, preferring instead to put some of it aside. Alternatively, suppose that, one week after receiving its usual £100 wages and profit, households decided to save £20 of their incomes rather than spend the whole of it on purchases of consumption goods and services. Then, instead of £100 coming back to the productive sector in purchases of goods and services, only £80 would come back. Consequently, since incomes can only be generated to an amount

Figure 8.1

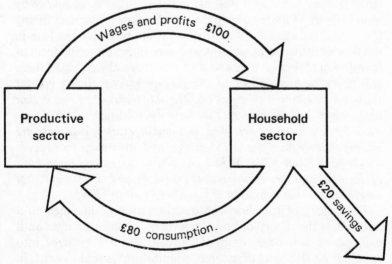

equal to final sales, only £80 of income (or value added) would be created in the productive sector and be available for distribution to households in the following week. In diagrammatic terms the circular flow of incomes would have a 'hole' in it at the point where the flow leaves the household sector, as shown in Figure 8.1.

With only two accounts in the picture, as above, there is nothing to stop the system from emptying itself. But if a capital account is introduced the situation changes. For this account represents, on the one hand, the absorption of the savings of the household sector, and, on the other hand, capital formation, which is an additional injection into the productive sector. For example, the system could be kept in equilibrium with £100 of income flowing round the circuit in the manner shown in the following diagram.

Figure 8.2 below will be recognised as simply an abridged form of the type of flow diagram already used to show the relationship between the production, household and capital accounts. And in the previous encounters with such accounting relationships it was already shown that both sides of each account, including the capital account, must balance and, in particular, savings were always equal to investment by definition. Hence, one might well ask what the fuss is about? Why worry about a failure to keep the circular flow of incomes at any given level on account of a possible failure to match the leak in the flow constituted by savings with a re-injection in the form of investment; for if savings and investment are always equal there can never be any danger of the savings leakage being greater than the investment re-injection. *The short answer to this is that the savings and investment that have been shown to be always equal by definition are actual savings and investment and these are not necessarily the same as the savings and investment that people would have liked to do, or had planned to do, at any given level of income, and are hence not the savings and investment that correspond to the definition of equilibrium given above.*

The theory of the short-run determination of incomes, in a nutshell, is the theory of how the level of incomes changes until *planned*, or *desired*, savings and investment are brought into equality. At this level of income 'equilibrium' is said to exist, in the sense that there is no inherent tendency for the level of income to change. The essence of the theory is that either planned savings or planned investment, or both, are related to the level of incomes (e.g. if incomes increase people wish to save more), so that a change in the level of income induces a change in planned savings or investment. Hence, if income is at a level at which the amount that people wish to save is not equal to the amount that other people wish to invest, the income level will change, thereby changing either planned savings or planned investment until the two are brought once more into equality. Thus the theory depends on the hypothesis that either savings or investment or both are, in fact, related to the level of income. If not, no variation in the income level could possibly help to

Figure 8.2

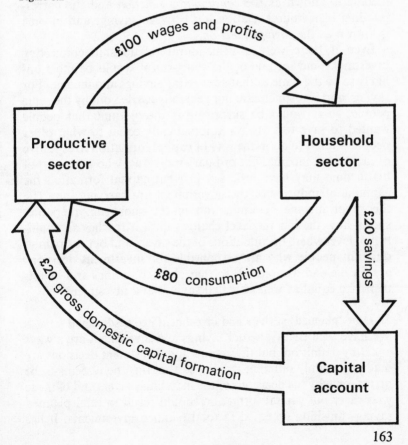

163

restore the equality of planned savings and investment since variations in income would not affect either of them.

The postulated relationship between savings (or investment) and income is a *behavioural* relationship, as distinct from an accounting relationship. For example, a possible behavioural relationship between consumption and income is shown on page 126. Since households' savings equal the difference between their consumption and their disposable income (i.e. their income after they have paid taxes), this equation also implies a behavioural relationship between savings and income of the following form:

$$S_h = -£5 + 0·2(Y_h + TP_g - T_h)$$

The behavioural relationship between consumption and income is known as the *consumption function* and the corresponding behavioural relationship between savings and income is known as the *savings function*.

Even if there were a behavioural relationship connecting investment and income in the short-run it would be most unlikely to be the same as that connecting savings and income. For savings and investment are not generally carried out by the same people, so it would be surprising if the amount that people wanted to save was always automatically equal to what other people wanted to do in the way of capital formation irrespective of the level of income. The ordinary individual who saves part of his income may have little say in what capital formation the captains of industry or the government are carrying out. The theory of income determination in the short-run, therefore, shows how the income level changes until it reaches an equilibrium level where the intentions of the savers and of the (mainly) different people who are responsible for investment decisions are, in the end, reconciled, so that planned savings and investment are equal as well as actual savings and investment.

3. How 'planned' savings and investment are made equal

We have seen that (i) actual savings and investment are always equal by definition, but (ii) savings and investment decisions are made by mainly different people, so that (iii) there seems to be no reason why the decisions of the individual savers and of those who carry out capital formation should result in total planned savings finishing up equal to total planned investments. It has further been alleged that it is a lack of equality between planned savings and investment that leads to short-run changes in the level of income. The reader may well ask, therefore, how, if actual savings are always equal to actual investment, planned savings and investment can be unequal. The answer is that if planned savings and investment are not equal then actual savings and investment, which are always equal, *must include some unplanned, or undesired*, savings or investment. The way that this will come about can best be seen by switching attention from savings and investment towards the corresponding market in goods and services, in the following manner.

(i) Possible effects of a rise in the savings ratio

Consider a simple economy in which there is no government sector and no foreign trade (i.e. no rest of world account). Suppose that, in some initial time period, say the first week, the economy is in equilibrium with no investment and with output at £100, representing the sales by firms to consumers of £100 worth of consumer goods. Since there is no foreign trade or government sector the whole of the value added of £100 is available for distribution, if the firms wish, to households. And let us assume that, in fact this £100 of value added is paid out entirely to households in the usual form of wages and profits, and that households saved nothing. But suppose now that, in the second week, households no longer want to spend the whole of their £100 income on consumer goods and prefer, instead, to save 20 % of it – i.e. their 'savings ratio' rises from zero to 20 % – so that they only spend £80 on consumer goods. What will happen in the firms' sector? Obviously firms will, if they had not anticipated the fall in demand, be left with £20's worth of unsold goods on their hands.[1] This will be recorded in our accounting system as an increase in stocks. Thus investment, which, it will be recalled, *includes changes in stocks*, will still be equal to savings.

Actual investment, including changes in stocks, now amounts to £20 and so is still equal to actual savings, which in this case are the same as planned savings, namely, £20. But actual investment now consisted of £20 of unplanned investment, namely the un-

---

[1] It will be recalled that, in the introduction to this chapter, we introduced the assumption that prices did not change. Thus firms will not dispose of their surplus goods by reducing prices.

intended increase of stocks by £20 which occurred only because dealers found themselves selling £20 less of goods than they normally sell.

But planned investment is still zero, and planned savings is 20% of income. We can now examine how this inequality leads to a change in the income level. As a result of the unexpected fall in consumers' demand and hence the unexpected rise in dealers' stocks, there will now be a tendency for firms to cut output, since if they went on producing at the old rate of £100 per week, with consumption now running at only £80 per week, unwanted stocks would go on accumulating. The excess of planned savings over planned investment has led to the demand for goods being less than the output. To avoid accumulating unsold goods producers will cut output and the reduction in output will, of course, mean a reduction in incomes and hence in demand and so on. The essential point to notice is that this adjustment in output has followed from the fact that the original supply of goods (£100's worth per week) has become too great given the new demand for goods, which has fallen from £100 per week to only £80 per week. This disequilibrium in the market for goods – i.e. this excess of the supply of goods over the demand for goods – arose because of an excess of planned savings over planned investment. Actual savings still equals actual investment at £20 each, but the £20 of actual investment is composed of £20 of unintended increase in stocks.

(ii) Possible effects of a fall in the savings ratio

In the last example, the disequilibrium between the demand and supply of goods arose because there was an increase in planned savings from zero to £20 without any increase in planned investment. Actual investment comprised £20 of unplanned investment. Conversely, a gap between demand and supply of goods can be seen in the reverse case of a deficiency of planned savings relative to investment rather than an excess. Suppose, for example, that the £100 of output had originated from the production of £80 of consumer goods and £20 of planned capital formation in the first week. Incomes would then equal £100, but suppose that, in the second week, householders wanted to spend all of their £100 of income on consumer goods rather than save any of their income. They would go along to the shops with their £100 to buy their consumer goods but would find that there were not enough such goods for them to buy. In the simple closed economy that we are assuming here, various things might then happen.

The consumers might simply be disappointed and be unable to spend all their £100, thereby being forced to save £20. In this case, demand exceeded supply, and producers will tend to raise production in order to satisfy the higher demand for consumer goods.[1] Looked at from the point of view of the equilibrium between savings and investment, what has happened is that the *actual* savings and investment are still equal, as always, but the £20 of actual household savings is more than was planned; it comprises £20 of unplanned savings.

Alternatively, instead of disappointing the consumers, firms might be able temporarily to satisfy the unexpected rise in consumer demand by running down their stocks by £20 below the usual level. This £20 fall in stocks amounts to a fall of £20 in capital formation, so that actual savings and investment are still equal, as usual, but this time it is planned savings that are satisfied (at zero) but the planned level of investment is lower by £20 than the actual level.

In both cases production will increase as firms try to meet the unexpected rise in demand for their products, whether their initial reaction had been to force consumers to save £20 more than they had wanted to save, or whether they had temporarily run down their stocks below the level that they had considered normal given the level of their output. The same applies if the outcome had been some combination of the two extreme possibilities mentioned above – i.e. if, say, consumers had been allowed to buy £90's worth of goods, thereby saving only £10 more than they had planned and firms ran down their stocks by £10 in an attempt partially to meet the unexpected rise in demand. In this latter case, the savings and investment account would show £10 actual saving and only £10 actual investment, for against the £20 of capital goods being produced to start with

---

[1] Again, our initial assumption of no price change precludes the possibility that firms will simply raise prices in response to the demand increase.

would have to be offset a negative item of £10 representing the running down of stocks by £10. In this case neither the savings nor the investment would be the desired or planned levels of savings or investment. The savings would be £10 more than was planned and the investment would be £10 less than was planned, on account of the £10 unplanned fall in their stocks.

Thus although actual savings and actual investment are always equal, a discrepancy between planned savings and investment will be reflected in a discrepancy between the planned supply and demand for goods. This will lead to a change in supply in order to adjust it to the new level of demand (given our initial assumptions of flexible supply and no change in prices).

4. How far does adjustment process go?

Still sticking to our simple economy we must now examine the next question, namely 'How far does the process of adjustment of output proceed before equilibrium is restored – i.e. before planned savings and investment are equal as well as *actual* savings and investment?' To answer this question precisely it is necessary to know a little more about the way that changes in income are related to changes in savings or in investment. That is to say we need to know more about the savings (or consumption) function and the investment function. In the last example we only knew that there was a shift in the amount that people wanted to save, when they were at an income level of £100 per week. Instead of continuing to save £20 at this income level they decided that they wanted to spend all the £100 on consumption. This led to an excess of demand over supply, with a consequent tendency to an increase in output, and hence, in incomes. Let us assume that the investment function takes the form that investment is constant – i.e. that it does not vary with income but is stable at the original level of £20 per week. Planned savings would then obviously only become equal to planned investment when incomes had risen to the point where households wanted to save £20. Only at that point would the leakage in the system be exactly offset by the re-injection in the form of investment, so only at that point would demand and supply be equal. But how far the process of adjustment goes before planned savings have been brought back into equality with planned investment depends, obviously, on how savings are related to changes in

168

income. That is to say, it depends on the specific behavioural relationship between savings and income.

Consider a situation in which total national output had been in equilibrium at £100, composed of £90 of consumer goods and £10 of capital formation. Suppose now that households had originally saved £10, indicating that the original behavioural relationship was that savings equal 10% of income. Assume now that in 'week' 1, households decide that they would like to save 20% of their incomes, so that at the £100 income level planned savings would be £20 instead of £10. Firms would then suddenly find themselves with £10 of unsold goods on their hands (constituting £10 of unplanned investment). Suppose that as a result, in week 2, they reduce output to £90,[1] comprising the same £10 of capital formation as originally but only £80 of consumers' goods, this being the new reduced demand for consumer goods. But we know that output is equal to income, so that incomes have also fallen to £90. Now, if households still persist in trying to save 20% of their incomes they will want to save 20% of £90, instead of 20% of £100 as before. This will mean that in the second week they will try to save £18 and to spend only £72. But this £72 is still less than the new and lower output of consumer goods, which had been cut from £90 to £80. So there will still be a disequilibrium in the market for consumer goods – supply having fallen to £80, but demand having fallen to £72. Thus firms will reduce output even further to eliminate the excess of £8 of supply over demand.

This sequence can continue for some time before equilibrium in the market is restored, as can be seen in the following table. In this table, the second column represents the situation in the second time-period (which we have assumed to be the second week) when firms had cut output from £100 (£10 capital goods plus £90 consumption goods) to £90 (£10 capital goods plus £80 consumption goods). But, as this column shows, if the behavioural relationship linking income to savings is such that, at any level of income, savings will be 20% of the income of that week, then at an income level of £90 savings will be £18, so that consumption will be £72. This means, as is shown in row 6, that the output of consumption goods, at £80 exceeds the demand

---

[1] They might reduce output to below £90 if they wanted not merely to adjust to the lower level of demand but also to be able to get rid of surplus stock.

for them by £8 – i.e. excess supply is £8. Similarly, as is shown in row 7 in terms of savings and investment, the excess of desired (i.e. planned) savings over planned investment is also £8.

WEEKS:	1	2	3	4	n
1 Output (=income)	100	90	82	75·6	50
2 Investment	10	10	10	10	10
3 Consumption goods produced (=consumption goods demanded in previous week)	90	80	72	65·6	40
4 Desired (planned) savings (=20% of row 1)	20	18	16·4	15·1	10
5 Consumption goods demanded (=80% of row 1)	80	72	65·6	60·5	40
6 ∴ excess supply (=row 3 – row 5)	10	8	6·4	5·1	0
7 Difference between planned savings and planned investment (=row 4 – row 2)	10	8	6·4	5·1	0

The third column of the above table represents the next step in the sequence. Output of consumer goods would be cut to £72 in view of the fall in demand to this level at the last stage, so that total output and total incomes in the second column would fall to £82 (including the £10 of investment on goods). At this level of incomes, the attempt to save 20% of their incomes would mean that households' demand for consumer goods would fall further to £65·6, with a further fall in output and so on and so forth. It should be noted that, at every stage, the disequilibrium in the market for goods, which is shown in row 6 and which equals the difference between the value of goods produced and the demand for goods is necessarily equal to the excess of planned savings over planned investment, which is shown in row 7. They are two sides of the same coin.

Where does this particular sequence of declining incomes and output come to an end? Other things being equal, this depends on whether the proportion of their income that the community wishes to save is 20% of income irrespective of the level of income. In the unlikely case that the savings function does take this form then the last column of the above table shows the final equilibrium position. It shows that when income has fallen to £50 the excess of supply over demand is zero, as is, of course, the excess of planned savings over planned investment. At this point, therefore, there will be no forces operating to bring about a further reduction in output – all the output produced has been sold.

5. A quick method of finding the equilibrium level of income and output

But it would be very laborious to have to find out at what income level the new equilibrium can be achieved by plodding through a whole sequence of calculations such as that shown in the above table. Fortunately this is quite unnecessary. For we have seen that equilibrium can only be achieved when planned savings equal planned investment. Only at this point will the leakage be offset by the re-injection. And so only at this point will the demand and supply in the market for the product of the economy be equal, since only at this point will that part of output that is composed of consumer goods be equal to that part of their income that people *want* to spend on consumer goods. If equilibrium is only reached at the point where planned savings is equal to planned investment there is a simple way of calculating the equilibrium level of income. For the equilibrium level of income must be that level which, when multiplied by the proportion of incomes that people desire to save, yields just that level of desired (or planned) savings that is equal to planned investment.

Using the same symbols as before, but with it being understood that the savings and investment referred to now are the *planned* savings and investment, the equilibrium level of income is such that when it is multiplied by the proportion of incomes that people wish to save, which is equal to S/Y, the resulting savings, S, is equal to planned investment I.

In the example shown in the above table, the savings ratio rose from 10% to 20% of income – i.e. S/Y rose from 0·1 to 0·2. Investment (I) was given as fixed at £10. Hence income would be in equilibrium when 0·2 of income equalled £10. This only occurs when income is equal to £50. At this level of income, 0·2 multiplied by Y is equal to I. In other words, income is in equilibrium when planned S equals planned I,

but $$S = \frac{S}{Y} \times Y$$

171

so income is in equilibrium when

$$\frac{S}{Y} \times Y = I$$

or when

$$Y = \frac{I}{S/Y}$$

which, in the above case, is when

$$Y = \frac{£10}{0 \cdot 2} = £50$$

As a check, with $S/Y = 0 \cdot 2$, and $Y = £50$, S must equal £10, which is equal to planned investment, and so this is the equilibrium level of income.

Thus, given the level of investment, the equilibrium level of income can be rapidly calculated by dividing it by the proportion of income that is saved – i.e. the 'average propensity to save' – *provided that this proportion remains stable irrespective of the level of income*. For example, if the level of planned investment were to remain at £10 as in the above example, but the average propensity to save were 15% instead of 20%, then the equilibrium level of income would be £10/0·15, which equals £66·66. For 15% of this is £10, so that this is the income level at which planned savings is equal to planned investment of £10. If, on the other hand, the average propensity to save were to be 0·2, as originally, but with planned investment at £20, instead of £10, then the equilibrium level of income would be £20/0·2, which equals £100. At this income level, planned savings, at 20% of £100, equals £20, which is equal to planned investment.

We have seen, particularly in the numerical example on page 170, that equilibrium is attained where planned savings equal planned investment, which is the same as where the demand for and supply of goods are equal. Corresponding to these two ways of looking at the equilibrium conditions, there are two diagrammatic methods of showing how the final equilibrium level of income is determined. The first concentrates on savings and hence on how this leak in the circular flow of incomes is offset by the re-injections into this flow constituted by investment. The second concentrates on consumption, rather than savings, and hence on the total demand for goods and services if consumption demand is added to investment demand. Since income is either spent on consumption or saved, the behavioural equation for savings used in the first presentation must correspond to a particular consumption function in the second presentation.

In Figure 8.3 below, the first type of diagram is shown. In this diagram, income is measured along the horizontal axis, and planned savings and investment along the vertical axis. The figure illustrates a situation in which investment is assumed to be fixed at £10 – that is to say, it does not vary with variations in the level of income. Consequently, the investment line I, is a horizontal line indicating that planned investment remains at the value £10 whatever the level of income measured along the income axis. The lines S_1 or S_2, however, illustrate two alternative savings functions.

Thus the line S_1 reflects a behavioural equation according to which people wish to save 10% of their income whatever their income level (an unrealistic assumption that will eventually be relaxed). It can be seen from the line that at the income level of £100 (as measured along the horizontal axis) planned savings is

Figure 8.3

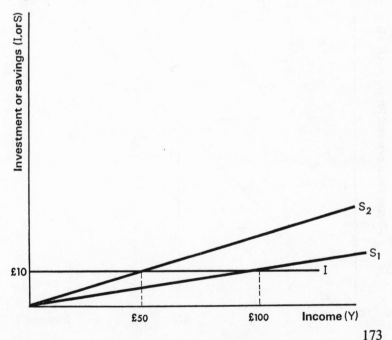

equal to £10 (measured along the vertical axis). Similarly, with the same S_1 line, at an income level of £50, planned savings would be equal to £5. If we start with the savings line S_1, indicating that people wish to save 10% of their income at any level of income, then it can be seen from the diagram that the planned savings line cuts the planned investment line at the income level of £100, and so this is the equilibrium level of income.

Suppose now that people decide to save 20% of their income (at any level of income). The savings line would then shift to line S_2. And it can be seen at a glance that this line cuts the investment line at the income level of £50, since it is at this level that planned savings is now equal to investment of £10.

The second type of diagram referred to above is the one in which the equilibrium process is looked at from the point of view of the balance of demand and supply in the market for goods and services.

One ingredient of such a diagram needs to be introduced at the outset. This is the '45° line'. In Figure 8.4 below, income is

Figure 8.4

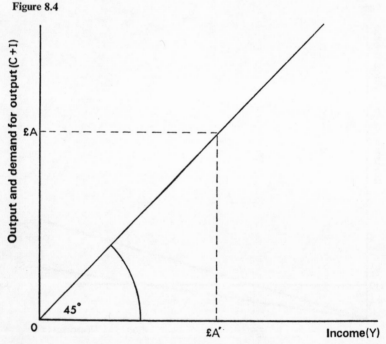

measured along the horizontal axis, and up the vertical axis are measured both (a) total output and (b) the amount of goods and services demanded at each level of income. Given that scales along both axes are equal, the 45° line has the property that given any level of output on the vertical axis, such as the point £A, one can read off along the horizontal axis, with the aid of the 45° line, the amount of income generated by the level of output £A. For income is equal to output, and by moving horizontally from the point A to the 45° line and then downwards vertically to the point £A' on the horizontal axis, the distance OA' must be equal to the distance OA. Hence, if output, which is shown on the vertical axis, is equal to OA, income, which is shown along the horizontal axis, must be equal to OA'.

In Figure 8.5 below we now insert the lines representing the two categories of output, consumption and investment, showing

Figure 8.5

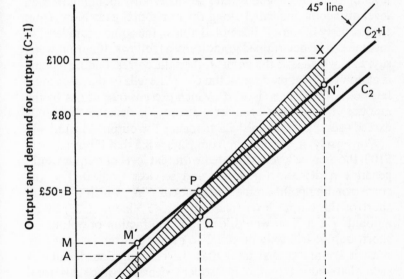

175

how they are related to the level of income. As in Figure 8.3, the investment line is a horizontal line indicating that the demand for investment goods is fixed at £10 per unit of time irrespective of the level of income. But the consumption line, C, which is now introduced, must show a level of consumption demand for every level of income that matches the planned savings line of Figure 8.3. For consumption demand is simply the difference between planned savings and incomes. The shaded area between the C line and the 45° line must therefore represent the savings associated with every level of income. If the S' line is steeper, the C line in Figure 8.5 would be correspondingly flatter, leaving a greater shaded area. Of the two S lines in Figure 8.3, the steeper is S_2, which will correspond to C_2 in Figure 8.5, which shows that consumption demand is always 80% of income.

If the consumption demand associated with every level of income as given by the C line is added to investment demand as given by the I line, then the resulting line, $C+I$, shows the total level of demand for goods (and services) corresponding to each level of income indicated along the horizontal axis. Now, from the property of the 45° line noted above, the equilibrium level of income can be determined graphically as follows. If output were, say, £25, which is at the point A, then the corresponding income is at point A'. But reading off the $C+I$ line tells us that at income level OA', the *demand* is $A'M'$, which exceeds output OA by the amount AM. As has been seen already, if demand for goods exceeds supply there will be a tendency for output to rise.[1]

Conversely, it can be seen from Figure 8.5 that if output were £100, the income level associated with that level of output would generate a demand for goods and services (indicated at the corresponding point on the $C+I$ line) of $C'N'$, which would fall short of the output level (read off the 45° line as $C'X$) by an amount $N'X$ and so would lead to a contraction of output. In short, output will only be equal to demand at the level of £50, since it is only at that level that the consumption demand is such that, added to the investment demand, it equals total output. That is, it is only at that income level that the $C+I$ line cuts the 45° line.

---

[1] It will be recalled that there is only a 'tendency' for output to rise in real terms: it may not be possible, in practice, to squeeze any more output from available resources, but we have assumed at the outset that output is flexible.

The numerical example of page 170 showed that the equilibrium position of income could be determined from two points of view, either from the point of view of what income level made planned savings equal to planned investment (where row 2 equalled row 4), or what income level made planned demand for goods equal to the output (where rows 2 plus 5 equalled row 1). Figure 8.3 illustrates the former approach and Figure 8.5 illustrates the latter approach. The answers must, of course, be the same, and the close connection between the two diagrams will be fairly obvious. For example, in Figure 8.5, at the equilibrium level of output and income of £50, it can be seen that the reason why planned $C+I$ equals output is that the savings represented by the gap between C and the 45° line, namely PQ, is just equal to investment at that income level, which is the same result as in Figure 8.3.

The Figure 8.5 type of diagram can also be used, like Figure 8.3, of course, to analyse how a change in the proportion of their incomes that people wish to save affects the equilibrium level of income. In Figure 8.3 an upward shoft in the proportion of their incomes that people wanted to save, from 10% to 20% was illustrated by the shift from S_1 to S_2 – i.e. to a steeper savings line. In Figure 8.5 this would involve a downward shift in the proportion of their incomes that people wanted to spend on consumer goods – like to a flatter C line, which would obviously also mean that the combined demand curve, $C+I$, would also have a flatter slope and so intersect the 45° line at a lower level of income.

EXERCISES 8

N B. In all the following exercises the symbols, S and I represent planned savings and investment respectively, and Y represents income (equals output).

1   If $S = 0.3Y$, what is planned savings when
     (i) $Y = 100$; (ii) $Y = 150$?
    Draw a graph, with savings on the vertical axis and income on the horizontal axis, from which planned savings can be read for any level of income over the range $Y = 0$ to $Y = 300$.

2   If $S = 0.2Y$,
    (a) what is Y when

(i) $S=15$; (ii) $S=20$; (iii) $S=35$?
(b) insert the line representing $S=0.2Y$ on the graph specified in question 1 and check your answer to part (a) of this question.
(c) still with $S=0.2Y$, what is the demand for consumer goods (i.e. planned C_h) when the level of income is (i) 100; (ii) 250?

3 If I is constant, at 15, at any level of income add the line representing investment to the graph requested in question 1 above and then
(a) at what level of income do the two lines intersect?
(b) what is savings at this level of income – both by reading off the graph and by the algebraic method used, presumably, in answering question 1?

4 With $I=20$ for any level of income
(a) what is the equilibrium level of income if $S=0.1Y$ and $S=0.2Y$?
(b) draw graphs similar to those mentioned above and check at what income levels the I line intersects the two S lines.
(c) with the same two S equations, what is the equilibrium level of income if, instead of $I=20$, $I=30$?
(d) insert the $I=30$ line on the graph for this question and check the answer to (c).
(e) from inspection of this graph, what happens to the equilibrium level of income if I increases, for any given S line?
(f) for any given I line, what happens to the equilibrium level of income as the proportion of their incomes that people wish to save gets smaller, in the sense that the S line gets flatter?
(g) given the I line, what happens to *actual* savings as the S line gets flatter, and what happens to income?
(h) given the S line what happens to actual savings as the I line rises horizontally? And what happens to the equilibrium level of income?

Chapter 9

What makes national product change? (II)

In the last chapter we have seen that the 'equilibrium' level of income is the one where the savings that would be desired at that income level are equal to the investment that is desired at the same level. Consequently, we have been able to specify exactly how this 'equilibrium' level of income may be calculated given the relationships between savings and investment on the one hand, and income on the other. In this chapter we will extend the analysis in three ways. First, we will drop the assumption that, whatever the precise proportion of income that people wish to save, this proportion remains stable over the whole range of income. Secondly, we shall examine the way income *changes* when one of the determinants of the equilibrium income level changes. This is known as 'multiplier' analysis. Thirdly, we shall relax the simplifying assumption that there is no foreign trade or government sector in the economy.

1. The consumption function and the equilibrium conditions
In the last chapter the bulk of the analysis was in terms of a proportionate relationship between income and savings that did not vary as income changed. For example, they took the form of relationships such as that planned savings would be 10% of income or 20% of income at any income level, which is the same as saying that people will want to spend 90% or 80% of their income whatever the income level. This, however, is probably a very unrealistic representation of the way that people's spending and saving habits are related to their incomes. The statistical evidence about this is not as unambiguous as one would like and the author's guess about the true relationship is probably hardly any better than the reader's. But it does seem fairly safe to say that the lower the income level, the greater is the *propor-*

tion of their income that people wish to spend, and hence the smaller is the *proportion* they wish to save. A very poor man will rarely save, and may have to borrow, whereas a rich man may save a substantial proportion of his income. Beyond such fairly vague generalisations, however, the precise relationship between income and consumption, or savings – which is known as the *consumption function* – is more difficult to identify. For example, little is certain about the way that savings habits are affected by the interest rate. Little is known for certain, either, about how they are affected by short period changes in income as distinct from more permanent changes – i.e. how long are the time lags before people adjust themselves to changes in their incomes, or in their environment. These aspects of the consumption function – and many others – are of considerable importance for the theory and practice of economics, and the reader can find many excellent discussions of them in the more advanced literature.

For purposes of this book, however, we will take account only of the hypothesis – which is fairly well established – that the smaller their income the greater will be proportion of their income that people wish to spend on consumption. This does not involve any significant change in the nature of the equilibrium conditions set out above, but it does mean that the equation expressing this condition is slightly more complicated than that shown above.

A reasonably realistic first approximation to the way that consumption, and hence savings, is related to the level of incomes may be shown in the following equation, in which C = consumption, Y = incomes, and a, c, are parameters,

$$C = a + c \cdot Y \qquad (1)$$

This equation states that, at zero levels of income (when $Y = 0$), consumption will be positive and equal to a. This would imply that there must be some borrowing or living on past savings. The equation also indicates that, for every £1 increase in income, consumption will rise by £c. The parameter c is known as the *marginal propensity to consume*, since it indicates what is the marginal increment of consumption for any marginal increase in incomes. It is not the same as the average propensity to consume, C/Y. The average propensity to consume will only equal the marginal propensity to consume if there is no constant term, a, in equation (1) – i.e. if $C = cY$.

In Figure 9.1(a) below, the line passing through the points C_1 and C_2 corresponds to a consumption function of the type shown in equation (1) above. It starts on the vertical axis at a distance of a from the origin, corresponding to the constant term a in the equation. For this indicates that when income is zero, and so is at the point O on the horizontal axis, consumption is equal to a. As income increases – i.e. as we move along the horizontal axis in measuring income – consumption rises by an amount equal to c times the increase in income. If income rises by £10, consumption will rise by £c10. The line corresponding to this thus rises from left to right with a slope corresponding to c. Because of the constant term a in this particular consumption function, the ratio of consumption to income must change as income changes. For example, at income level Y_1 consumption is equal to $Y_1 C_1$. The ratio of consumption to income at this point can be seen as the slope of the line OC_1, which joins the origin to the point C_1, since the slope of this line reflects the ratio of the amount of consumption (the height of $Y_1 C_1$) to the distance along the income axis, $O Y_1$. At a different level of income, say, Y_2, the slope of the line from the origin to the corresponding point on the consumption line C_2, is clearly flatter than at the first income level. As can be seen from the right-hand Figure 9.1(b), in which the consumption function does not contain any constant term, the slope of the line joining the origin to any point on the consumption function must always remain unchanged. Since the ratio of consumption to income is the same thing as the 'average propensity to consume', the difference between the two consumption functions illustrated in the diagrams is that in the case where there is a constant term in the function, the average propensity to consume changes as income changes, whereas in the case where there is no constant term the average propensity to consume remains the same whatever the income level. In the last chapter only the latter type of consumption function was used – as illustrated by the line OC_2 in Figure 8.5.

Since consumption and savings have been defined in such a way that they exhaust income, $Y = C + S$, so that $C = Y - S$, so that substituting for C as given by equation (1) we have that

$$S = Y - (a + c \cdot Y),$$

i.e.
$$S = -a + (1 - c) Y \qquad (2)$$

Figure 9.1(a)   **Figure 9.1(b)**

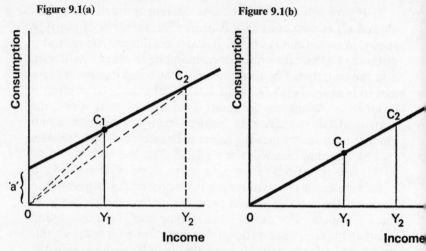

This equation indicates that the *marginal propensity to save* is equal to $(1-c)$, and that the savings ratio, or the '*average propensity to save*' is no longer constant for any level of income but is equal to

$$\frac{S}{Y} = \frac{-a+(1-c)\,Y}{Y} = \frac{-a}{Y}+(1-c) \qquad (3)$$

With these more realistic equations for the propensity to consume or save, the equilibrium condition that income must be such that planned savings at that level of income are equal to planned investment, must now be expressed in the form of the following slightly more complicated equation:

$$S = -a+(1-c)\,Y,$$

so   (planned) $I =$ (planned) S

when $I = -a+(1-c)\,Y,$

or

$$Y = \frac{I+a}{1-c} \qquad (4)$$

This last equation is, in fact, simply a slight modification of the equation on page 172 which stated that, provided the average propensity to save is constant, income was in equilibrium when

$$Y = \frac{I}{S/Y} \qquad (5)$$

For if the proportion of their incomes that people save is

182

constant, this means that, as their incomes rise, they always save (and hence consume as well) the same proportion of the *extra* income. In other words, if the average propensity to save is constant, it must be equal to the marginal propensity to save. And again, since income is either consumed or saved, the marginal propensity to save, s, is equal to $(1-c)$, where c is, as before, the marginal propensity to consume. Hence if the average propensity to save is constant, the equilibrium condition, which is that (average propensity to save) times $Y=I$, can be replaced by the condition (marginal propensity to save) times $Y=I$; i.e. $(1-c)\,Y=I$, so that $Y=\dfrac{I}{(1-c)}$. Hence, equation (5) above could have been written as

$$Y = \frac{I}{1-c} \tag{6}$$

It will be seen that the only difference between this equilibrium condition under conditions of constant average propensity to consume (and hence to save also) and equation (4) is that in equation (4) the constant term a has been added to the numerator. The equation (4) equilibrium condition is thus of more general applicability, since it applies also to conditions in which the consumption function is of the more realistic form given in equation (1). If, however, the more restricted but simpler situation of Chapter 8 – in which the average propensity to consume remains constant – is the relevant one, equation (4) still applies, since one merely sets a at zero, thereby obtaining equation (6), which is the same as equation (5), which is the one used in Chapter 8.

Equation (4) enables the equilibrium level of income to be calculated at once given the level of investment and the parameters of the 'consumption function'. For example if $I=20$, and $C=5+0.8\,Y$, then the equilibrium level of

$$Y = \frac{20+5}{1-0.8} = 25/0.2 = 125$$

The equilibrium condition expressed in equation (4) can be used to see immediately how income is affected by a change in (i) investment or (ii) in the constant term of the consumption function without any change in the slope, so that the average propensity to consume changes without any change in the marginal propensity to consume, or (iii) in the slope of the consumption function, so that both the marginal and average propensities to consume change (or any combination of the three). For example, if I increases, it is clear that the equilibrium level of income will rise. If, on the other hand, constant term a in the consumption schedule falls, which means that the proportion of their incomes that people wish to save has risen for any given level of income, the numerator in the equation (4) will be smaller, leading to a lower equilibrium level of income. The same result would follow, of course, from a rise in the denominator, so that one can see that the equilibrium level of income would also fall if there were a fall in c, the marginal propensity to consume, since the denominator in the equation, $(1 - c)$ would then be greater. (See diagrammatic analysis in next section.)

These conclusions emphasise that whatever individuals would *like* to save for each income level, the level of income only reaches equilibrium when both total planned and actual savings equal planned and actual investment. In other words, people can save what they like as individuals, but what they will all save in the end, taken together, will be governed by the level of investment.

Changes in the propensity to save will change the level of income, since income will only be in equilibrium when planned savings have become equal to planned investment. Given investment, desired savings will always tend to equal investment, whatever people's propensity to save. Changes in the latter merely change the income level at which this equality is brought about.

EXERCISES 9.1

1   What is the marginal propensity to consume when the marginal propensity to save is: (a) 0·1; (b) 0·3?

2   What is the average propensity to save if the average propensity to consume is 0·8?

3   What is the savings function corresponding to each of the following consumption functions:
    (a) $C = 5 + 0·9Y$;

  (b) $C = 10 + 0.7Y$;
  (c) $C = 5 + 0.8Y$?

4 If $C = 10 + 0.6Y$, what is planned consumption and planned savings when (a) $Y = 100$; (b) $Y = 50$; (c) $Y = 200$?

5 If $S = -5 + 0.1Y$, what is planned consumption and planned savings when (a) $Y = 100$; (b) $Y = 200$; (c) $Y = 500$?

6 In question 4, (i) what is the average propensity to consume and the average propensity to save at each of the three income levels indicated? (ii) How does the average propensity to consume vary as incomes rise?

7 In question 5 what is the average propensity to consume and the average propensity to save at each of the income levels indicated?

8 (i) If I is given as constant at a level of 10, and $C = 10 + 0.8Y$, what is total demand (consumption plus investment) when (a) $Y = 100$; (b) $Y = 200$; (c) $Y = 400$?

  (ii) At which of the three income levels is total output equal to total demand, and what is the relationship between planned savings and investment at that income level?

9 (i) If I is given as constant at 20, and $C = 10 + 0.8Y$, what is total demand and savings when output (and hence income) is (a) 100; (b) 200; (c) 300?

  (ii) Which, if any, of the three income levels shown is the equilibrium level, and if none of them is, what *is* the equilibrium level of income?

10 (i) If I is given as constant at 10 and $C = 20 + 0.7Y$, is income in equilibrium at any of the following income levels? (a) 80; (b) 100; (c) 200?

  (ii) At other income levels among those shown what is the gap between planned investment (I) and planned saving?

11 If $C = 10 + 0.8Y$, what must investment be if income is in equilibrium at (a) $Y = 100$; (b) $Y = 150$; (c) $Y = 300$?

12 If $I = £20$, what is the equilibrium level of income when
  (a) $C = 5 + 0.9Y$;   (b) $C = 15 + 0.9Y$;
  (c) $S = -10 + 0.2Y$;   (d) $S = -10 + 0.1Y$;
  (e) $S = -20 + 0.2Y$;   (f) $C = 15 + 0.8Y$?

The results obtained algebraically can be presented in the same sort of diagram as in Figures 8.3 and 8.5. In the left-hand diagram below, income is measured along the horizontal axis and (planned) savings and investment are measured up the vertical axis. If it is assumed, for purposes of simplicity at this stage, that planned investment is fixed – i.e. it does not vary with income – then investment can be represented by the horizontal line I. The amount of saving that the community wishes to do at any level of income will rise with income in accordance with the equation (2) above. Thus, in the Figure 9.2(a) the savings curve cuts the vertical axis at a distance from the origin equal to $-a$, and the slope of the curve is equal to $(1-c)$. From the diagram, it can be seen that equilibrium will be at the point Y_e, where the savings line cuts the investment line, since at any other point desired savings, as given by the savings line, will not be equal to desired investment. It can be seen that the equilibrium point is now determined not only by the *slope* of the S line, but also by the distance from the origin at which the S line cuts the vertical axis – i.e. by the value of $-a$.

In Figure 9.2(b) the process is looked at from the point of view of the demand and supply for goods. As in Figures

Figure 9.2(a)   Figure 9.2(b)

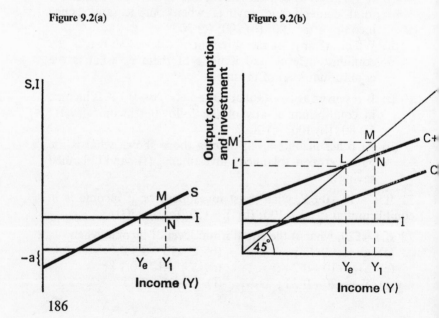

8.3 and 8.5, the C line is related to the S line – the equation for the latter having been derived from the equation of the former. The 'gap' between the C line and the 45° line in Figure 9.2(b) is equal to the savings at each income level shown on Figure 9.2(a), since the C line shows the consumption demand at each income level, and consumption plus savings equal total income. Total demand for goods at any income level is, again, simply the sum of the demand for consumption goods and investment goods, so this can be expressed on the diagram by adding, vertically, the I line (which has been assumed to be horizontal) to the C line – as was done in Figure 8.5 – to obtain the $C+I$ line. It will then be clear that, say, income level Y_1 cannot be an equilibrium level since total demand for goods is equal to Y_1N at this income level, whereas the total output that gave rise to that income was Y_1M (as this is the output, measured up the vertical axis that equals the income OY_1 measured along the horizontal axis). There is a deficiency of demand equal to the gap MN, which is the same as the excess of planned savings over investment in Figure 9.2(a) at the same income, Y_1.

From the diagram, it is obvious that equilibrium can only exist at the income level OY_e, since only at this level is total demand, which is composed of C plus I, i.e. (the height of the $C+I$ line) just on the 45° line and so equal to total output.

The diagram also illustrates the conclusions reached algebraically already such as that the equilibrium level of income is determined not only by the slope of the C line – i.e. the marginal propensity to consume – but also by a change in the constant term. For example, if the constant term a increases then the whole $C+I$ line will shift upwards, parallel to its initial position in exactly the same way as if I had increased, and this will lead to a higher equilibrium level of income. Similarly, if the constant term in the equation of the consumption function remained unchanged but the slope became steeper, indicating a rise in the marginal propensity to consume, there would also be a rise in the equilibrium level of income. The same results have been obtained just as well, of course, from the algebraic equations (4) above, in which the effect of a change in the constant term in the consumption function or the marginal propensity to consume or in I has been seen.

If, however, we were interested not in the way that equilibrium is determined given the whole schedule of savings and investment but in the way that income *changes* following some change in the level of investment or in the constant term, *a*, in the consumption function, *the constant term in* the *consumption function is no longer relevant, and all that matters is the marginal propensity to consume* (*or save*). To analyse the effects of such changes we must make use of the concept known as the *multiplier*.

2. The multiplier

It is clear from the equilibrium condition expressed, say, as in equation (4) that, given the level of investment, the equilibrium level of income depends on the constant term and the slope of the consumption function. Suppose, however, that *starting* from the level of income on the following diagram indicated by point Y_1, as given by the intersection of the line S_i and I_1, there is an upward shift in the investment line to I_2. Then it can be seen that income must rise to Y_i. And it can be also seen simply by looking at the diagram that the amount of the consequent rise in income depended solely on the *slope* of the *S* line. If, for

Figure 9.3

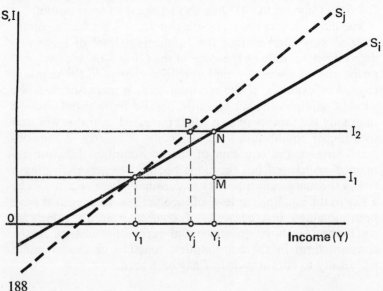

example, the savings function had been S_j instead of S_i, the new equilibrium position reached by a shift to I_2 would have been OY_j. That is, the increase in income resulting from the same increase in investment, would have been only Y_1Y_j instead of Y_1Y_i. With the initial S line of S_i the upward shift of investment by the amount MN has led to an increase of income of Y_1Y_i, which is also, as can be seen, equal to LM. The three points, L, M and N are the three corners of a triangle. The ratio of the increase of investment, MN, to the resulting rise in income LM, can be seen to depend on the slope of the third side of the triangle, namely LN. It can be seen by inspection that the slope of this line, LN, determines the ratio MN/LM, and the slope of LN is, of course, the marginal propensity to save s. As we have already seen, this is equal to $(1-c)$, where c represents the marginal propensity to consume. In other words, given an increase in investment, the resulting increase in income depends only on the marginal propensity to save (or the marginal propensity to consume).

In less diagrammatic terms the reason for this is as follows. Starting from a given equilibrium income, if there is a change in investment, income will have reached a new equilibrium when there has been a change in savings equal to the change in investment. How much income needs to change in order to reach its new equilibrium level will depend solely on how savings change as incomes change. In other words, it depends solely on the marginal propensity to save, i.e. the *slope* of the savings schedule, $(1-c)$. The absolute height of the schedule no longer enters into the calculation.

The same argument can be presented algebraically. For what is required is that the change in savings equals the change in investment, and using the symbols:

$dY=$ a change in income,
$dS=$ a change in savings,
$dI=$ a change in investment,

income will be in equilibrium, following a change in investment when $dS=dI$.

But from equation (2) above it follows that $dS=(1-c)dY$, so income has reached a new equilibrium when

$$dI = (1-c)\,dY,$$

189

or when
$$dY = \frac{dI}{(1-c)} \qquad (7)$$

This latter equation can be transformed to express the relationship between any change in investment and the consequent equilibrium change in income as follows:

$$\frac{dY}{dI} = \frac{1}{(1-c)} \qquad (8)$$

From this it can be seen that the ratio between a change in income and the change in investment which generates the change in income depends only on the *marginal* propensity to consume (in this simple model).

Exactly the same conclusion could have been arrived at by another very short route. We have seen, from equation (4), that income is in equilibrium when

$$Y = \frac{I+a}{1-c}$$

This could have been written as

$$Y = (I+a) \times \frac{1}{1-c} \qquad (9)$$

In this form it is obviously stating that, to obtain the equilibrium level of income, the numerator $(I+a)$ has to be multiplied by $\frac{1}{1-c}$. From this it is obvious that if there is any change in the numerator – either an addition or a subtraction – the value of the change has to be multiplied by $\frac{1}{1-c}$ to arrive at the resulting equilibrium change in income.

Equation (9) also emphasises that a shift in the constant term a, in the consumption function would have the same multiplicative effect on income as a change in investment. This, too, is obvious from the diagrams, where we have seen that a parallel shift in the consumption function must affect the total $C+I$ line and hence the final equilibrium level of income in exactly the same way as a shift in investment.

The right-hand side of equation (8) is known as the *multiplier* (usually indicated by the symbol k) for the very good reason that it indicates by how much any change in investment has to be multiplied in order to find out how much income will change. For example, if investment rises by £10 per year, and the value of the marginal propensity to consume, c, is 0·8 so that the marginal propensity to save is 0·2, then it is clear that for savings to rise by an amount equal to the rise in investment it is necessary for income to rise by £50, since this is the amount which, when multiplied by 0·2, is equal to £10. The value of the multiplier in this case is $\dfrac{£50}{£10}$, or 5. And this is, in fact, equal to $\dfrac{1}{(1-c)}$, or $\dfrac{1}{0·2}$.

In general, therefore, the multiplier is the amount by which any change in investment (in the simple economies we are dealing with so far), has to be multiplied in order to arrive at the final equilibrium change in income (and output). It depends on the marginal propensity to consume (or save) and its value can be expressed as follows:

$$\text{Multiplier} = k = \frac{1}{1-c} = \frac{1}{s} \tag{10}$$

3. The 'static' and the 'dynamic' multipliers

So far we have obtained the formula for the multiplier by calculating what the final change in income has to be in order that the associated change in savings is once more equal to the change in investment that gave rise to the initial displacement from the equilibrium position. This is a sort of 'instant' multiplier. But in practice, of course, the process of adjustment to the new equilibrium level of income may take some time. In the simple example of page 170 above, it was seen that equilibrium was only restored after a process of successive adjustments and, according to the time lags in the process of income circulation, the series of adjustments may take months or even years to make significant progress.[1]

Consider a situation in which the marginal propensity to consume is 0·8 and there is a rise in investment of £10. At the first stage incomes will rise by £10, and consumers will then spend a further £8 on consumption. The increased output of £8 of consumers' goods (given the assumption which we have

[1] Theoretically, infinite time is required for completion.

adopted that output is flexible) will lead to a further rise in incomes of £8 which will bring forth a further rise in the demand for, and supply of, consumption goods of £6·4. In due course, this will lead to successive increases in consumption of £(6·4 × 0·8), and so on. The series of additional consumption expenditures will look like the following:

$$10 + 8 + 6·4 + \ldots, \text{etc.}$$

which is derived as follows:

$$10 + 10(0·8) + 10(0·8)^2 + 10(0·8)^3 + \ldots + 10(0·8)^n$$

Symbolically, where c = the marginal propensity to consume, and dI = the initial change in investment, this series is of the form

$$dI + dIc + dIc^2 + dIc^3 + dIc^4 + \ldots + dIc^n$$

The sum, to infinity, of such a series is

$$\frac{dI}{(1-c)} \quad \text{or} \quad dI \times \frac{1}{(1-c)}$$

so this is the sum of the final total rise in incomes. This expression, it will be no surprise to learn, is the same as the expression for the multiplier given in equation (7) above. If the question 'What is the final total increase in incomes resulting from the initial increase in investment?' is answered by summing the series of gradually diminishing increments of income, the answer is in terms of the 'dynamic' multiplier, since it is arrived at by concentrating attention on the gradual changes that take place over time. The same answer arrived at in equations (7) or (8) is known as the 'static' multiplier since it is obtained by calculating directly what the eventual final increase in incomes must be for the associated final increase in savings to be equal to the initial increase in investment, without passing through all the intermediate changes that must take place before this final outcome is arrived at. In practice, it may often be vitally important to distinguish between the two forms of the multiplier. In the first place, the marginal propensity to consume may change during the time period concerned. Secondly, the policy makers may be interested in what will be the effect of some measure during the next three months. If a Finance Minister asks his pet economist how much income will rise if investment is raised by £100 million, and the economist has learnt only about the static multiplier, he might give a quite misleading answer.

The reason why the static multiplier does not involve the constant term in the consumption, or savings, function but only the marginal propensities was illustrated graphically in Figure 9.3. And the reason why the dynamic multiplier also involves only the marginal propensities can be seen graphically by using the alternative form of diagram involving the consumption function instead of the savings function. In Figure 9.4 below, the consumption function is denoted by the line C, and the initial investment function is denoted by the horizontal line I_1. Then, as usual, the equilibrium level of income will be at Y_1, where $C+I_1$ cuts the 45° line. Suppose now that investment demand rises to I_2, so that the total demand for goods and services will, in the first instance, rise from Y_1M to Y_1N. There is now an excess of demand over supply equal to MN. If output then rises to Y_1N in response to the demand being at this level, income will rise to OY_j (equal to Y_1N). But at income level OY_j, total demand will be equal to Y_jQ, which exceeds total output by PQ. This is a smaller excess of demand over supply than at the first time round, but will still tend to lead to a rise in output

Figure 9.4

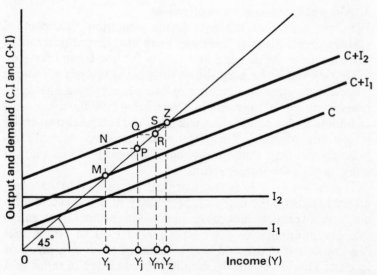

193

to Y_jQ, which corresponds to a rise in income to OY_m, leading to a further rise in demand to Y_mS, leading to an excess of demand over supply of RS and so on. The successive increments of output, incomes and the excess of demand over supply are smaller and smaller, as in the numerical sequence on page 192. The sequence written out on page 192 corresponds, in fact, to the distances, on the diagram, MN, PQ, RS ..., and so on.

It can be seen from the Figure 9.4 that the successive changes converge at the equilibrium income level OY_z, where, as usual, the total demand as given by the $C+I$ line at this income level is equal to the total output that gives rise to that income level. But it can also be seen from this diagram that the extent to which income rises, given any increase in investment, depends solely on the slope of the C line – i.e. the multiplier depends solely on the marginal propensity to consume. For example, if the C line were steeper in the above diagram (but the initial equilibrium was at the same point) this means that the $C+I$ line passing through point N would be steeper, and it is obvious from inspection that the amount of convergence before final equilibrium is reached would be greater. If the $C+I_2$ line is tilted upwards through the point N, it will clearly cut the 45° line at a higher level of income, implying a greater multiplier.

4. More about leakages and injections

We have seen that the equilibrium condition that planned savings equals planned investment can also be put in terms of equilibrium in the demand and supply for goods (and services, of course). It has also been shown that, in the analysis of *changes* from any position of equilibrium caused, say, by a change in investment, all that matters in determining how far the process of finding a new equilibrium will go is the marginal propensity to consume (or save). This latter result has been reached algebraically and diagrammatically, but it is important to see how it links up with the former result.

The reason why it is the marginal propensity to *consume*, rather than, say, the marginal propensity to invest (i.e. the increase in investment induces an increase in income), that enters into the multiplier, in the simple model used so far, is that it is consumption demand that is assumed to be a function of income. This links with the equilibrium condition in terms of a balance between the supply and demand for goods in the following manner. Suppose, for example, that there is an upward shift in investment demand; then the analysis of the process by which a new equilibrium is eventually reached assumes that, on account of the rise in incomes generated by the rise in the output of capital goods there is a newly-created additional demand for consumer goods, *but no further additions to the demand for capital goods*. The subsequent series of adjustments, such as those in Figure 9.4 between the points P and Z, are the successive steps by which the output of consumer goods gradually expands to match the increments in the demand for consumer goods.

In Figure 9.5 below, if investment demand rises by an amount AQ, from I_1 to I_2 (so that the $C+I_1$ line shifts upwards to $C+I_2$) we assume that this leads to a corresponding increase in the output of investment goods. Thus total output rises to Y_1N, which means that income rises to OY_2. The market in investment goods will then be in equilibrium, but the rise in incomes corresponding to the increased output of investment goods

Figure 9.5

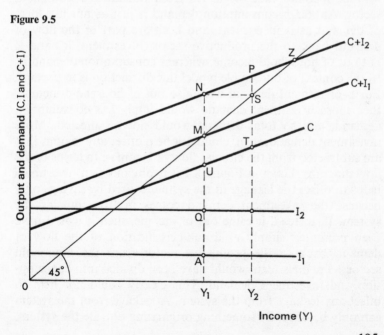

195

means that the demand for consumer goods, which had been Y_1U, has now risen to Y_2T, with the result that total demand, instead of remaining at Y_1N (equals Y_2S) has risen to Y_2P and so is still above total output (Y_2S). The whole of the gap, PS, in this sort of sequence is in the demand and supply for consumer goods. And, given our assumption that only consumption, and not investment, increases as income rises, all the subsequent steps in the sequence of convergence to the new equilibrium point, Z, reflect the gradual elimination of disequilibrium in the demand for consumer goods. This is another aspect of the fact that, on our assumption, it is the slope of the C line alone that determines the amount of the final equilibrium change in income, even though it is a change in investment which, in our example, sets off the process of change in income. In short, therefore, the slope of the C line alone enters into the multiplier because consumption has been assumed to be a function of income but investment has not.

A similar reason explains why, in the flow diagrams used earlier, we treated investment as a re-injection into the circular flow of incomes that originates from outside the household sector. Although consumption demand is just as much a form of demand as is investment, and both are part of the flow of demand back to the productive sector, investment demand is not out of household income, whereas consumption demand is. In the context of our simple model this distinction is important. For if investment demand were also out of household income, then more investment demand would imply less consumption demand, and so total demand would not be affected. More investment demand, then, could not help offset any savings that are subtracted from the circular flow of incomes. In terms of the flow diagram shown in Figure 8.2 it is obvious that investment helps to offset the leakage in the system caused by savings only because the investment demand comes in from outside the system. If, instead, it came out of income, then it would have been presented simply as a sub-classification of the flow of demand back to the productive sector from the household sector – i.e. the stream would have been divided into consumption and investment demand. This clearly could not help to offset any leakage from the system. A leakage from the system can only be offset by something originating outside the system.

196

Thus the special expansionary character of investment in our model is that it is a form of demand that is not out of income, but it gives rise to incomes for the people involved in the production of investment goods, and these incomes will then give rise – according to our assumptions – to some demand for consumption goods. Unless, therefore, some consumption goods are now produced as well, total demand will exceed total supply. The mere fact that investment demand may be matched by supply of investment goods does not prevent investment having a net expansionary effect.

Imagine an economy in which all output consisted of £100 of investment goods, such as machines and roads. The persons acting in their capacities as producers might be quite happy but in their capacity as private individuals – i.e. as consumers – they would be less so. Suppose, for example, that the productive sector distributes £90 in wages and profits. When the housewives go to the shops to spend most of this on food and clothing they would be told that, unfortunately, there was no food or clothing to sell – all output had consisted of machines and roads. Thus, because £100 of investment goods are demanded and produced, it would be necessary also to expand output to include some consumer goods if total demand is to be matched by total supply.

Given our assumptions, and the simple model of no government or foreign trade, the same sort of imbalance could not possibly arise in an economy in which output consisted solely of consumer goods. For suppose that, in such an economy, total output consisted only of £80 of consumer goods. Now we have assumed that the demand for these goods has come out of incomes, so that income must have been at least £80 (unless incomes were very low and everybody was living partly on borrowing from abroad). Since no investment goods were being produced, this £80 (at least) of income must have originated from the production of consumer goods. Hence the output of consumer goods must be enough to meet the demand for them.

To summarise, therefore, in the simple model we have been using, the marginal propensity to consume is in the multiplier because consumption demand is assumed to be a function of income. Investment is treated as the 'multiplicand' – namely, the item whose changes are multiplied by the multiplier to find out the final equilibrium change in income. Savings is a 'leakage' because it subtracts from the demand – namely the consumption demand – that is a function of income. The higher is the propensity to save, therefore, the lower will be the equilibrium level of income – given the other variables. A higher marginal propensity to save will also reduce the multiplier, because it reduces the rise in consumption demand caused by a rise in income. Investment is an 'injection' into the flow of incomes because the demand for investment goods originates from outside the system and hence does not directly reduce the flow of demand for consumer goods. For the same reason investment does not enter into the multiplier.

Thus looked at from the point of view of leakages or injections into the flow of incomes, savings and investment are counterparts. Savings leak out of the system and investment comes back into it from outside. But from the point of view of their place in the multiplier analysis, they are not analogous; the marginal propensity to save affects the multiplier because saving is functionally related to income and determines how much extra consumers' demand is created as a result of extra income. But in this simple model investment is not a function of income and so does not enter into the multiplier.

More complicated models exist, of course, which do not make the assumption that only consumption rises when income rises. In particular, the essence of modern trade cycle theory is the way that investment, too, is related to changes in income.[1]

A variable appearing in any model is either determined by the other variables in the model or is not. In the former case it is known as an *endogenous* variable, and in the latter case as an *exogenous* variable. In the context of the simple model described so far, without government or foreign trade, the only variables

---

[1] If we had assumed that consumption was not a function of income – i.e. that it remained constant – but that investment was a function of income, taking the form, say, $I = a_i + vY$, then the multiplier formula would be:

$$\frac{dY}{dC} = \frac{1}{1-v}, \quad \text{instead of} \quad \frac{dY}{dI} = \frac{1}{1-c}$$

Thus the familiar multiplier formula simply reflects the particular behavioural relationships assumed to apply to income, on the one hand, and consumption or investment on the other. If one were to assume different behavioural relationships one would derive different multiplier formulae. Thus the appropriate multiplier formula depends on the particular 'model' of the economy that one is using.

were income, investment and consumption (or savings, which amounts to the same thing, since given income and consumption, savings is also determined). Of these, we have assumed that investment was not a function of income, and so investment appears as an 'exogenous' variable. Income is determined by investment and the consumption function, and is therefore an endogenous variable, as is also consumption, being simply a function of income.

5. Introducing government and foreign trade into income determination

We shall now change our model and relax the assumption that there is no foreign trade or government sector. This means that allowance has to be made for imports and exports and for government expenditures and taxation. We shall also assume that imports and taxes are 'endogenous' items that are related to incomes in the same sort of way as were savings. Thus, a rise in income will lead to an increase in tax payments either by households or by firms, and to an increase in imports.

On the other hand we shall retain the assumption that a rise in income does not lead to increased domestic capital formation, at least not in the same time period. We shall also assume that a rise in incomes does not lead to a rise in government consumption or in exports – again, in the same time period. These assumptions are fairly realistic as far as the short-run goes. Most investment is generally determined by longer run prospects, and anyway cannot be varied from day to day with the same flexibility as can consumption. As for exports, these are obviously determined more by variations in *overseas* incomes.[1] Finally, government purchases are also, by comparison with private consumption, relatively unaffected by short period changes in income.[2] Thus, we shall regard government consumption and exports as 'exogenous' items.

In the light of the preceding discussion of what is a leakage and what isn't, and of the nature of the items that enter into the multiplier, we can now examine how the equilibrium conditions

[1] We abstract here from the questions of whether a high *pressure* of domestic demand (not the same thing as rise in demand) hampers exports.

[2] Some government transfer payments, however, are automatically but negatively related to changes in income, such as unemployment benefits which tend to rise when national income falls and vice versa.

governing the income level and how the multiplier formula have to be amended to allow for the changes we have made in the model.

(i) The impact of government

One of the reasons why the household sector may not pass back to the productive sector, in the form of demand for goods, all the income that it received is that in addition to its desire to save it may have to pay taxes to the government. Such taxes will, therefore, constitute another leak in the circular flow of income from the productive sector back to the productive sector. But governments also purchase goods and services, as well as make transfer payments. But given our assumption that government expenditures are exogenous items that are not related to incomes they must constitute injections into the circular flow of incomes in much the same way as investment. The analogy is complete, in fact, as regards government purchases of goods and services. Consider, for example, an economy in which all output consisted of goods and services that the government purchased. The resulting incomes would be paid out to ordinary private households in the usual way and when the housewives went round to the shops the following Monday to buy some food and the like, they would be told by the shopkeepers that they were very sorry but all the output had been bought by the government. There would clearly be an excess of demand over supply as a result.

In the same way that government expenditure resembles investment in the sense that it raises the demand for consumer goods without adding to the supply of them, so government tax receipts have the same sort of impact on demand as savings. That is to say, they act to reduce the circular flow of incomes; they constitute a 'leakage' in the flow. They reduce the amount of household incomes that find their way back to the productive sector in the form of final demand – i.e. for consumer goods. Whether or not all taxes (including company taxes) are regarded as being paid by households in the last analysis is – as pointed out in Chapter 5 (page 95) – a matter about which opinions can differ, but this does not change the role of taxes in the income determination mechanism. They tend to reduce demand for consumer goods without reducing the supply of them. Like investment and savings respectively, therefore, government expenditures tend to be expansionary and taxes tend to be contractionary.

But this does not mean that, if public expenditures and taxes rise by the same amount, the net impact on demand is zero. An equal rise in government expenditures and taxes may have – and probably will have – an expansionary impact on demand. There are various reasons for this. The first is the distinction that has to be made – and which we emphasised in Chapter 2 – between government purchases of goods and services, on the one hand, and transfer payments, on the other. In general, the latter have less multiplier impact on incomes than the former. If, say, the government increases its purchases of goods and services by £10, this increases final output, and hence national product, by £10 in the first instance (assuming no supply limitation). The corresponding rise in national income is then also equal to £10. This will lead to a rise in demand for consumer goods for, say, only £8, and so on, the series being then: £10 + £8 + £6·4 + ... +, which will sum to £50.[1] But if the government had spent an extra £10 on transfer payments, such as family allowances rather than on goods and services, then assuming that the marginal propensity to consume were still 0·8, the first impact on the demand for final output would be only £8 and the series of successive increments in national income would be the same as the above series except that the first term – the £10 – would be lacking. It would then sum to only £40, not £50.

Now taxes are merely negative transfer payments – as became clear in our discussion, in Chapter 2, of the treatment of indirect taxes and subsidies. Hence, assuming that the marginal propensity to consume of tax-payers is the same as that of the recipients of transfer payments, a rise in taxes of £10 will have an equal numerical final impact on demand as a cut in transfer payments by £10. That is, it will have a final impact on demand of £40. Thus, if the government increased its purchases of goods and services by £10, which has a final upward impact on demand of £50, and raises taxes by £10, which reduces demand by £40, there will be a net upward impact on demand of £10. This result,

---

[1] If, as indicated, the marginal propensity to consume is 0·8, the multiplier equals $\frac{1}{1-0\cdot8} = \frac{1}{0\cdot2} = 5$; and $5 \times £10 = £50$.

which derives from the elimination of the first term in the series of increments of income shown above, is the essence of what is known as the 'balanced budget multiplier theorem'.

Of course, if, to start with, the government's increase in expenditure of £10 had been on transfer payment, not on goods and services, the impact of the increase in taxes would have fully offset that of the rise in expenditures. Thus, without even having to take account of further distinctions that one might want to make between different kinds of government expenditures or taxes, the net impact on demand of a government budget deficit or surplus must depend on the extent to which its expenditures are composed of transfer payments rather than of goods and services.[1] In the rest of this chapter, however, we shall ignore government transfer payments (TP_g) and take account only of government consumption (C_g). Since taxes are negative transfer payments we shall net out these government transfer payments against the corresponding tax payments, so that we are dealing here only with purchases of goods and services by the government and the taxes remaining after deducting from total taxes an amount equal to the transfer payments.[2] But quite apart from 'balanced budget theorem' considerations and the precise net impact on demand of the government's budget, there is no doubt about the direction of the impact on demand, of changes in government taxes and expenditures taken separately. Any rise in taxes constitutes a greater leakage in the income flow and so reduces demand relative to supply. And increased expenditures by the government on goods and services constitute an increased re-injection. Whatever the balance of the budget and the impact of the whole budget on demand, a rise in government expenditure is therefore analogous to a rise in investment, and a rise in the tax rate is analogus to an upward shift in the savings schedule – like a rise in the S line in Figure 8.3 above.[3]

[1] For example, a rise in the salaries of government employees would count as an increase in public expenditure on goods and services, yet its impact on demand might not be very different, if at all, from an equal rise in transfer payments. On the other hand, government purchases of foreign military equipment would have a negligible impact on *domestic* demand.

[2] This follows the procedure adopted in an excellent and simple survey of this particular problem in William A. Salant 'Taxes, Income Determination, and the Balanced Budget Theorem', *Review of Economics and Statistics*, 1957.

[3] Apart from qualifications to the impact of a change in the budget surplus or deficit on account of the composition of the expenditure and payments, we

Furthermore, whether the government happens to be running a surplus or a deficit and irrespective of the impact of the government budget on demand, it is necessary to allow, in the multiplier, for the fact that taxes are related to incomes. Insofar as tax payments resemble savings, being a form of leakage, their relation to incomes rise will affect the multiplier in the same way as does the marginal propensity to save. If, say, incomes rise in response to a rise in government expenditures or a rise in investment, some of the increased incomes that would have been converted into a rise in demand for consumer goods will be syphoned off in tax payments instead, thereby reducing the multiplier effect of whatever began the initial rise in incomes.

(ii) The role of foreign trade
The impact of foreign trade is similar to that of the government. Exports, like government consumption, clearly add to the incomes out of which people will demand consumer goods. But, like investment or government purchases, exports lead to demands in the given economy for consumer goods without adding to the supply of any goods *to the same economy*. In an economy that produced only exports, housewives would clamour in vain for the consumer goods that they wanted, thereby exerting an expansionary influence on output. Exports, therefore, act on demand in rather the same way as investment or the output of goods and services that are absorbed by the government.

Imports, by contrast, represent the supply of goods to the given economy without any corresponding incomes being created *in the same economy*. It is the producers of the overseas economies from which the imports have been bought who will derive the incomes. Imports are thus a leakage in the flow of incomes of the given economy. If, out of domestic incomes, citizens of the given economy demand imported goods, this is reducing their demand for nationally produced goods, and is

---

have not taken any account of the monetary impact of changes in the budget. For example, a government deficit may involve government borrowing that could have the effect of leading to a shortage of liquidity or a rise in interest rates that would have some contractionary effect, thereby tending to offset the expansionary impact of the deficit. Our exclusion of these considerations is part of our general exclusion of monetary considerations throughout this and the preceding chapter.

hence causing a leakage out of the circular flow of incomes of the given economy.

Similarly, as with savings or taxes, imports are probably linked to incomes so that as incomes rise, some of the increased demand for consumer goods represents increased demand for imported goods. Thus, the strength of the link between incomes and imports will determine the size of the multiplier. For example, suppose there is a rise in incomes in some foreign country and that this causes a rise in their demand for the exports of the given country. This is an exogenously produced increase in exports of the given country, and would be represented by an upward shift in the exports schedule just like an upward shift in the investment schedule in, say, Figure 9.3 or 9.4. In the same way it would tend to lead to a cumulative rise in incomes, for the increased incomes created at home by the rise in exports will lead to increased demand for consumer goods. But some of this increased demand for consumer goods will take the form of an increased demand for imported goods, and so will not be passed back to the productive sector of the given country. This will obviously dampen the multiplier effects of the rise in incomes. The marginal propensity to import is – like taxes and savings – a way of reducing the marginal propensity to consume home products, and it is this that determines the size of the multiplier.

In this respect, the items entering into foreign trade are somewhat like government expenditures and taxes. The main difference is that, unlike taxes or private savings the import leakage is only a leakage from the given system. It is not a leakage if one adds together the various countries involved. The imports that constitute a leakage for one country must constitute an injection for the exporting country. This is of some importance in a full treatment of the multiplier, since the expansionary effect of the exports of the other country on its own income may lead to some feed-back in the form of increased exports for the given country. However, this would be going much farther than we need to go in this book.

6. The full equilibrium conditions

Armed with the above analysis of the essential character of leakages and injections, as well as some further insight into the way that these have to be incorporated into multiplier analysis, we can now rapidly proceed to derive the full algebraic conditions for the equilibrium level of income, and for the multiplier effect on the income level of any change in the exogenous determinants of income. This can be approached in either of two ways. First, from the point of view of the equality between the leakages and injections – i.e. the planned savings and investment approach. Secondly, from the point of view of the equality between the planned demand and supply of goods.

(i) The leakage–injection approach

If government expenditure on goods and services and exports can be regarded as exogenous direct additions to the flow of demand for final output (i.e. injections from outside the system), like domestic capital formation, and if taxes and imports can be regarded as endogenous leakages in the circular flow of incomes, like savings, and since we know that equilibrium in the flow will only be obtained when the sum of the (planned) leakages equals the sum of the (planned) injections, it follows that equilibrium will only be obtained when government consumption, exports and domestic investment equals taxes, imports and savings. Furthermore our assumptions are that only the leakages are endogenously related to the level of income, not the injections.

Let us assume that the leakages are related to income in the following manner:

$$\text{Tax payments} = T = a_t + tY;$$
$$\text{Savings} = S = a_s + sY;[1]$$
$$\text{Imports} = M = a_m + mY.$$

Now we have that income will be in equilibrium when

$$GDCF + C_g + X = T + S + M$$
$$\text{(injections)} \qquad \text{(leakages)}$$

so that income will be in equilibrium when

$$GDCF + C_g + X = a_t + tY + a_s + sY + a_m + mY,$$

i.e. when $GDCF + C_g + X = a_t + a_s + a_m + Y(t + s + m)$

---

[1] It would be much more realistic to make savings, and hence consumption, a function of income *after* taxes – i.e. 'disposable income'. But this complicates the algebra slightly without adding to the few points being made here. It does, however, lead to different equilibrium conditions.

i.e. when $$Y = \frac{GDCF + C_g + X - a_t - a_s - a_m}{t + s + m} \qquad (11)$$

The relationship between this equilibrium condition and that used in the last chapter is as follows. In the simple model it was seen that if c is the marginal propensity to consume, the marginal propensity to save, s, must be equal to $(1-c)$, since consumption is merely the difference between income and savings. Now that tax payments have been introduced into the model, however, an additional leakage from income has to be allowed for before consumption expenditures can be carried out. Consumption will now be the difference between income, on the one hand, and both savings and taxes, on the other. Hence, with t representing the marginal propensity to pay taxes, we now have the equation:

$$t + s = (1 - c) \qquad (12)$$

Substituting this equation in equation (11), we have that income is in equilibrium when:

$$Y = \frac{GDCF + C_g + X - a_t - a_s - a_m}{(1 - c + m)} \qquad (13)$$

The reader should check the similarity between this equation and equation (4) of this chapter. It will be seen that equation (13) differs from equation (4) in that (a) in the numerator of equation (13), the other injections (government consumption and exports) have been added as well as the constant terms from the equations of the other leakages (taxes and imports), and (b) in the denominator, too, allowance has been made for these other leakages. The marginal propensity to pay taxes is allowed for in that, as in equation (12), it determines the size of the marginal propensity to consume. The marginal propensity to import has been added, but with opposite sign to that of the marginal propensity to consume, since it reduces the amount of the extra consumption that goes back as demand in the economy concerned.

Alternatively, the normal marginal propensity to consume, c, that has been adopted so far and which relates to the total consumption demand by households irrespective of whether they are trying to buy domestically produced consumer goods or not, could be replaced by an adjusted marginal propensity to

206

consume, c', which would relate only to the marginal propensity to consume *home-produced* goods and services. For purposes of the multiplier this is what matters, since it is only the propensity to consume domestic output that leads to a flow of demand back to the productive sector of the given country. Thus, c' would equal $(c-m)$. Although we shall not adopt this device here, since it might mean overlooking the role of imports, it will be seen later to be useful for diagrammatic purposes.

(ii) The demand and supply for goods approach

It will be recalled that when adopting the demand and supply of goods approach to find the equilibrium conditions in the simple case of a closed economy with no government sector the only demands that were involved were (i) private consumption and (ii) investment (domestic). The problem then was to find the level of output (and income) at which the sum of these two forms of demand at that level of income was equal to the output. In the more complicated model with which we are now concerned, therefore, the problem must be to find the level of output which can satisfy the sum – at *that* level of output and income – of *all* the categories of demand now taken into account. These demands are now recognised as comprising, in addition to private consumption and domestic investment, government consumption and exports less imports. But it is not necessary that national output be equal to all these demands on it since some of this demand can be met by imports. Equilibrium will thus be obtained when national output *plus* imports is equal to the sum of private consumption, investment and government consumption. This is expressed in the following equation:

$$Y + M = C_h + GDCF + Cg + X$$

which can be re-arranged in the more familiar form:

$$Y = C_h + GDCF + C_g + X - M \qquad (14)$$

In the simple model of the last chapter the only one of these components of final demand that was determined by income was private consumption, and it was not necessary to allow for the possibility that some of this demand did not feed back as demand for domestic output on account of it being siphoned off as demand for imports. Now, however, in attempting to relate demands to income it is necessary to make a deduction from the consumption demand corresponding to the propensity to import. Thus, given our assumptions that only private consumption and imports are functions of income (the former depending on the income-determined taxes and savings), taking the following form:

$$C_h = a_c + cY \quad \text{and} \quad M = a_m + mY$$

we have that the total demand at any income level will be composed of:

$$GDCF + C_g + X + a_c + cY - a_m - mY$$

(exogenous demand injections) (income induced additions or subtractions from demand for *national* output)

Hence output (and income) will be in equilibrium when it is equal to the demands generated at that level of output (income), i.e. when

$$Y = GDCF + C_g + X + a_c - a_m + Y(c - m) \qquad (15)$$

i.e. when

$$GDCF + C_g + X + a_c - a_m = Y - Y(c - m) \qquad (16)$$

i.e. when

$$Y = \frac{GDCF + C_g + X + a_c - a_m}{(1 - c + m)} \qquad (17)$$

But since $C \equiv Y - T - S$; $a_c = -a_t - a_s$ and $c = 1 - (t + s)$, so substituting for a_c and c in (17) we come back to equation (11) above.

If this equilibrium condition is split up in the same way that equation (4) was split up in equation (9) – i.e. separating out the numerator and the denominator – it is obvious that any change in the numerator has to be multiplied by the denominator to give the equilibrium change in income. In other words, in the same way that the multiplier in the simple model was

$$k = \frac{1}{(1 - c)} \quad \left(\text{since equilibrium } Y = \frac{I + a}{1 - c}\right)$$

so, from the equilibrium condition as given in equation (11) the multiplier in the present model will be

$$k = \frac{1}{(t + s + m)} \qquad (18)$$

This result matches the earlier argument in terms of the character of leakages and injections. For it is clear that, given an increase in any of the injections, such as government consumption, the final effect will depend on how much extra demand is created for consumer goods and this will depend not only on the marginal propensity to save and pay taxes, which together determine the marginal propensity to consume, but also on how much of this extra consumption demand feeds back to the domestic economy rather than leaking off in the form of demand for imports. The bigger is the taxation, savings or imports 'leakage' the smaller will be the impact on incomes of a change in any of the autonomous injections into the flow of incomes.

7. Diagrammatic presentation of full equilibrium conditions

In the following diagram the exogenous – i.e. the independent (of the system) – demand elements are shown as horizontal lines indicating that they do not vary with the income level. Whereas in the simple model only investment appeared in this way, it is now necessary to add such lines for government consumption and for exports. Private consumption, as usual, is shown as

Figure 9.6

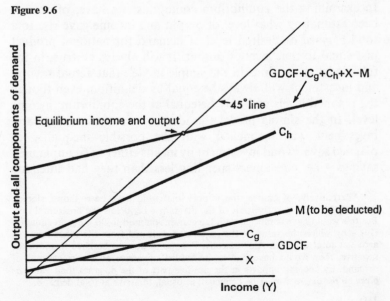

rising to the right, indicating that it is greater the greater is income. But before one can proceed to add vertically all the demands at any level of income in the usual manner, it is now necessary to allow for the fact that some of these demands may not be demands for domestic output, since they may be met by imports. Hence, if we are assuming – as is the case – that import demand is a function of income, a line representing this demand has to be inserted sloping up to the right (if imports rise with income). But since imports, as shown by such a line, *reduce* demand for domestic output, total demand at any income level indicated along the horizontal axis will be equal to (a) the vertical sum of all the lines except imports, minus (b) the height of the import line. Another procedure would be to replace the line C_h by a line relating to consumers' expenditure on home-produced goods and services only; i.e. the lines C_h and M would be amalgamated into a net line C'_h, which would be lower than C_h. This procedure has not been adopted here, however, in the interests of retaining a diagrammatic presentation that matches the accounting equation used earlier to define the components of GNP.[1]

8. Planned and actual savings and investment in the full model

In examining the equilibrium conditions, we have, of course, been estimating what level of output and income gave rise to a total *planned* or desired level of demand for national product just equal to that level of output. It will always be true, in the full model as much as in the simple model, that actual savings and investment will always be equal by definition, even though the planned levels will only be equal at the equilibrium income level. In the simple model the identity of actual savings and investment was reconciled with the possible inequality of planned savings and investment by means either of (i) unplanned savings – i.e. consumers spending less than they had intended

---

[1] Alternatively, of course, the import line could have been shown sloping downwards in the negative part of the diagram – i.e. below the horizontal line. But this would have conflicted with the convention used so far – e.g. in equation (14) – by which the value of the imports is deducted from the other items to arrive at total demand. Algebraically, if imports were to be already shown as negative, they would have had to be 'added' to arrive at a correct total of demand. By keeping imports in the positive part of the diagram their value *as given on the diagram* must be deducted, as usual, to arrive at total demand.

to spend – or (ii) unplanned investment in the form of unplanned changes in stocks (or some mixture of the two). In the full model, however, the number of possible ways by which this reconciliation may be effected is much greater. This is because the number of items now appearing in the savings–investment identity is much greater than in the simple model. In fact, the model of income determination that we have arrived at corresponds to the full savings–investment identity expressed in the capital account of the economy. This was seen in Chapter 5 (page 108) to be:

$$GDCF + (X - M) = S_f + S_h + S_g \tag{19}$$

For bearing in mind that the savings of government are merely the difference between the injection provided by government consumption (C_g) and the leakage of taxes $(T_f + T_h)$,[1] the last equation could have been written as:

$$GDCF + X + C_g = T_f + T_h + S_f + S_h + M \tag{20}$$

Suppose now that, starting from a position of equilibrium, households decide that they would like to save less for any given level of income and spend more on consumption goods. We know that when they try to buy the greater quantity of consumer goods they will, at first, tend to be disappointed. Perhaps they will be forced to carry out some unplanned savings. Alternatively, their increased demands for goods may be met by running down stocks – i.e. unplanned investment as in the simple model. In this case, the fall in actual S_h on the right-hand side of the last equation has been matched by a fall in actual $GDCF$ on the other side of the equation. But now that the equation contains more terms than in the simple model, it can be seen that many other combinations of events could have retained the equality of the two sides of the account.

For example, firms might meet the suddenly increased demand for consumer goods by increasing imports, so that M would rise, offsetting the fall in S_h and leaving the right-hand side of the equation intact. Alternatively, some of the goods and services destined for the government or for exports might be

[1] We are continuing here with the procedure adopted on page 202 of this chapter by which government transfer payments are netted out against an equivalent amount of the receipts, so that T_f and T_h are net of this amount. Obviously, an equal deduction from both sides of the government account cannot affect the net balance of the account and hence government savings, S_g.

diverted to the use of private households, in which case, the C_g or the X on the left-hand side of the equation would have fallen to match the fall in the right-hand side. In practice, of course, some combination of all these and other changes may have taken place, being accompanied, all the time, by a discrepancy between demand and supply until income has reached the point where planned savings equals planned investment, so that planned demand is equal to planned supply.

EXERCISES 9.2

1 What is the value of the multiplier, k, when the marginal propensity to *save* is (a) 0·2; (b) 0·1?

2 What is k when the marginal propensity to consume is (a) 0·5; (b) 0·6?

3 What is k when
(a) $C = 5 + 0·75 Y$;   (b) $C = 15 + 0·75 Y$;
(c) $S = -5 + 0·4 Y$;   (d) $S = -10 + 0·2 Y$;
(e) $C = 0·9 Y$;   (f) $S = -50 + 0·25 Y$?

4 What is the change in income (dY) when the change in investment (dI) is 10 and
(a) $C = 10 + 0·8 Y$;   (b) $C = 5 + 0·9 Y$;
(c) $S = -10 + 0·4 Y$?

5 What is dY when $C = 5 + 0·8 Y$ and
(a) $dI = 10$;   (b) $dI = 20$;
(c) $dI = -5$;   (d) $dI = -15$?

6 What is k when
(a) $C = 5 + 0·6 Y$ and M (imports) $= -10 + 0·2 Y$;
(b) $C = 10 + 0·6 Y$ and $M = -20 + 0·1 Y$?

7 What is k when
(a) $S = -10 + 0·2 Y$, $M = -5 + 0·1 Y$ and
 T (taxes) $= -5 + 0·2 Y$?
(b) $S = -20 + 0·2 Y$, $M = -5 + 0·3 Y$ and $T = 10 + 0·1 Y$?

8 With the multiplier of question 6(b), what is dY when
(a) $dI = 10$ and dX (the change in exports) $= 5$;
(b) $dI = 5$ and $dX = 20$;
(c) $dI = -10$ and $dX = 15$;
(d) $dI = -5$ and $dX = -5$;
(e) $dI = 15$ and $dX = 15$?

9 With the multiplier of question 6(b), what is dY when the import function changes from $M=10+0\cdot3Y$ to
   (a) $M=20+0\cdot3Y$;   (b) $M=-10+0\cdot3Y$?

10 If $GDCF=10$ and $X=15$, and there is no government sector, what is the equilibrium level of income when
   (a) $S=-15+0\cdot2Y$ and $M=-5+0\cdot3Y$?
   (b) $S=-10+0\cdot1Y$ and $M=-5+0\cdot3Y$?
   (c) $S=-10+0\cdot1Y$ and $M=5+0\cdot3Y$?
   (d) $S=10+0\cdot1Y$ and $M=-20+0\cdot4Y$?

11 If $GDCF=10$, $X=10$ and C_g (government consumption of goods and services) $=20$, what is the equilibrium level of income when
   (a) as in 10(a) and $T=-6+0\cdot1Y$;
   (b) as in 10(b) and $T=5+0\cdot1Y$?

12 With $S=-15+0\cdot2Y$, $M=-5+0\cdot3Y$ and $T=-6+0\cdot1Y$, what is dY if
   (a) $dC_g=6$;
   (b) $dC_g=-9$;
   (c) the tax function changes to $T=+3+0\cdot1Y$;
   (d) the tax function changes to $T=-12+0\cdot1Y$;
   (e) with the same exogenous injections as in question 11, and the same savings, import and tax functions as in the first line of this question, what is dY if the tax function changes to $T=12+0\cdot3Y$?

13 If the value of the multiplier is $2\cdot5$, what is dY when
   (a) $dI=5$, $dX=10$ and $dC_g=-5$;
   (b) $dI=15$, $dX=-10$ and $dC_g=-5$;
   (c) $dI=-10$, $dX=+10$ and $dC_g=+5$?

Chapter 10

What is a 'change' in national product?

1. What is the problem?

So far we have discussed what national product consists of and how its equilibrium level is determined, in the short-run, in the context of a very simplified model of the way that the economy behaves. In examining what determines a change in national product we have taken for granted that we know what we mean by 'a change in national product'. After all, if we know what goes into national product, surely we must know what we mean by an increase in it; it must mean more of whatever it is that goes into it. In a sense this last, rough and ready, definition of an increase in national product happens to be almost as close as one can get to a definition of what constitutes an unambiguous increase in national product, namely an increase in some of the constituents of national product without any decrease in any of the others. But in practice such a definition would be too restrictive, for in the real world the output of some items increases and of others it decreases. If national product changes from 5 apples and 10 pears to 10 apples and 5 pears, knowing that both apples and pears are included in national product does not help tell us whether the sum of the apples and pears has increased or not.

Apples and pears cannot be added together unless they are converted into some common units. For example, we could convert them into tons, and so might find that the total weight had risen from three tons of combined apples and pears to four tons. But this would still not be a satisfactory measure of the increase for purposes of the sort of questions that economists are supposed to be concerned with, since a ton of pears may be worth much more than a ton of apples. For purposes of answering the usual economic questions that arise, it is necessary to combine the apples and pears together by means of an indicator of their relative contribution to some aggregate, such as output or welfare, that one is interested in. This might appear, at first sight, to raise no special difficulties, since the prices of apples and pears can presumably be used for this purpose. But prices are not necessarily the same in different situations. For example, the cost of living may have changed, if we are interested in comparisons over time, or the price level in France may not be the same as that in Britain, if we are interested in comparing these two countries' standards of living. Money income may rise from one year to another, but if the cost of living has risen just as much there is no increase in *real* income. Similarly, the value of the economy's production may rise from one year to another, but if prices rise just as much there would be no increase in *real* output. Furthermore, not only may the price level of output as a whole be different in two situations, but the relative prices of the individual components of total output may have changed. Not only may the prices of both apples and pears have risen, but the price of one may have risen more than the other. Which set of relative prices of apples and pears should be used for combining the collections of apples and pears together for purposes of comparing total output or income?

And when we leave simple products like apples and pears yet other difficulties emerge. For example, how do we compare the output of this year's automobiles with that of, say, thirty years ago? Today's apples of a given type are probably not very much different from the same type of apple of thirty years ago. But one could not make the same statement about today's automobiles. Hence, in addition to the problem of which year's prices should be used in order to link together the collections of goods in any year, there is the problem of whether a unit of a commodity such as an apple or an automobile in one year is equivalent to a unit of the 'same' commodity in another year, and, if they are different, how to convert units of, say, 1930 automobiles into units of 1960 automobiles. This is a very complex subject which gives rise to much controversy. Furthermore, it is a subject that is of some practical importance, and not just a matter of academic quibbling. For example, a major American governmental study of the problems of inflation came to the conclusion that price indices tend to exaggerate the rise in

215

prices over time (and hence to under-estimate the rise in national product in 'real' terms). The reason given was that the price indices fail to allow for 'improvements' in the quality of goods and services, such as shorter length of stay in hospital to cure certain illnesses or 'In the case of goods, changes in styling, improvements in design and durability . . .', etc. Hence, it is maintained that price indices overstate 'the costs to the consumer of acquiring an equivalent level of satisfaction'.[1] In fact, as will be shown in this chapter, whilst both are important, and whilst they are usually related to each other, the measurement of *output* changes must be carefully distinguished from changes in *satisfactions*. Some kinds of changes in styling, improvements in design and so on, may add to satisfactions but may have nothing to do with changes in output.[2]

Similar problems are often encountered in the area of international comparisons of income levels. It is sometimes argued, for example, that the poor countries of the world are not really as poor as they would appear from available measures, since their needs are not as great as those of people in rich countries.

On account of the practical importance of the problem of how to measure changes in national product the assumption that we all know what is meant by a change in national product must now be dropped and in this chapter we shall explore the concept of a change in national product a little further.

The question of what constitutes a change in 'real' income or output, should, strictly speaking, be replaced by the question 'What constitutes a difference in real income or output between two situations?' For we are as much interested in the difference between the income (or output) levels of two countries as in the difference between the income (or output) levels of two years, and the former can hardly be examined under the heading of 'What constitutes a change in incomes?' Conceptually the comparison between the income levels of two countries at the same point of time is exactly the same as a comparison between the income levels of the same country at two different points of time. In fact the analytical problems are essentially the same

[1] Joint Economic Committee of Congress *Staff Report on Employment, Growth and Price Levels*, December 1959, 86th Congress, 1st Session, page 108.

[2] Though it might be argued that the notion of 'output' unrelated to the satisfactions derived from it is of little value for policy purposes. This question is discussed in detail in Chapter 3 above.

even if we are trying to compare two completely hypothetical situations that may never exist at all; such as if we were asking a consumer which, out of two hypothetical collections of quantities and prices and incomes, he would prefer.

But bearing this in mind, it is probably easier to continue the discussion in terms of 'changes in income or output', though the whole argument would apply, *mutatis mutandis*, if put in the more general terms of 'differences in income or output'. In practice it is very simple to transpose conclusions about intertemporal comparisons into the field of international comparisons.

2. The analytical tools

It is possible to discuss the concept of changes (or differences) in income and output without recourse to technical tools of analysis, such as the 'indifference curve' or the 'transformation curve'. But whilst the reader can learn the rules of the game without the aid of these analytical tools he is never likely to obtain a clear view of the object of the game or of its underlying logic. Hence, some aspects of these techniques of analysis will be explained briefly at the beginning of the chapter before going on to draw the implications of them for the rules of the game. Readers who find that this technical material is rather tough going are advised to supplement their reading on this point with a more general textbook on economic theory, including the theory of consumers' behaviour and the theory of price determination.

(i) The indifference curve

The first concept to be grasped is that of the *indifference curve*. The basic idea of this curve is very simple, and it is only in the context of complex questions in 'welfare economics' that difficult issues crop up, such as the extent to which one can add the indifference curves of different individuals in order to derive an aggregate indifference curve for the community as a whole, or the extent to which evidence of preferences constitutes evidence of 'satisfactions'.

The starting point in the concept of the indifference curve is, as its name suggests, the establishment of alternative collections of goods between which the consumer is indifferent. For example, we could start by presenting him with, say, 10 apples and 5 pears, and then ask him to say how many extra pears he would need to leave him just as well off if we took away one apple. The answer would indicate what is known as *the marginal rate of substitution* of apples for pears at that particular collection of apples and pears. 'The marginal rate of substitution' of X for Y can be defined as the additional amount of X, from a given combination of X and Y, needed to leave the consumer just as well off if one unit of Y is taken away from him. In this case, for example, if he answered that he would require 2 extra pears to compensate him for the loss of one apple, his marginal rate of substitution of pears for apples, *at that particular collection of apples and pears*, is 2. We could then ask him how many more pears he would need to leave him just as well off if we took away yet another apple, and the answer might now be 3 more pears. Thus we would have a third combination of goods between which he was indifferent, giving us the following three collections:

10 apples plus 5 pears

9 apples plus 7 pears

8 apples plus 10 pears

These three points can be represented on a diagram in which apples and pears are shown along the two axes, as in Figure 10.1. The three points represent different collections of the two goods between which he is indifferent. This is the beginning of an 'indifference curve'. We could obviously continue discovering the whole range of collections of apples and pears which are just as acceptable to the individual concerned as the initial collection of 10 apples and 5 pears, thereby constructing a complete indifference curve. Furthermore, we can start with another collection, say, 20 apples and 15 pears, which he would presumably prefer to the first collection[1] and then proceed in the same way as before, finding out all the collections of apples and pears which give him as much satisfaction as 20 apples and 15 pears, thereby constructing another indifference curve. Similarly, we might start with a collection that was less satisfying to him than the original collection, such as 5 apples and 3 pears, and proceed to find out all the collections that gave him the same satisfactions as this lower collection. By constructing a whole

---

[1] If he did not prefer 20 apples and 15 pears to 10 apples and 5 pears then the products concerned would not be 'goods' but 'bads'.

218

family of such curves, we can draw what is known as his 'indifference map'. A movement from one point on any curve to another point on the same curve leaves his satisfaction unchanged, since he is indifferent between any collection on that curve, but moving from one curve to a higher one at any one moment of time indicates that, other things being equal, his satisfactions are increasing and he is 'better off'.

Figure 10.1

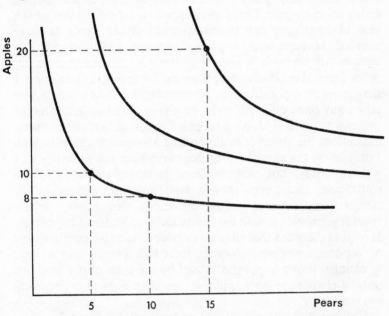

The qualification, in the last sentence, about 'other things being equal' is one which need not concern us much in this book, although it is very important in the more fundamental issues of welfare economics. For example, if it can be known with certainty that as between yesterday and today I have moved from one indifference curve to a higher one, it can still not be known that I am happier today than I was yesterday. All that can be concluded is that, *on today's tastes*, etc., I prefer today's collection of goods to the one I had yesterday. There may have been no change at all in my preference patterns in the sense in which the indifference curves describe them – i.e. in terms of how much

219

of one good I would require to compensate me for giving up a unit of another. But this tells one nothing about how happy any collection of goods makes me. Thus, even if my preference patterns have not changed, I may have woken up today with a hangover or have found that my wife had run off with the milkman.

It may well be that observations could show that my zest for life was not the same as it had been yesterday. Yesterday, when asked how many pears I would need to compensate me for giving up one apple, I may have appeared very distressed at the idea of sacrificing one delicious health-giving apple and demanded at least one more scrumptious beautiful pear to compensate me for it. Today, by contrast, when asked how many pears I would need to compensate me for giving up one apple I may listlessly reply: 'Apples, schmapples, I should worry if you take away one apple. All right, so give me a pear, but don't do me any favours, I don't like pears much either.' From such indications the observer might be able to conclude that although I may be on the same indifference curve I am not as happy as I was yesterday, but such evidence is rarely available to the statistician. Thus, even though tastes may not change at all, comparisons between actual situations can never, strictly speaking, provide a basis for comparisons of states of happiness. It might be argued that they do provide a basis for comparisons of 'economic welfare', however, since this is not a matter, say, of changes in my happiness caused by the state of my liver but only of changes in my happiness *caused by changes in economic circumstances.*[1]

Unfortunately, this does not entirely resolve the difficulties, since, with exactly the same income and prices and quantities today as yesterday, and without any change in my tastes as defined by my preference patterns expressed in the indifference curves, I may still be less happy today than yesterday on account of some change in external economic circumstances, such as a rise in the income of everybody else, which may make me dissatisfied with what I had yesterday.[2] But again, as long as it is recognised that, strictly speaking, comparisons of economic

---

[1] See I. M. D. Little, *A Critique of Welfare Economics*, 2nd edition, Oxford University Press, page 6.
[2] *Ibid.*, page 44.

welfare between different dates or places or people cannot easily be transposed into comparisons of happiness or even of the satisfactions that are derived from collections of goods, the more philosophical issues surrounding the interpretation of such welfare comparisons can be ignored and we can concentrate on the manner in which certain fairly non-controversial properties of the indifference curve affect the use that can be made of them.

In particular, it will be noted that we have drawn the curves in Figure 10.1 with a special curvature (known as convex to the origin). This follows from an assumption, which is probably a very reasonable one, namely that as our consumer gets more and more pears relative to apples, he values each successive pear less and less (the law of diminishing marginal utility), and as he is deprived of more and more apples he values the apples more and more. From this assumption it follows that as he gives up more apples he will want more pears per apple to compensate him for the loss of each marginal apple – i.e. his marginal rate of substitution of pears for apples will increase as he has more pears and less apples. For example, when he is going from 20 apples and 15 pears to 19 apples he might be prepared to accept only one extra pear to compensate him for the loss of the 20th apple. But if we move round the same curve we are likely to find that when he is left with only 5 apples he would want 3 pears to compensate him for giving up the 5th apple. It is clear that this will make the curve get flatter and flatter as we give up apples and add pears – i.e. as we move down the curve from left to right.[1]

Given this model of how a consumer's preferences will be represented, and given a further assumption, namely that the consumer will act rationally, in the sense that he will try to move to preferred positions, we are now able to describe how he will behave when faced with any particular income and set of relative prices of apples and pears. To do this we have to introduce the concept of the 'budget line', which is also a vital concept in the measurement of income changes.

[1] If the two goods are *very* close substitutes the curvature will not change much as one moves along the curve. In other words the greater the substitutability between goods the less does the marginal rate of substitution change as one moves along an indifference curve.

(ii) The 'budget line'

Given a certain amount of money that the consumer can dispose of, it is obvious that if he spent it all on apples the amount of apples he could buy would depend on their price. Suppose that the price of apples and his income were such that he could buy the quantity of apples shown by the point A_1 in Figure 10.2 below. And similarly, suppose the price of pears is such that, if he decided to spend all his income on pears rather than apples, he could buy the number of pears shown by the point P_1 on the diagram. If we now connect up the two points the resulting line, known as the *budget line*, indicates all the possible combinations of apples and pears that his income allows him to buy. He can buy A_1 apples or P_1 pears, or any combination lying along the line A_1P_1. For the slope of the line must represent the relative price of apples to pears since it indicates how many apples he would have to give up in order to buy more pears, and this depends, of course, on the relative prices of the two goods. Consider, for example, one of the two possible extreme cases, namely where he buys no apples and spends all his income on pears, obtaining P_1 of pears. Clearly, if we doubled the price of pears the slope of the line would become much steeper. For he would now be able to buy only half as many pears as before in place of the apples, so that the budget line would have to cut the pear axis at P_2.

Now if the consumer is acting in such a way as to maximise his satisfactions, he will move along his budget line in such a way as to get on to the highest possible indifference curve. As can be seen from the following diagram, this will be at the point where his budget line is tangential to an indifference curve and therefore at the point where the relative prices of the goods (equal to the slope of the budget line) equals the marginal rate of substitution between them (equal to the slope of the indifference curve at the same point). Any other point along his budget line would be at a lower indifference curve. At such a point of tangency, at the highest possible indifference curve, he is in a position of stable equilibrium and he would only move to another point if one of two things happened. First, the relative prices of the two goods might change, in which case he would move along the new budget line until he was once again at a point of tangency between the new budget line and an indifference curve.

Secondly, without any change in the relative prices of the two goods, his income might change. If, say, his income rose without any change in the prices of the goods then his budget line would simply rise parallel to the original line, and he would move to a point where the new and higher budget line is tangential to an indifference curve. The latter type of movement would express the effect on his consumption pattern of a rise in his *real* income.

Figure 10.2

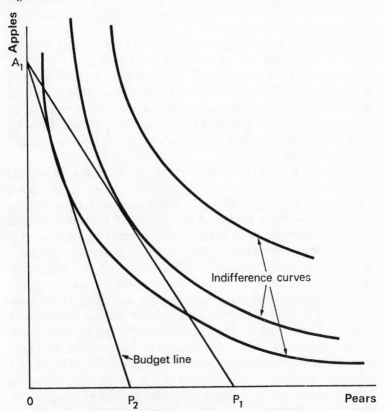

The common sense of the equilibrium condition is as follows. The amount of one good, *X*, that a consumer needs in order just to compensate him for giving up one unit of *Y* has been defined as the marginal rate of substitution of *X* for *Y*. As we have seen, this changes as he moves round his indifference curve. Now if, at

223

equilibrium, the ratio of the prices of the goods is equal to the marginal rate of substitution, then it is easy to show that he cannot possibly re-arrange his consumption pattern in a way that will make him better off. For example, suppose he is at a point where the marginal rate of substitution of X for Y is three – i.e. he would need three X to compensate him for losing one unit of Y and vice versa. Suppose that X costs £1 per unit and Y costs £5 per unit. Then clearly he would be well advised to give up one Y, thereby saving £5 and using this to buy $5X$, since with only 3 more X he would have been just as happy after giving up 1 unit of Y.

However, he would not go on indefinitely substituting X for Y, because as he gives up more and more Y and buys more and more X he would get relatively less and less satisfaction from X relative to Y. When, eventually, his marginal rate of substitution has changed to the point that he requires 5 more X to compensate him for giving up yet another Y he will have no further interest in saving another £5 by giving up one more Y in order to buy 5 more X.

Finally, we have to switch attention from the individual consumer to the community as a whole. If we draw up an indifference map for the whole community corresponding to that which we have drawn for an individual consumer we can define the community as having a higher real income when it is on a higher community indifference curve. Strictly speaking, when one is using *community* indifference curves, rather than *individual's* indifference curves, for analytical purposes many dubious assumptions often have to be made. This is the case, for example, when it is assumed – as it has to be for some analytical purposes – that the community indifference curve remains unchanged as the distribution of income changes. However, we shall abstract from such complications in this book, and define an increase in real income, or in economic welfare, as being represented by a move from one indifference curve to a higher one. Simple comparisons of money income can clearly not indicate when *real* income, in this sense, has increased; for there may have been changes in the price level, which prevented the community from moving to a higher indifference curve. For example, if money income doubled but all prices doubled as well, the community's budget line would remain in exactly the same position, since the higher money income would still not permit it to buy any more of the goods measured along the axes. Hence the community would not have been able to move to a higher indifference curve, and therefore would not have experienced an increase in real income in the sense in which it has been defined.

It should, however, be emphasised that although we shall discuss, in this and the next chapter, how to measure differences in *real income*, which we will equate with economic welfare, such measures must not be interpreted as corresponding, in any way, to measures of the degree to which one indifference curve exceeds another. In the first place, as the reader can verify for himself, it is easily possible to draw a pair of indifference curves in such a way that the gap between them varies over the length of the curves, so that no meaning can be attached to the notion of how much one indifference curve lies above another. In any case, indifference curve maps have only *ordinal* value – i.e. they indicate the ranking, or *order*, of different combinations of goods. They do not have *cardinal* value, in the sense that one could say that one indifference curve represents 1,000 units of happiness or satisfaction whereas another represents only 800, so that if the community (or an individual) is on the former curve today and was on the latter curve yesterday, today's satisfactions must be 25% higher than the satisfactions obtained from yesterday's collection of goods.

Thus, what we set out to measure is 'real income', not satisfactions, even though the indifference curve is the basic concept underlying the measurement. For example, suppose that as a result of a change in an individual's money income and in the absolute and relative prices of the goods he buys, he moves to a lower indifference curve. Then we would say that the fall in his 'real income' could be measured by the amount his money income would have had to have fallen – assuming prices had remained the same – to have made him move down to the lower indifference curve. Alternatively, one might define his fall in real income as the amount of extra income that he would now have to be given in order to bring him back up again to his original indifference curve.

(iii) The transformation curve
Corresponding to the concept of the indifference curve, a family

of curves can be drawn to represent 'equal collections of *output*'; the definition of 'equal' being implicit in the way the curves are constructed, in exactly the same way as the definition of what constituted an equal level of satisfactions to the consumer was implicit in the manner in which we constructed the indifference curve. In the case of output we can construct a family of curves, each one of which indicates the alternative combinations of output that the economy could produce for any given level of capacity, equipment, employment, skills and education and so on. Such curves, are called *transformation curves* (also often known as 'production possibility curves').

In the Figure 10.3 below, for example, we may start with the point I, in which the economy is producing, say, 5 automobiles and 100 washing machines. We could then ask how many more washing machines could be produced *by the same resources* if we cut production of automobiles by one unit. In other words 'What is the marginal *cost*, in terms of washing machines, of producing cars?'. If the answer is 30 washing machines, then we can plot a. new point, II, representing 4 automobiles and 130 washing machines. These two points thus constitute 'equal' amounts of output in the same sense that two points on an indifference curve represent equal amounts of satisfactions. If we continue we would construct a whole schedule of the possible combinations of products that the economy could produce with the same amount of resources, knowledge, skills and so on. Unlike the indifference curve, however, such a transformation curve would have a slope that was concave to the origin. The reason for this is that, in general, since most factors of production have been specially designed or trained or combined together to perform a special kind of activity they will not be so productive – at least in the short-run – if they are switched from the activity for which they were designed to another activity. Thus, *given resources* and so on, the *marginal opportunity costs* of producing one product instead of another, increase as one produces more and more of it and less of the other.[1] In the extreme simple case, such as that used for describing consumers'

---

[1] Roughly speaking, the concave curvature of the transformation curve is associated with the law of diminishing returns in the same way that the convex curvature of the indifference curve is associated with the law of diminishing marginal utility.

indifference curves, namely apples and pears, it would be quite impossible to produce more apples simply by giving up a few pears. The goods concerned may be good substitutes in consumption, but not in production. A pear tree cannot produce apples. Hence, if our diagram below had been in terms of apples and pears it would have no curvature at all. It would appear like the line *AXP*, indicating that, starting from some combination of apples and pears output such as that at *X*, the mere giving up of some pear output, which would be illustrated by a movement down the vertical pear axis, would not help at all to move along the horizontal axis to produce more apples.

Figure 10.3

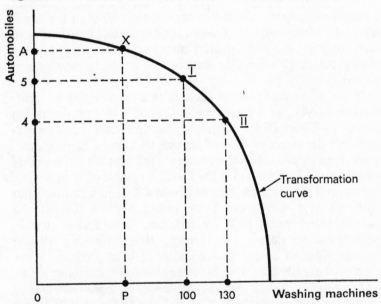

With manufactured products the scope for using the factors of production that were engaged in some line of activity to produce, instead, some other products is much greater, though it will depend on the precise products concerned. For example, giving up some electricity output would not contribute much to the resources available for producing more textiles. Not much manpower would be released and the capital equipment or raw materials used for producing electricity would be of little use in

227

producing textiles. By contrast, reducing the output of, say, sports clothes, would certainly increase the scope for producing blankets. Hence, in general, there is some substitutability between the different goods produced in any large and complex economy, but, at the same time, as resources are switched from one use to another the extent to which they will continue to be just as productive in their new use will probably diminish.

Because of these technological limitations on the extent to which resources used in the production of some goods can be switched to the production of other goods, the transformation curve will generally be of the shape indicated, since this corresponds to the fact that as one gives up more and more of the product measured up one axis it becomes increasingly difficult to use the resources released to expand the output of the goods along the other axis – i.e. the *marginal opportunity costs* of X in terms of Y increases as one substitutes resources from producing Y to producing X (given the state of techniques, knowledge and so on).

In the same way that we have drawn up a family of indifference curves, so we can draw a family of transformation curves. In Figure 10.4 opposite, for example, the curve T_1 represents all the combinations of output that could be produced, with a given amount of resources, etc., equal to the actual combination I. If we had started with a combination of output comprising the same amount of product X as in situation I but with, say, less of product Y, the resulting point II would lie exactly below point I. We could then have drawn another transformation curve, T_2, through II representing all the combinations of output that could have been produced if we employed exactly the same resources as used for combination II. *In other words, we are implicitly defining two 'equal' amounts of output as being amounts of output that could be produced with the same resources.* In other words, we are not defining equal amounts of output in terms of whether people like them equally or not. That is a matter of indifference curves and of equal satisfactions, not a matter of production. And of two collections of goods the one that represents 'greater' output is the one that is on the higher transformation curve. Point I represents more *output* than point II because it is on a higher transformation curve than point II.

Figure 10.4

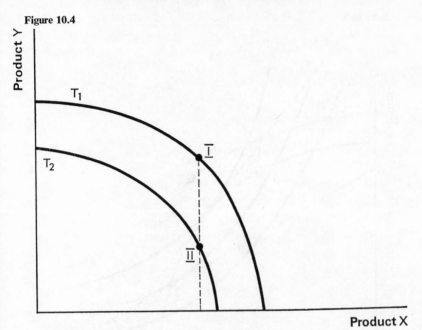

(iv) Optimum output

In Figure 10.5 opposite, we have put together some transformation curves and indifference curves. This diagram can be used to show some characteristics of the particular *pattern* of output – not *level* of output – at which the economy will be in equilibrium in the sense that, if its productive capacity is fully employed, it would not have wished to produce a different *pattern*. Suppose, for example, that the economy has transformation curve T_1. Clearly, since it can (by definition of a transformation curve) produce at any combination of output on the curve T_1, it would be preferable to move round this transformation curve until it reached the point I, since at this position it has reached the highest indifference curve (IC_1) attainable with the given transformation curve. This is the 'optimum output', given the production possibilities open to this economy. It would be unfortunate, for example, if the economy produced the pattern of output shown at point II, since it is quite capable of transforming its resources into the pattern of point I, at which point it is obtaining a higher real income, although output is no higher.

229

Figure 10.5

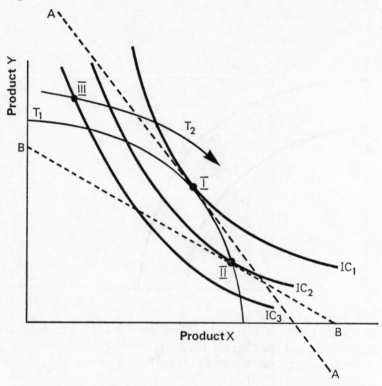

Fortunately, subject to various assumptions and qualifications (particularly concerning the degree of perfect competition), the price mechanism is such that forces will be set up to ensure that the economy will, in fact, move round to the optimum output of point I. Without going into the operation of the price mechanism – which is the subject of many excellent textbooks – the following rough explanation may give an intuitive idea of the way that the mechanism works.

Suppose, for example, that the economy produced at point II, instead of point I. Now if, say, consumers were in equilibrium, this would imply that the ratio of prices at that point was equal to their marginal rate of substitution – i.e. that the price ratio between the two goods X and Y was as shown by the line BB, since this is the only line that is tangential to the community indifference curve at point II. But this line cannot then be tangential also to the transformation curve at the point II, since at this point the transformation curve *cuts* the indifference curve and is not tangential to it. Hence, the price ratio of the two goods at point II cannot be the same as the cost ratio of producing the two goods at point II, which we have seen is measured by the slope of the transformation curve at this point.

In this particular case, at point II the *price* of product Y relative to X is higher than the *cost* of producing Y relative to X. This can be seen from the fact that the price line, *BB*, is flatter than the slope of the transformation curve at point II. Thus producers would find it profitable to expand the production of Y and to contract the production of X – i.e. to move round the transformation curve in the direction of the point I. Only when this point is reached will relative prices equal relative costs, so that there will be no more incentive for producers to switch from producing one good to producing more of the other, and both will be equally profitable to produce. In short, subject to various assumptions with which we are not concerned here, equilibrium can only be attained when the economy is at the point where the transformation curve is tangential to – i.e. has the same slope as – the highest indifference curve, at which point relative prices and relative costs are the same, being both equal to the slopes of the two curves (which are the same) at this point.[1]

We are now able to see the connection between propositions about economic welfare (or real income) and propositions about output. The former are about whether one collection of goods is on a higher indifference curve than another. The latter are about whether it is on a higher transformation curve. As can be seen in Figure 10.5, in the absence of any assumption about the working of the price mechanism preventing such perverse behaviour, it would be possible to find points that represent higher output but lower real income. For example, point III is on the transformation curve, T_2, that constitutes greater output than the curve T_1, but it is a non-optimum point and is on an indifference curve, IC_3, that is lower than the one attained at the

---

[1] It is usually maintained that relative costs have to be measured in terms of factor cost prices, whereas relative prices, for purposes of welfare comparisons, have to be measured in market prices – i.e. including indirect taxes – since these are the relevant prices from the point of view of the consumer. But, for various reasons, this distinction is not as clear cut as might appear at first sight.

point I. This means that if we were to compare points I with III solely on the output test we would find that point III is higher, but we would be mistaken if we deduced from this that point III also meant a higher amount of economic welfare than point I.

But the danger of drawing such false conclusions need not worry us very much. For the price mechanism will – subject to certain assumptions – ensure that no such points can be equilibrium points. Hence, points such as point III are simply not observable points. The community would not stop at that pattern of output. Given this assumption, if we observe that, on the output test, one point is higher than another, we can also conclude that it also represents greater economic welfare – i.e. it represents greater real income.

(v) *Changes in tastes*

There is, however, one important qualification to this conclusion, namely that it rests on the assumption that the indifference curves do not change when moving from one situation to another. For example, in Figure 10.6 opposite, suppose that point I is the output of year 1 and that point II is the output of year 2. Now it can be seen that in year 1 the community was better off at the output pattern I than it would have been at output pattern II, since, given year 1's preference patterns, point I is on a higher indifference curve than point II. But in year 2, when output has moved to point II, this is now a preferred position to point I since, *in terms of the new indifference curve pattern*, point II lies on a higher indifference curve than point I. In other words, if we forget the transformation curves in the diagram and concentrate on the two indifference curves it is clear that, since they cut one another, it is meaningless to maintain that one of them is 'higher' than the other. At some parts of the curves IC_2 will be higher than IC_1 and at other parts the reverse will hold true. Such a crossing of indifference curves can occur only if, in fact, the curves have shifted so that the indifference map of one period no longer applies in the other period. In short, tastes have changed.[1]

Thus if tastes have changed from one period to the other, it is meaningless to talk about real income being higher in one situa-

[1] In terms of inter-country comparisons, as distinct from inter-temporal comparisons, this corresponds to saying that tastes differ between the countries being compared.

Figure 10.6

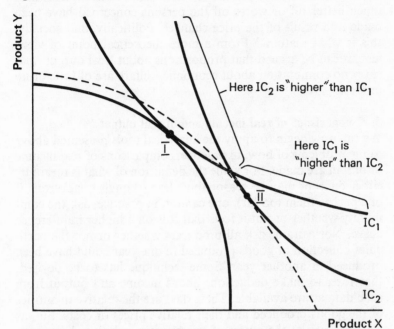

tion than another, even in the narrow sense of real income being used here in which any comparison of well-being is excluded. And we have seen that if tastes have not changed – i.e. if the pattern of indifference curves has not changed – then the price mechanism will ensure that an increase in real output implies an increase in real income, in the sense of having moved to a higher indifference curve.

Now tastes have either changed or they haven't. If they have changed then it is not, strictly speaking, possible to say whether there has been any increase in real income and economic welfare. And if they have not changed, then an increase in real output implies an increase in economic welfare. This suggests that one can forget welfare for some purposes and concentrate on output since either no firm proposition can be made about welfare or such conclusions as can be made can be made simply on the basis of output comparisons. But for certain practical purposes, the welfare considerations may be all-important. For example, adjustments in social security benefits or in wages to take

233

account of changes in prices need to be made in the light of how much better off or worse off the persons concerned have been made as a result of the price changes. Politically, and socially, this is what matters.[1] From a more theoretical point of view, also, it can be argued that propositions about 'real output' that carry no connotation about economic welfare are of little or no interest.

3. Comparisons of real income and of real output

We can now begin to apply the analytical tools presented above to the problems of how, in practice, comparisons of real income or output are made. For while the definition of what is meant by either concept may be reasonably clear (though treacherous if one pushes them too far), one cannot, in practice, ask the community whether or not it feels that it is on a higher indifference curve. Nor can one ask all producers whether or not the particular collection of goods produced in one year could have been produced in another year. Some technique has to be devised, therefore, to make deductions about income and output from such data as are available. These data are the relative quantities of the goods produced and their relative prices or costs. But, as we have seen at the outset of this chapter, prices and costs are not necessarily the same in different situations. Hence rules are needed for dealing with the differences in relative prices between situations.

(i) Real income comparisons

We have seen that, in comparing two collections of goods, if we merely wish to know which collection represents a higher real

---

[1] It should be noted, moreover, that even if it is assumed that tastes have changed, it may be useful to find out by how much a consumer feels better off this year, on this year's tastes, with this year's collection of goods, by comparisons with how well off he would have felt this year with last year's collection of goods. Whether or not he is better off than last year in any more fundamental sense will, of course, still remain indeterminate. But, as we have seen, this is so even if tastes have remained unchanged in terms of the shape of the indifference curves on account of possible changes in the capacity of goods to provide satisfaction. It is not the change in tastes which rules out comparisons of happiness. Changes in tastes rule out comparisons of real income between two situations. But they do not prevent consumers, say, in one situation, and given the tastes of that situation, saying how much income they would need to compensate them for the changes in prices that have taken place relative to some other real or hypothetical situation.

income then the problem is to know which one is on the higher indifference curve. If, in addition, we wish to know *by how much* real income in one situation is higher than real income in the other then the problem is to know by how much income would have to be raised to enable the community (or the individual) to have moved from the lower indifference curve to the higher one. In this chapter we shall make a start on the first question.

In Figure 10.7, overleaf, it would be obvious that the collection of goods at point I must lie on a lower indifference curve than the collection at point II, even if we had no information whatsoever about the indifference curves or the relative prices prevailing in the two situations. For point II has all the goods that are available at point I plus some more. Hence, as long as we are talking about 'goods' and not 'bads', collection II must represent greater real income than collection I, since it must be on a higher indifference curve. If, for the sake of brevity, we use the terms 'better' or 'worse' to represent 'greater real income' or 'less real income' respectively, we can say that the only completely unambiguous case of one situation being better than another, in the absence of any information about the indifference curves, is when it contains all that is available in the other plus some more (of one or other of the goods concerned). In other words, if we draw lines due North and East of point I, as in Figure 10.7, any point lying in the resulting North- East quadrant of point I must be 'better' than point I since it must contain all that is available in point I plus some more. Point III, however, does not lie in this quadrant and so one cannot say, without further information, whether or not it is on a higher indifference curve than point I.

To know whether III is better than I we need to know whether the indifference curve passing through III lies above (to the North-East of) point I or, alternatively, whether the indifference curve passing through I lies 'below' (to the South-West of) point III. This obviously depends on the shape of the two curves – i.e. on the amount of one product that has to be given up, over the relevant range, to compensate for more of the other product. Over a very small range this has been defined as the 'marginal rate of substitution'. Over a wide range, however, the concept of the marginal rate of substitution no longer applies, so that it is preferable to use the term 'conversion ratio'

Figure 10.7

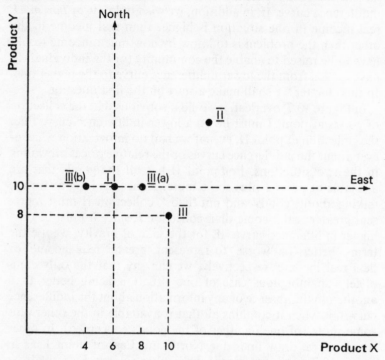

when describing the amount of one product that has to be given up to offset the addition of large amounts of the other product whilst remaining on the same indifference curve. This 'conversion ratio' will vary with the particular range over which we are measuring it.[1]

In other words, given two collections of goods, if one is North-East of the other then it is unambiguously better and it must be on a higher indifference curve. Hence, when faced with two collections of goods such as points I and III above, where III is South-East of I, the problem of deciding whether or not III is better than I can be looked at in either of two ways – they amount to the same thing in the end. One is that we are trying to find out whether III is on a higher indifference curve. The other is that we are trying to find out whether III can be

[1] The marginal rate of substitution will also vary as one moves round an indifference curve – apart from the extreme case of perfect substitutes.

converted into an equally satisfactory collection of goods (equal to the original III collection) that can be shown to be either North-East of I, and hence unambiguously better than I, or South-West of it, and hence unambiguously worse than I. To do this we clearly need to know the relevant 'conversion ratio', as given by the indifference curve passing through III, over the range from III to some point in either the North-East or the South-West quadrant of I.

(ii) Choice of conversion ratio for real income compensations
But there are at least two possible 'conversion ratios' that would have been relevant in order to compare any two points. For example, in Figure 10.8, in which we have reproduced points I and III from Figure 10.7, we have now inserted the two indifference curves that happened to pass through these two points,

Figure 10.8

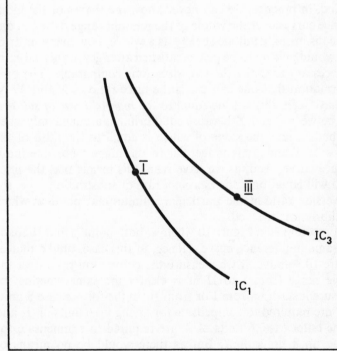

namely IC_1 and IC_3. It can be seen that, indeed, point III is 'better' than point I since the indifference curve passing through point III does, in fact, 'lie above' (i.e. passes North-East of) point I. But it can also be seen that the same conclusion could have been reached by asking ourselves whether the curve passing through I passed below III. This would have amounted to asking, not how to convert III into a collection comparable with I, but how to convert I into a collection that was un-ambiguously comparable with III. The conversion ratio is not the same when we are starting from I and trying to find out whether I definitely passes North-East or South-West of III as it is when we are starting from III and trying to find out whether the move through III passes North-East or South-West of I.

Now in this particular example, if we knew the shapes of the two indifference curves over the required range, the point III would represent a greater real income than I whichever curve we used. But this is not always the case.

And, in practice, we can never know the shapes of the indifference curves over the whole of the relevant range. Nor can one ask consumers, let alone society as a whole, how many units of X it would give up to be just as satisfied after getting all the extra Y necessary to make the two situations comparable. The only information that one can use is the price ratio of X and Y. As we have seen, this will be equal to the *marginal rate of substitution* between X and Y, because equilibrium is attained only when the budget line, the slope of which is equal to the ratio of the prices of X and Y, is tangential to the highest possible indifference curve. And, as we have seen, this means that the price ratio will equal only the *marginal* rate of substitution – i.e. the conversion ratio at the particular infinitesimal point at which equilibrium is reached.

For example, in Figure 10.9 below, both points I and II are on the same indifference curve. Hence, in this case, unlike that of Figure 10.8 above, if we measure the conversion ratio over the whole range from I to II, it is clearly the same whether we measure it starting from I or from II: in the former case 8 units of X are required to compensate for giving up 6 units of Y, and in the latter case, 6 units of Y are required to compensate for giving up 8 units of X. But as there would be no means of discovering this conversion ratio in practice, all that can be

Figure 10.9

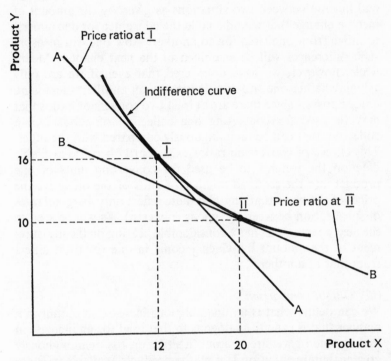

observed is the conversion ratio *at the points* I or II as indicated by the price ratios that happened to prevail at those points. For example, when the economy was at situation I, the price ratio must have been equal to the slope of the line *AA*. When it was at situation II, the price ratio must have been equal to the slope *BB*. In this case, therefore, if the implied conversion ratio of point I was used to compare point I with point II, we would find that point I was inferior to point II since the indifference curve through point I would appear – judging by the line *AA* – to pass below point II. But conversely, if we were to use the price ratio *BB* as an index of the conversion ratio over the whole range from II to any other point, then we would find that II was inferior to I, since, judging by the line *BB*, point II comes out 'below' (i.e. to the South-West of) point I.

To summarise, therefore, we have seen that the size of the distance between two indifference curves is not measurable in

239

principle, and all one can aim at is to measure the difference in real income between two situations as given by the amount of income change that would enable the consumer (or consumers) to move from one situation to another. How one can measure such differences will be examined in the next chapter. Meanwhile, however, we have discovered that even if we are only asking whether one situation is better than another, there is no unique answer since there are at least two conversion ratios that may be used for converting one collection of goods into a collection that can be unambiguously compared with the other. This choice of conversion ratios exists partly because available data on the weights to be used for converting units of one product into the required number of units of the other are the prices of the two situations, and these reflect only *marginal* rates of substitution between the goods converted. As will be seen in the next chapter, this has a considerable bearing on the measurement of the amount by which income in one situation differs from that of another.

(iii) Output comparison

We can define what is an unambiguous increase in output in a manner that is exactly analogous to that used for an increase in real income or welfare. Output in situation I is unambiguously greater than in situation II if all the products available in II are available in I plus more of one or the other products. There is no doubt whatsoever that 5 apples and 5 pears is greater output than 5 apples and 4 pears. More generally, if we start from any point on a transformation curve, such as point II in Figure 10.10 below, we can say that any point that lies in the quadrant to the North-East of point II must, unambiguously, represent greater output. For example, point III lies in this quadrant and clearly contains more of both products X and Y. Point IV also lies just in this quadrant; it does not contain any more of product Y but it does contain more of product X, since it lies further out on the X axis.

But these particular cases are too easy; in practice one may often be confronted with the need to compare point II with, say, point V, and point V lies outside the North-East quadrant subtended by point II. As with the welfare analysis, the whole problem, therefore, is to know whether one can convert point V

Figure 10.10

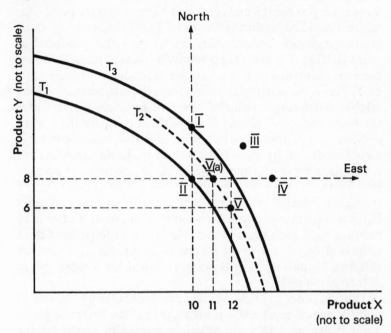

into an equivalent point *inside* this quadrant. Alternatively, what one wants to know is whether, if it had so wished, the community *could* have produced some combination of goods inside this quadrant instead of producing the combination at point V. This obviously depends on how much of good X would have to be given up in order to produce more of good Y.

As can be seen in Figure 10.10 this depends on whether the transformation curve passing through point V goes through points such as V(a) or I, both of which are in the North-East quadrant relative to point II, or whether, instead, it would pass to the South-West of point II. If the transformation curve that passes through point V is the curve T_2, indicating that with the same resources as employed at point V the economy *could* have produced the combination of goods shown at point V(a), then it is clear that point V represents a greater output than point II, since point V(a) is in the North-East quadrant subtended by point II – it represents as much of product Y as does point II and more of product X. In numerical terms, it can be seen from the

241

diagram that the economy could, if it wished, move from point V, where it produced 6 units of Y and 12 units of X, to point V(a) where it could be producing 8 units of Y and 11 units of X, which is unambiguously greater than the $8Y$ and $10X$ produced at point II. That is to say, the economy, if it was at point V, would have to give up one unit of X in order to produce two more units of Y. This is the conversion ratio – from the relative cost, not the relative satisfactions, point of view – of products X and Y *over the range indicated*. Hence, if we wish to compare the output combination of point II, which is $8Y$ plus $10X$, with the point V combination, of $6Y$ plus $12X$, we can make an unambiguous comparison by converting some of the X produced at point V into 2 units of Y, thereby having as many Y as at point II, and seeing if this leaves us with more or less units of X than at point II. In this particular example, when it costs only 1 unit of X to produce the 2 extra units of Y needed in order to go from the 6 units of Y of point V to the 8 units of Y of point II, we are left still with 11 units of Y, as at point V(a), which is 1 more unit of Y than at point II.

Thus, in order to know whether any particular point, such as point V, would represent a greater output than the given point, point II, we need to know whether, instead of producing the output combination point V, the economy could have produced a combination in the North-East quadrant of point II, where output is unambiguously greater than point II output. To do this we need to know whether the transformation curve passing through point V lies above point II or not. This, we have seen, is solely a matter of the conversion ratio of X into Y – i.e. how much of one product one must give up in order to produce an extra unit of the other product. In other words it is solely a matter of the relative costs of producing X and Y. In brief, this year's automobile is 'more than' last year's automobile if, and only if, one would have to give up more than one of last year's automobile in order to produce, instead, one of this year's automobile.

(iv) Choice of conversion ratio for output comparisons

There is, however, the same difficulty in output comparison as in real income comparison, namely that there is more than one conversion ratio that might be used. This is particularly important when we want to know *by how much* output in one period differs from that of another period. And, as with the real income comparisons, the reason why there is a choice between alternative conversion ratios for making one situation un-ambiguously comparable with the other is not that one could use the transformation curve of either situation for measuring the conversion ratio. The real reason is that one does not actually possess information about the shape of the transformation curves over the whole of the relevant range. All that one can use is the information about the relative costs (i.e. factor cost prices) that prevailed at each situation. And, as with price information as indicators of the conversion ratio of indifference curves over a wide range, relative costs only indicate the *marginal opportunity cost* of products – i.e. their conversion ratio *at the margin*. And this is generally supposed to change as one moves round a transformation curve. Relative costs at any point will measure only the conversion ratio at the infinitesi-mally small point on the transformation curve at which the economy happens to be producing in that situation.

Hence, even if we were comparing two situations that happen to be on the same transformation curve, the relative costs of giving up one product in order to produce more of the other will be different in the two situations.

Thus we arrive at conclusions that are exactly analogous to those we reached in the case of real income (or economic welfare) comparisons, namely that, in comparing any two situations, at least two alternative conversion ratios may be used, since

(i) on any one transformation curve the cost ratio will differ from one point to another, and

(ii) comparisons may be between points on two different trans-formation curves, so that even over the whole range con-cerned the conversion ratio given by one curve will not necessarily be the same as that given by the other curve.

4. Quality change

We can now proceed to examine how the analytical apparatus that we have developed can be applied to specific problems, particularly those concerning changes in the quality of goods – a problem which is still wide open and about which it would be wrong to lay down any hard and fast agreed view. To illustrate what the problem is all about let us take one frequently quoted example of the quality problem, namely the shift in purchase patterns from metal to plastic buckets. It is often argued, for example, that the usual indices of price (and hence the related indices of volume of production) of buckets fail to allow for the fact that consumers prefer the plastic buckets to the metal ones; they may be lighter or more attractive to look at. Suppose that, in Figure 10.11 below, plastic buckets were measured along the vertical axis and metal buckets were measured along the horizontal axis. And suppose that in the first time period, say a year, consumers bought the combination at point V, namely 12 metal buckets and 6 plastic buckets. Now assume that in the second year they have moved to point II, where they buy only 10 metal buckets and 8 plastic buckets. We can see that this represents a move from T_2 to T_1 – i.e. from a higher to a lower transformation curve. Point II lies inside the transformation curve T_2 from

Figure 10.11

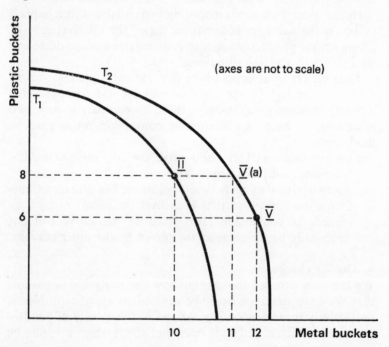

which the consumers started. This is clearly a fall in output. To acquire the extra two plastic buckets they need have given up only one metal bucket – i.e. by moving from V to V(a) – and instead they have given up two metal buckets; thereby reducing total output. There is little point in saying that people *like* plastic buckets more than metal buckets, since this cannot detract from the conclusion that there has been a movement from the initial position to a point inside the transformation curve, so that real output has fallen in the sense in which a transformation curve defines output. If the transformation curves for the economy had not changed at all, then in terms of its contribution to the measurement of real output a metal bucket is still twice the 'output' of a plastic bucket, since one of the former can be converted into two of the latter.

But in equilibrium, the relative costs of production are equal to the relative preferences, since we have seen that the equilibrium condition is that the marginal rate of transformation is equal to the marginal rate of substitution. A position in which consumers would need two metal buckets to compensate them for giving up one plastic bucket, but in which it still takes two plastic buckets to make one metal bucket is not a possible equilibrium position in the longer run. Such a position might prevail in the short-run, when it would indicate that either consumers or producers were not in equilibrium.

For example, a sudden shift of tastes in favour of plastic buckets would mean that consumers would reach equilibrium only if the relative prices of plastic buckets rose. But if, even after the relative output of plastic buckets had increased, it still required only half the resources used to make a metal bucket in order to produce a plastic bucket, producers of plastic buckets would start making very high profits on the plastic buckets. *The rise in the price of the plastic buckets would be pure price rise, not a genuine economic improvement in the 'quality' of buckets* so far as the measurement of *output* is concerned, even though consumers would be quite happy to pay the extra price. In the short-run, therefore, if the relative preferences of consumers were used as a guide to the change in the quality of buckets there would be some over-estimate of the rise in 'real output'; production may have moved to a point such as point II, which is inside the old transformation curve. In this case, consumers may well derive more satisfaction from the new pattern of output on account of the shift in their tastes, but they are obtaining more satisfaction from a lower volume of 'real output'. If the transformation curve has not changed there is no doubt that output has fallen.

It may also be true that, *on the new set of tastes*, the new collection of goods is preferred to the old collection, so that *on the new set of tastes* 'real income' is higher. There must be some amount of income that consumers would need to compensate them for going back to the old mixture of plastic and metal buckets and this can be taken as a measure of the rise in their real income. This may be significant for many practical purposes, but it is still not the same as an output comparison. Nor is it even a comparison of 'real income' between the two situations in the same sense as is possible when tastes have not changed. If changes in the total amount of satisfactions derived from any collection of goods are indiscriminately taken to indicate a change in 'real output' it would be impossible to distinguish between a change in output in the sense of an expansion of the transformation curve, and a change in tastes (or even a change in the satisfaction derived from a given collection of goods but without a change in tastes).

A nice example of the consequences of failing to distinguish between a rise in *satisfactions* and an economic increase in *quality*, which corresponds to an increase in output, has been suggested by Milton Gilbert.[1] This is as follows: suppose that the satisfaction obtained from swimming costumes has remained the same over the years in spite of – or because of – the fact that they have become progressively smaller and smaller. Now, if one takes this trend towards ever smaller bikinis to the limit, and if one used the satisfactions from them as the measure of the amount of 'output' that they are supposed to represent, then one would arrive at a situation in which the output of swimming costumes, in terms of satisfactions, would be the same (or possibly greater) whilst there would not be a single swimming costume producer left in the business! Like the plastic bucket example, this is an example where the change is in the nature of the product's ability to provide satisfactions; and clearly this

[1] Milton Gilbert, 'Quality Changes and Index Numbers' in *Economic Development and Cultural Change*, Vol. IX, No. 3, April 1961; and 'Quality Changes and Index Numbers – A Reply', *Monthly Labour Review*, May 1962.

cannot be taken as a justification for regarding the output of the product concerned as being as large as before. What has happened is that people now derive the same (or more) satisfaction from a smaller amount of bathing costume: there has been no *economic* increase in their 'quality'.

In Figure 10.12 below, the transformation rate of nineteenth-century swimming costumes into modern bikinis is put at a constant rate of one of the former for two of the latter. To simplify the argument we can begin by assuming that this rate does not change, even over time. In 1860 consumers' tastes are such that they purchased collection I, which contains much less bikinis, even though bikinis are cheaper. In 1960 their tastes have changed – as illustrated by indifference curve 1960 – and so, even if they bought the same total of all swimming costumes as before, the proportion of bikinis in the total has risen. It can be seen that, whatever has happened to relative prices, there is no doubt that, *at 1960 tastes, their real income is*

Figure 10.12

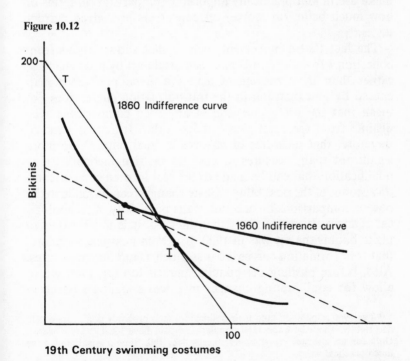

19th Century swimming costumes

higher than if they had been obliged to continue buying the 1860 collection of goods. For the indifference curve that they are on in 1960 clearly passes above the old collection of goods at point I. Nevertheless, collection II, which they buy in 1960, is equally clearly less *real output* than collection I since it lies well inside the transformation curve *T*.

But, as always when there has been a change in tastes, although it is legitimate to say that, *on 1960 tastes*, consumers are enjoying higher real income, it is not legitimate to say that their real income in 1960 is higher than it was in 1860 in a more fundamental sense, namely one that implied that if they had been given the choice, *in 1860 also*, between the two collections of goods they would still have selected the 1960 collection. It is obvious from the diagram that in 1860, given the tastes they had then, they would have preferred the 1860 collection. Thus, when tastes have changed real income comparisons are not strictly possible in the strong sense, though it may still be possible to make useful and practically important comparisons in terms of how much better (or worse) off consumers are, given current tastes.[1]

The fact that a movement such as that shown above from collection I to collection II has been produced by taste changes, rather than by a movement across a given preference map caused by an expansion in the transformation curve, does not mean that the preference side of any such comparisons – as distinct from the costs side – is less valid. It does not mean, therefore, that measures of changes in 'real output' are more significant than measures of changes in 'real income'. Every qualification that can be made to the real income comparisons, on account of the possibility of taste changes, can be made to the output comparisons on account of the possibility of technological changes. It may well be that, in 1960, it is much easier to make bikinis than it was in 1900. It is even possible, therefore, that transformation curves cross as much as indifference curves. Also, before pushing the bikini argument too far, the need to allow for equilibrating changes in prices should be borne in

[1] The 1960 population (and their political leaders) probably don't care much, and rightly, about how the 1860 population would have liked today's bikinis. Only for an ancestor worshipping society does this 'time-reversal' test have much practical value.

mind. For example, in Figure 10.12 above, if consumers are in equilibrium at point II in 1960, relative prices must have adjusted themselves so that they correspond to the dotted line tangential to II. Hence, either relative costs have, in fact, changed correspondingly or producers are not in equilibrium and bikini manufacturers are making exceptional profits. In the former case, the costs approach shows that 'real output' has fallen after all; the new transformation curve is the dotted line and from this it follows that output at point II is, in fact, greater than at point I. Since relative costs equal relative prices at point II, it will also be found that real income at point II exceeds that at point I, when measured in terms of the prices prevailing at point II, by the same amount as does real output.

Nor can the superiority of the cost approach be defended on the grounds that changes in tastes are more likely than changes in technology. In fact, the reverse may be true. Some estimates suggest that international differences in tastes are slight and that most international differences in relative consumption patterns reflect differences in incomes and relative prices.[1] At the same time, it would not be denied that the differences in technologies between the countries covered were substantial – since they ranged from the USA to Italy, and related to 1950 when the gap between the USA and the other countries covered in the comparisons was probably even greater than it is now. This suggests that tastes are fairly stable, whereas there is no doubt that technologies are changing constantly.

It may not always be possible to draw a transformation curve in terms of both qualities of the product concerned. For example, with changes in automobile design, when a new model car is introduced, production of the old model may cease immediately. And even in the case of the buckets, although both the plastic and the metal buckets may be on sale when plastic buckets are introduced it is not possible to incorporate them in a transformation curve for the period when only metal buckets were produced. This means that one can only apply the transformation curve test to the transformation curve of the current period in which both types of bucket are available. This is, of course, a limitation on the strength of the conclusions that can

[1] Milton Gilbert and Associates, *Comparative National Products and Price Levels* (O E E C, Paris, 1958), Chapter 6.

249

be drawn from the comparison, in the same way as a change in tastes limits 'real income' comparisons. In other words, one can only say whether, given present techniques and knowledge, it is possible to produce one plastic bucket by giving up the production of one metal bucket. If it requires two metal buckets to produce one plastic bucket, then one plastic bucket is equivalent, in terms of output, to two metal ones and so, in economic terms, represents higher quality. But one cannot carry out this test in terms of the base year production possibilities.

It will be noticed that we have excluded from an increase in output a 'costless' improvement in the goods concerned, such as a reduction in the size of bikinis. If, however, consumers got more satisfaction out of bikinis because they were made of costlier materials or were handpainted by Picasso, then this may be a perfectly genuine increase in 'output' as well as 'real income' since it represents an increase in the amount of resources absorbed in producing the bikinis and therefore the sacrifice of a greater amount of alternative output if the resources now used to produce the bikinis had been left to produce other things instead. Thus the acid test of whether today's bikini represents as much 'real output' as the swimming costume of fifty years ago is whether or not giving up the production of one modern bikini would enable us to produce one of the fifty-year-old type of swimming costume. The output test is *not* whether or not people are just as happy with present day bikinis as with the older variety. If a wave of puritanism were to sweep over the world they would be less happy with bikinis.

The distinction between costless improvements in quality and those that involve extra resources and that, therefore, represent an economic increase in quality which is equivalent to an increase in output, may be better appreciated in the case of automobiles. For example, suppose that in terms of performance (say acceleration, road holding, braking, etc.) today's automobile is much better than one produced twenty years ago. Is it more or less automobile? There are two extreme possibilities. First, the improvement is entirely due to the use of, say, more steel, rubber and other inputs. Secondly, without any increase in the inputs, the improvement is due to a gradual improvement in the art of design. The second case would be a 'costless' improvement in quality, whereas the former is not. In the case of the costless improvement in automobiles, if one asks the question 'How many old-fashioned automobiles could one produce in the place of one of today's automobiles?', the answer is 'one', so that if the same number of automobiles is being produced, output has not changed. But in the case where the improvement in the performance of the automobiles has been due to an increase in the inputs used to make them, then the answer to the above question may be that instead of producing one of today's automobiles one could produce two of the old-fashioned ones. In this case, if the same actual number of automobiles were being produced, we would have to say that the output of automobiles had doubled.

This doctrine sometimes puzzles people on the grounds that if we are only to count an increase in output as taking place when it is not costless, then how can one ever have an increase in productivity, which surely means that output can be increased at no cost? But there is no real difficulty in reconciling increases in productivity with the view that output only increases when, *if produced today*, more resources would be required to produce today's good than yesterday's good. Consider, for example, the case where labour productivity suddenly doubles in the production of automobiles in 1961. If, in 1961, 1960 automobiles could also be produced with half as much labour as before, which is likely, there has been no change in the relative costs of one 1960 automobile, from the point of view of the amount of 1961 automobiles that they represent. Suppose that the amount of labour being employed does not change, so that, thanks to the doubling of productivity, twice the amount of automobiles are produced in 1961. Now, it might be asked, since this is achieved thanks to the productivity increase it is 'costless', so should it not be counted as an increase in output? But this is a mistaken view of what costs have to be compared with what. In this particular example, it still costs just as much *after* the productivity increase to produce one 1961 automobile as to produce one 1960 automobile – the conversion factor between them has not changed at all. Hence, if we now produce twice as many automobiles in 1961, as in 1960, they have to be counted as twice the amount of output. For this year's total output still costs twice as much to produce this year as if only last year's total output were to be produced. The point is that *both* last

251

year's and this year's cars can be produced at lower cost, so that the *opportunity* cost of one of this year's automobiles in terms of one of last year's is left unchanged.

Another way of looking at it is as follows. The problem, in comparing one year's output of automobiles with another, is to reduce the automobiles produced in both years to the same units of output. There is no difficulty in comparing, say, this year's bananas with those of ten years ago, since they are equivalent. But this year's automobiles may not be the same as last year's, and in order to say whether more or less cars are being produced, it is essential to reduce the two vintages to a common unit of output. That is, we want to find the *conversion factor* that enables us to say, for example, that one of this year's automobiles is equal to, say, two of last year's automobiles. *Only* if we have such a conversion factor is it possible to compare this year's output with last year's. Now, even without recourse to technical concepts such as the 'transformation' surface it is intuitively obvious that, from the point of view of their contribution to output, one of this year's automobiles is only equal to two of last year's if, instead of producing one of this year's one could, in its place (i.e. with the same resources) produce two of last year's.

If, on account of improvements in productivity or in the arts and sciences of design, it is now possible to produce both with half the resources previously used this does not change the *conversion factor*; one of this year's automobiles will still be equal to two of last year's, though productivity will have risen according to the extent to which both may be produced with less resources than hitherto. And the criterion of the conversion factor, that is, the amount of the old product that could be produced with the same resources needed to produce one of the new product, is clearly nothing to do with the question of whether one likes the old product more or less than the new one. This, as we have seen, may be a question of changes in satisfactions or tastes or 'needs'. The conversion factor is simply the cost, in terms of the commodity given up, of producing more of the other commodity. The relative costs have nothing to do with relative satisfactions derived from them.

The practical applications of all this apparently rather academic discussion are considerable. For example, it was often argued that our concern with so-called 'inflation' was excessive since prices really rise much less than is commonly supposed. The reason for this, it was argued, was that the price indices exaggerate the true rise in price, and underestimate the true increase in real income, on account of a failure adequately to allow for the improvements in *quality* – such as that plastic buckets are better than the old ones. The strength of this argument, as well as its limitations, should now be apparent.

Many other examples are constantly being raised which may be less convincing. One such popular example concerns the improvements in medical science. It is argued that although one may now spend much less time in hospital being treated for some ailment or operation than twenty years ago, this improvement in the quality of medical service is not taken into account in computing the price of such services. But if, as a result of, say, improvements in medical science, we want much less medical service to get the same health then it may be that there has been a shift in our tastes in the sense that, in order to be as 'happy' as before, we now require less medical service defined in terms of units of output.

So it is not simply a question of how much more satisfaction one obtains from a day's stay in hospital. The whole question of the equilibrating price and cost changes in response to the shift in tastes also has to be taken into account. Another aspect of the problem is the extent to which the increased efficiency of the medical services was obtained as a result of costs that were incurred in the past – e.g. research costs into new drugs – and whether some allowance should be made for these past costs, even though they do not enter into the relative opportunity costs facing the economy today. Against this, it might be argued that, if there is no limit to how far back in time one can go in computing costs, then, if one were to go back to Adam and Eve, the costs of the apples introduced at the start of this chapter have been incalculable; we are still paying for them.

Thus, one way or another, the quality problem is still a complex issue and there is no universally agreed doctrine. From a practical point of view, the allowance for quality changes applied in national accounting depends largely on the extent to which the statistician can enter into detail, and not count all automobiles as simply automobiles. But one need not stop there. Much work is being done to take account of the fact that an automobile is really not a single 'product' at all but a collection of sub-products, such as an engine, so much tyres and glass, and so on. How far the statistician distinguishes between different grades and qualities of the more conventional concept of a 'product' by re-defining them in terms of their components in this manner, is one of the determining factors, in practice, of the adequacy of allowance for changes in 'quality'.

Chapter 11

The measure of changes in national product

1. Real income and the budget line

In the last chapter we have seen that it is convenient to identify an increase in 'real income', as distinct from money income, with a rise in economic welfare, and that the latter, in turn, can be interpreted as a shift from one indifference curve to a higher one. We could also modify this proposition so as to eliminate the element of time that enters into it, and say that, as between two alternative collections of goods, the one that represents the higher 'real income' is the one that is on the higher indifference curve.

However, we are usually not interested merely in whether or not real income in one situation is higher than in another. We usually also want to know *by how much it is higher*. For example, we may want to know whether national product is 2% or 4% higher than last year, or how far national product per head in the USSR falls below that in the USA. But we have seen that this sort of question raises certain difficulties. First, no meaning can be attached to the degree to which one indifference curve is higher than another. This is basically because indifference maps describe only an ordinal system, not a cardinal system. But although one cannot measure the amount of satisfactions that people derive from any particular collection of goods and so one cannot say how much more satisfactions they derive from one collection rather than another, one can measure the income spent on each collection. Hence, our measure of how far real income in situation I exceeds that of situation II is approximately a measure of how much more income they must have had in order to buy the collection of goods bought in I by comparison with the income they must have had to buy the collection of goods in situation II.

(*i*) *Real income differences as measured by differences in the 'budget line'*

In the last chapter it was seen that this can be roughly interpreted in terms of the distance between the 'budget lines' of the two situations. But it was also seen that the slope of the budget line depends on the relative prices prevailing in the two situations. We must now examine in slightly more detail how this affects the measurement of real income differences.

Figure 11.1 represents a situation in which apples cost £1⅓ per ton and pears cost £2 per ton, and a total income of £20 is spent on 6 tons of apples (making £8) plus 6 tons of pears (making £12). This collection of goods is marked as collection I. Suppose now that, in another situation, collection II, representing 8 tons of apples and 3 tons of pears, is bought, and that prices are exactly the same as in I. A simple calculation shows that this must represent less income (ignoring savings), since the 8 tons of apples will cost £12 and the 3 tons of pears will cost £6 giving a total of only £18. Thus income has fallen by 10%, from £20 to £18. The ratio of the second to the first year's income is 18:20, or 0·90. This same result is usually expressed in the form of an 'index number' – that is, a value for one year relative to some other year which is taken as equal to 100. In this case, if situation II's real income is 0·90 of I's real income, it will be shown as 90% of I. If II had represented 20% more real income than I, then with I = 100, the index of real income in II would have been 120. For the sake of brevity in subsequent formulae, however, we shall usually omit to multiply the ratio of one year's income to another by 100, since this is just a change of scale. The ratio 0·90:1·00 is the same as 90:100.

In the particular example given, the fall of 10% in real income corresponds to the amount by which a line drawn through II, parallel to I, has fallen below I. Such a line would represent the budget line in situation II if prices had remained the same as in I – which is why it is parallel to the budget line passing through I. If income had been only £18, instead of £20, and the prices had remained unchanged, the consumer could clearly not have bought *OB* pears even if he had wanted to, since 10 tons of pears at £2 per ton would have cost more than the £18 he could dispose of. The maximum number of pears he can buy is indicated at the point *C*, namely 9 tons of pears. Similarly, the

Figure 11.1

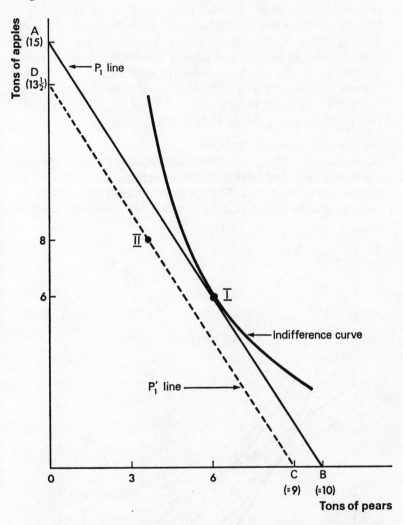

maximum number of apples he can buy with an income of only £18, and with apples at £1⅓ per ton is 13½ tons, as indicated at the point *D*. The line *CD* is his new budget line and represents, by comparison with the original line, how much his real income had fallen. The 10% fall in real income, for example, could be measured either in terms of the fall in the amount of pears he can buy – i.e. the ratio of *OC* to *OB* (which is 9:10, or 0.9) or in terms of the fall in the amount of apples he can buy (which is 13.5:15, or 0.9). Or it can be measured in the terms in which we first measured it, namely by seeing how much the actual II collection would have cost compared with the I collection, when we arrived at the result that the respective costs of the two collections was £18 and £20. Whichever way it is done the result is the same, namely, that II is 0·9 of I, or, taking I as 100, II is equal to 90 – a fall of 10% in real income.

(*ii*) The '*index number problem*'

But in this simple example, the comparisons of the income levels could give only one answer because there was only one set of relative prices to be used. The price ratio in collection II was the same as in I. In Figure 11.2, by contrast, we show a situation in

Figure 11.2

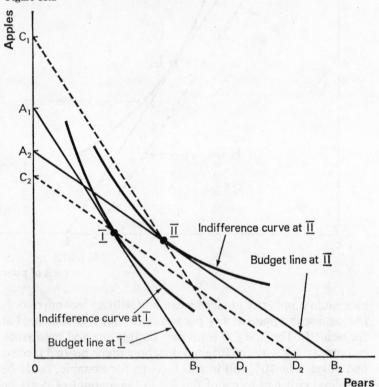

which the relative price of apples has risen considerably from situation I to situation II. In II, the budget line, as given by the line A_2B_2 has a very different slope from the budget line A_1B_1 which is tangential to collection I. The I collection can be valued *at the prices of II*, by passing a line, through the I collection, that is parallel to A_2B_2, since this represents the relative prices at point II. The I collection will then appear as having been bought with the income indicated by the line C_2D_2. This implies that the income spent on the II collection, which is represented by the line A_2B_2 is slightly higher than the income spent on I. The gap between the two incomes is measured by the gap between C_2D_2 and A_2B_2.

However, it would be equally possible to compare the two collections of goods by valuing them both in the prices of the I collection. The actual income of I, at the prices prevailing at I is, of course, given by the budget line passing through I and having the slope, A_1B_1, corresponding to the actual price ratio prevailing at point I. If collection II is valued at the same prices, this would be represented by a line, parallel to A_1B_1, passing through collection II, namely the line C_1D_1. This line is clearly well above A_1B_1, indicating that, at the I prices, collection II represents far more real income than the I collection, whereas at II prices, collection II appears to be only a little more real income than collection I.

The problem of which measure to use – if either – and of how to select a 'true' measure is the essence of the 'index number' problem. The difference between the two measures of the difference in real incomes results from the 'index-number spread'. Thus the problem encountered in the last chapter of alternative conversion ratios for finding out how much better one situation was than another can be looked at as the problem of which set of prices to use to measure how far a 'budget line' has shifted. As we have seen, since the distance between indifference curves is, in principle, immeasurable, it is the amount of shift in the budget line that we are taking as our measure of the change in real income. And, given any two points, different slopes of the pair of parallel lines drawn through them must yield different measures of the distance between the pair of parallel lines. This is a purely abstract proposition that has nothing to do with whether we are measuring any economic phenomenon at all. In

Figure 11.3

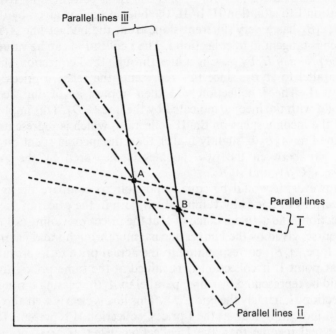

Figure 11.3, irrespective of the meaning of the axes, it is obvious that, as we change the slope of any pair of parallel lines through the two points *A* and *B*, so the gap between the pair will change its size and even its algebraic sign (with set I, for example, unlike sets II and III, the line through *A* is higher than the line through *B*).

2. Choice of prices and the bias in real income comparisons

(i) *The direction of the bias*

In Figure 11.4(b) below, two collections of goods are compared in terms of the prices of collection II. This is done, in the usual manner, by passing a line through both collections parallel to the slope of the actual budget line that prevailed in situation II. The measured difference in real income is then, as usual, the gap between the two budget lines derived in this manner. As can be seen, if the indifference curves had the shape indicated, then over the range of the curves indicated, the gap between the

Figure 11.4(a)   Figure 11.4(b)

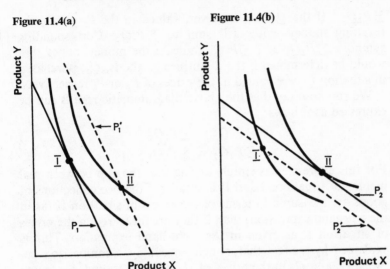

curves appears to be larger than the gap between the two budget lines (namely P_2 and P_2'). Hence, though this is not a rigorous argument (on account of the above-mentioned limitations on the meaning that can be attached to the concept of the 'gap' between two indifference curves), it is a useful intuitive way of seeing that, measured in II's prices, the excess of II's real income over I's real income will be measured as less than the 'true' gap between the two indifference curves on which the two collections happen to lie. In Figure 11.4(a), by contrast, it can be seen that if the two collections of goods are compared in terms of situation I's prices – i.e. if a line parallel to the I budget line is drawn through II – then the gap between the two budget lines (P_1 and P_1') appears to be much greater and to exceed, in fact, the 'true' gap between the indifference curves on which the two situations lie.

For convenience, the above results can be translated into the simple symbolic short-hand used for the analysis of index-numbers. Q_1 and Q_2 will be taken to refer to the collections of goods purchased in situation I or II respectively, and P_1 and P_2 indicate the set of prices in the two respective situations. Thus, if the various goods bought in II are valued in the prices of II, the resulting money value of the goods purchased will add to

261

$\sum P_2 Q_2.$[1] If the Q_2 are, however, valued in the P_1 prices, the resulting money value will sum to $\sum P_1 Q_2$. Corresponding symbols, $\sum P_2 Q_1$ and $\sum P_1 Q_1$ indicate the money values that would be determined if the quantities of goods, Q_1, purchased in situation I, were valued in the prices of P_2 or P_1 respectively.

We can now say that the above diagrammatic results can be expressed as follows:

$$\frac{\sum P_2 Q_2}{\sum P_2 Q_1} < \frac{\sum P_1 Q_2}{\sum P_1 Q_1} \tag{1}$$

For this expression is simply saying that the gap between real income of situations I and II is smaller if the two collections of goods are measured in terms of the prices of situation II (as in the left-hand expression) than if they are measured in the prices of situation I, as given in the right-hand expression. This is explained by the fact that, roughly speaking, a comparison between Q_1 and Q_2 in the prices of II, will tend to under-estimate the 'true' gap between the indifference curves on which they lie (as in Figure 11.4(b)), whereas a comparison at the prices of I will over-estimate the 'true' gap. Thus, in II's prices, Q_2 does not exceed Q_1 by as much as it does at I's prices. This is all that the expression above indicates. It is a conversion of the real income comparison into the form of an index-number formula, in which the 'weights' in the index number that are used to combine the quantities together are the prices of one situation or another.[2]

Before discussing an exception to the general rule about which way the choice of price weights will bias the index-number comparison, the rule can be put in words as follows. In comparing two collections of goods, the aggregate quantity represented by one collection will appear to be relatively greater if the comparison is in the price of the other collection than if the comparison is in its own prices. Whether or not it will appear to be *absolutely* greater than the other situation is irrelevant; it is

[1] The $\sum$ sign indicates that we have summed the values of expenditure on all the goods. Thus if, for example, the collection of goods, Q_1, comprises two goods, Q_i and Q_j, so that there are two prices, P_i and P_j, the value of expenditure on them will sum to $Q_i P_i + Q_j P_j$. If the quantities and prices in situation I were, say, 5 tons and 10 tons and £2 per ton and £1 per ton, the value of $\sum Q_1 P_1$, would amount to £$(5 \times 2) + $£$(10 \times 1) = $£20.

[2] The two algebraic expressions shown only differ from index-number formula in that we have omitted to multiply them by 100 in order to change them from their original simple ratio to a percentage form.

merely that the comparison is *relatively* more favourable to a situation on the other situation's prices than on its own prices. For example, in Figure 11.2 above, although collection I was found to be absolutely smaller than II on either set of prices, it is not so much smaller than II on II's prices as it is on its own prices.

The common sense of this result is as follows. We have seen that the problem is to compare, in quantitative terms, two collections of goods, say apples and pears, which have to be combined together by their prices, since it is these which, in the context of a real income comparison (not an output comparison), indicate the relative contribution of the goods to economic welfare. But, if the prices change from one year to another, the consumer will adapt the proportions in which he buys the two goods to allow for the change in their relative prices. In general he will buy less this year of the goods that have risen in price and more of the goods that have, relatively, fallen in price. Thus, in comparing, say, this year with last year, he will tend to consume relatively more this year of the goods that are relatively cheaper this year and vice versa. If the various goods consumed in both years are linked together by price weights the price 'weight' that will be given to those goods that have risen in price will be greater (and the weight given to those that have fallen in price will be smaller) if this year's prices are used than if last year's prices are used. But the goods whose prices are *relatively* greater this year will be those whose consumption has, relatively, fallen. Hence this year's prices will tend to give greater weight to the items whose consumption has risen less, and vice versa. Hence, on the whole, this year's price weights will tend to underestimate the rise in the aggregate quantity consumed, in the manner demonstrated in Figure 11.4(b) above.

The difference between a base-weighted and a current-weighted index according to the weights used, which has been referred to above as 'the index-number spread', is also sometimes known as the Paasche–Laspeyres spread, in recognition of the originators of the two alternative indices. The Paasche index is the index in which II is compared with I on the basis of the weights of situation II (current-weighted index), and the Laspeyres index is the index in which II is compared with I on the basis of the weights of situation I (base-weighted index).

The index-number spread can be seen in the arithmetical examples shown in the following table. In this table, the prices of apples have trebled between years 1 and 2, and the price of pears has risen only by one-third, from £3 per ton to £4 per ton. Total expenditure (assumed to be equal to money income) has also risen considerably, from a total of £18 in the first year to a total of £35 in the second year. At the same time, on account of the relative rise in the apple price, the quantity of apples consumed has fallen off, whereas the quantity of pears consumed has risen. If the two collections of goods, Q_1 and Q_2, are valued at II's prices, we have the current-weighted index of real income, $\sum P_2 Q_2 / \sum P_2 Q_1 = 35/34 = 1 \cdot 03$, indicating that real income has risen by only 3%. In the usual index-number form, with I as the base year $(= 100)$, year II $= 103$.

If, however, the two collections of goods are valued in terms of year I prices, we have the base-weighted index of real income $\sum P_1 Q_2 / \sum P_1 Q_1 = 20/18 = 1 \cdot 11$, indicating that real income has risen by 11%.[1] The 'index-number' spread is the difference between the two indices, 111 and 103.

QUANTITIES (tons)				PRICES (£ per ton)			
year 1 (last year)		year 2 (this year)		year 1 (last year)		year 2 (this year)	
apples	pears	apples	pears	apples	pears	apples	pears
6	4	5	5	1	3	3	4

Thus, once again, given the assumption that relative consumption patterns respond to relative price changes in the direction postulated – i.e. the goods whose prices have risen relatively will have fallen relatively in consumption – we find again that any situation compares relatively more favourably with another situation in terms of the prices of the other situation. In the

[1] The various estimates can be obtained from the above table as follows:
$\sum P_1 Q_2 = (1 \times 5) + (3 \times 5) = £20$ (equals the Q_2 collection valued in the prices of year 1)
$\sum P_1 Q_1 = (1 \times 6) + (3 \times 4) = £18$ (equals the actual amount spent in year 1)
$\sum P_2 Q_2 = (3 \times 5) + (4 \times 5) = £35$ (equals the actual amount spent in year 2)
$\sum P_2 Q_1 = (3 \times 6) + (4 \times 4) = £34$ (equals the Q_1 collection valued in the prices of year 2)

above example, situation II is 11% better than I if Q_2 is valued in I's prices, and only 3% better off if valued in II's prices.

(ii) The exception of 'inferior' goods

The critical assumption, however, is that consumption patterns do respond to changes in relative prices in the manner indicated. Thus if the comparison were between situations such as those shown in Figure 11.5 below, the usual bias would not hold. We have here an indifference map in which one of the goods is an 'inferior' good – this being a good the demand for which falls off as real income rises (such as margarine, since people buy butter as they become wealthier). In the diagram, commodity Y is so inferior that, as its price falls, less of it tends to be consumed.[1]

Figure 11.5

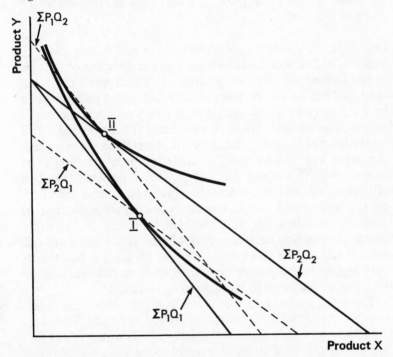

[1] The fall in its price implies a rise in real income. In the case illustrated, the negative effect of this rise in real income outweighs the tendency for its price decline to increase demand for it.

In this case, the index-number bias is the reverse of those obtained above. It is clear that $\Sigma P_2 Q_2$ exceeds $\Sigma P_2 Q_1$ more than does $\Sigma P_1 Q_2$ exceed $\Sigma P_1 Q_1$. In other words, II is better off relative to I *on its own prices* than it is on I's prices. In this particular case the rise in real income consequent upon a fall in its price will then tend to reduce consumption of Y, instead of raising consumption of Y as in the more normal case. Hence, at the new higher income, less will be consumed of the good whose price has fallen (Y's), so that the new situation will give a smaller price weight to the fall in consumption of Y than would be the case if the earlier higher price of Y of year 1 had been used as the weight. In practice, general laws about the index-number spread might also be broken on account of changes in tastes leading, for example, to a rise in the demand for some products the price of which rises in response to the demand increase.

(iii) Sufficient conditions for an increase in real income

From what has been said already about the direction of the bias in real income comparisons according to which year's prices are used, deductions can be made about which set of prices have to be used in order to be certain that one year's real income is greater than another. We have seen that if II is compared with I on the basis of II's prices (i.e. if a current-weighted index is used) the index will tend to under-estimate the 'true' position of II relative to I. This means that if II appears to be better than I on II's prices, we can be confident that it is, in fact, better than I. If, on the other hand, we had used I's prices, we could not be similarly confident, for we know that I's prices tend to exaggerate II's position relative to I. II will not really be so well off, relative to I, as the index might suggest. Hence, the fact that II may appear to be greater than I on such an index cannot be taken as a sure guide to its superiority relative to I.

These deductions from the previous results about the index-number spread can be illustrated, or proved, in Figure 11.6 below.

In Figure 11.6(a), Q_2 is compared with Q_1 at the prices that applied to Q_2. That is, a line parallel to the price (budget) line that passed through Q_2 is also passed through Q_1. This, as we have seen, amounts to valuing the collection Q_1 in the prices that applied to Q_2. In this case it is found that $\Sigma P_2 Q_1$ is less

Figure 11.6(a)

Figure 11.6(b)

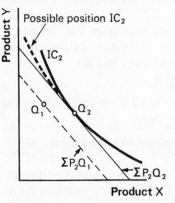

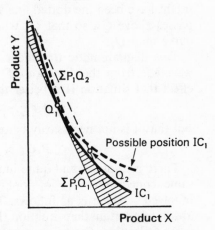

than $\sum P_2 Q_2$. In diagrammatic terms this corresponds to the fact that the $\sum P_2 Q_1$ line is below the $\sum P_2 Q_2$ line. Now, from our earlier assumptions about the law of diminishing marginal utility and hence the assumption that indifference curves have roughly the shape shown in the diagram, such as IC_2, it is clear that whatever the precise shape of the indifference curve that passed through Q_2, it must pass above Q_1 (and hence be a higher indifference curve than the one that passed through Q_1). For whether the indifference curve that passed through Q_2 is the solid line IC_2 or the dotted line version of it as shown, or some similar curve, the mere fact that it curves upwards away from the $\sum P_2 Q_2$ line is quite sufficient to ensure that it must be better than the Q_1 point which lies below the $\sum P_2 Q_2$ line. Hence, if we know that $\sum P_2 Q_2 > \sum P_2 Q_1$ we can be sure that Q_2 is on a higher indifference curve than Q_1.

Suppose, however, that we had merely found that Q_2 represented a greater amount of expenditure than Q_1 in the prices applicable to Q_1. That is, suppose we had compared the real incomes of the situations in terms of the prices of Q_1 and had found that $\sum P_1 Q_2$ was greater than $\sum P_1 Q_1$, which is the comparison illustrated in Figure 11.6(b). In this case we could *not* be sure that Q_2 was really on a higher indifference curve than Q_1. For although the indifference curve passing through Q_1 might have been the solid line IC_1, in which case it would

267

have been true that Q_2 was better than Q_1, the indifference curve might have been the dotted line version of IC_1, in which case it passes above Q_2, so that Q_2 would be on a lower indifference curve than Q_1.

This diagrammatic treatment thus reinforces the deduction we made from the direction of the index-number bias to the effect that situation II is better than situation I if

$$\Sigma P_2 Q_2 > \Sigma P_2 Q_1,$$

but that it is not necessarily better than I if we find merely that

$$\Sigma P_1 Q_2 > \Sigma P_1 Q_1$$

There is another, and quite important, way of arriving at the same conclusion – or of looking at the point of principle involved – which is as follows. The only way that one can be absolutely certain that situation II is preferred to situation I is if, when collection Q_2 was purchased, the consumers *could* have bought collection Q_1 if they had wanted to but didn't, and bought Q_2 instead. For this demonstrates that Q_2 is definitely a preferred collection. Now it can be seen in Figure 11.6(a), that when they bought Q_2 they could have bought the Q_1 collection of goods; for this collection lies below the budget line at their disposal at Q_2, and we know that consumers can buy any collection on, or inside, this budget line. Hence, if they bought Q_2 when they could have bought Q_1, it must be concluded that they preferred Q_2 to Q_1.

The converse does not apply, however, in Figure 11.6(b). Here, all that can be deduced from the fact that $\Sigma P_1 Q_1$ is less than $\Sigma P_1 Q_2$ is that in situation I, consumers could not have bought Q_2 even if they had wanted to. It lies above the budget line at their disposal in situation I. But this does not prove that they would have bought it in preference to Q_1 if they had been able to buy it. There must be a very large number of collections of goods that we cannot buy but which we would not want to buy even if we could do so. If IC_1 happens to be the true indifference curve, then *any* point in the shaded area between this curve and the budget line represents a collection that they could not buy but would not want to buy anyway. Hence, merely proving, as does Figure 11.6(b), that Q_2 could not be bought at the income and price combination that prevailed in situation I does not prove that it would have been bought if it could. This is shown by the fact that although Q_2 lies above the budget line of situation I, the indifference curve passing through Q_1 might – as with the dotted version of IC_1 – pass above the Q_2 collection of goods.

Thus the condition $\sum P_2 Q_2 > \sum P_2 Q_1$ is sufficient to establish that situation II is better than I, since any collection of goods that could have been bought in situation II but which was not bought must be inferior to the collection that the consumers actually did buy in that situation. On the other hand, the condition that $\sum P_1 Q_2 > \sum P_1 Q_2$ does not suffice to establish that situation II was better than situation I, since not all the collection of goods that could not be bought when collection Q_1 was bought are necessarily preferable to the Q_1 collection.

(iv) Averaging alternative measures

The fact that we can state which of the alternative weighting bases provides a sufficient condition for saying whether or not one situation represents higher real income than another is not, unfortunately, the end of our troubles with the index-number spread. For we have seen that this property of the indices arises because one index tends to exaggerate the gap between the real income of two situations whereas the other index underestimates the gap.[1] So, for purposes of finding out *by how much* (if at all) real income in one year is higher than the other, neither index is very good – each having a bias in one direction or the other. For some purposes, therefore, it seems desirable to take an average of the results that would be obtained by the two indexes. How exactly one should do this has long been the subject of much discussion and controversy in the literature on the subject. It is not proposed to go into this controversy here. Suffice it to say that, for most practical purposes, when there is a choice between the two measures no great harm will be done by taking a simple 'geometrical average' of them – that is the two index numbers are multiplied together and the square root of this product is taken to be the best answer to what is essentially an unanswerable question.

---

[1] This should not be interpreted as saying that one index provides a maximum, and the other a minimum, estimate of the 'true' difference between a pair of indifference curves, insofar as any meaning can be attached to the notion of the 'true' difference between two indifference curves.

3. The index-number spread in output comparisons

One of the methods used above to demonstrate some implications of the index-number spread was the diagrammatic approach of Figure 11.6, in which the crux of the argument turned on the particular curvature that indifference curves were generally assumed to possess. For example, having established that Q_1 would be below the budget line through Q_2 if both Q_1 and Q_2 are valued at the prices P_2, it could be safely concluded that Q_1 must be less real income than Q_2 because the indifference curve passing through Q_2 could be assumed to slope upwards away from the budget line passing through Q_2. Hence, since Q_1 must lie below this budget line, the indifference curve passing through Q_2 must pass above the point Q_1. If, however, we could not assume that the indifference curve passing through Q_2 curved upwards away from the budget line this conclusion would no longer follow. If the indifference curve passing through Q_2 took, instead, the shape shown by the solid line in Figure 11.7(a) below, for example, then the fact that $\Sigma P_2 Q_2$ was higher than the line $\Sigma P_2 Q_1$ no longer ensures that the point Q_2 is on a higher indifference curve than Q_1. For if the indifference curve passing through Q_2 can slope downwards then in the absence of further information it might be the dotted-line version of T_2, in

Figure 11.7(a)   **Figure 11.7(b)**

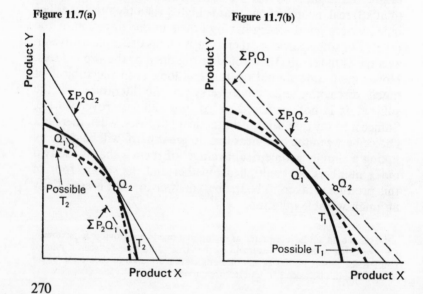

270

which case it would pass below Q_1. It will now be recognised that although indifference curves cannot, in fact, slope in the manner shown by the solid line T_2 (on account of the law of diminishing marginal utility), *transformation curves can*, and generally do.

Thus, since transformation curves have, in general, the opposite slope to indifference curves, all the conditions that apply to indifference curves have to be reversed when applied to transformation curves. In Figure 11.7(a), it can be seen that, since the transformation curve passing through Q_2 could be the solid line or the dotted line versions of T_2, or any such downward sloping curve, the condition $\sum P_2 Q_2 > \sum P_2 Q_1$ no longer guarantees that Q_2 is on a transformation curve that passes above Q_1 and hence no longer guarantees that Q_2 is greater *real output* than Q_1.

In fact, when we are dealing with transformation curves, the sufficient condition for Q_2 to be greater real output than Q_1 now requires to be in the prices of situation I, namely that:

$$\sum P_1 Q_2 > \sum P_1 Q_1$$

This can be seen in Figure 11.7(b). In this diagram Q_2 has been valued in the P_1 prices, and it is found that it must be on a higher 'budget line', since $\sum P_1 Q_2$ is greater than $\sum P_1 Q_1$. Now, since transformation curves, contrary to indifference curves, slope *downwards* from the budget line in the manner shown, if Q_2 is definitely above the budget line passing through Q_1, it can be safely concluded that whatever the precise slope of the transformation curve passing through Q_1 it must fall below Q_2. Hence Q_1 *must* be less real output than Q_2. This clearly holds true whether the transformation curve passing through Q_1 is the solid line or the dotted line version of T_1 – i.e. it holds true without our knowing the exact shape of the transformation curve.

Similarly, all the propositions discussed above, in the context of a real income comparison, concerning the direction of the bias according to which prices are used, must be reversed when applying them to output comparisons. In particular, the output of any given situation will always appear to be greater, relative to another situation, if the comparison is made on the basis of its own prices than if it is made on the basis of the prices of the other situation. This is why, in the case of output, being better than some other situations at one's own prices is no guarantee that one is really better than the other situation, since one's own prices tend to be favourable in an output comparison.

Before leaving this topic, the reader should be warned that, in practice, the importance of the index-number spread depends on the magnitude of the difference being measured. For year to year changes in income or consumption, for example, it probably does not make much difference which index one uses since the pattern of relative prices does not change significantly from year to year. Similarly, the changes in tastes which, as was seen in the last chapter, impose a theoretical limitation on the interpretation of measures of real income changes, are probably not important from one year to another. However, if it is a question of comparing consumption levels in 1960 with those of 1860, or real income per head in the USA and India, all these problems become much more important and it is futile to expect accurate and precise measure of the differences.

4. The relationship between quantity indices and price indices
So far we have been concerned only with indices of quantity, or 'volume indices' as they are sometimes called. This is because we have posed the problem in terms of what is meant by greater *real* income or *real* output. We have wanted to eliminate that part of the comparison between two aggregates of money income or value of output that might reflect differences in price in order to isolate that part that was purely a difference in the quantity of goods consumed or produced. But while differences in real income or real output may be more naturally approached via a discussion of indices of quantity, or volume, of output and income, there is no reason why they could not have been approached via a discussion of how one should construct indices of prices. For it is everyday experience that, if we know by how much a person's (or a community's) money income has changed, we can calculate the change in his 'real income' by dividing the change in his money income by the change that has taken place in the price level of the goods that he buys. If, this year, a housewife has 20% more to spend in the shops than last year, she will not be able to buy any more goods if all prices have risen 20%. Dividing the change in her money income, then, by the change

in the price level shows that she is no better off. If, however, with the 20% rise in her money income, prices have only risen by 10% she will be nearly 10% better off.[1] When any series at current prices is corrected by a price index in this way, it is said to be *deflated*.

In terms of a consumer's budget line, it is obvious that if, say, his money income doubles but all prices also double, his budget line will not have moved at all. The intercept of his budget line on either axis will be just the same for he will only be able to buy the same amounts of each good as before. And since we have seen that a rise in real income should be measured by the amount of rise in the budget line, it is clear that this can be interpreted as the amount by which the change in money income has been offset by any change in prices.

Thus in order to measure the change in real national product or income from year to year, one way of proceeding would be simply to take the value of national product in each year in the prices of each year – i.e. the readily available figures of national product *at current prices* – and deflate it by the price index of national product. This gives the index of real national product, which is also often known as the index of national product at *constant prices*, for it is an index of the way that national product would change if it were measured in the prices of only one of the years covered. Indices that have been adjusted for price changes, such as the indices of real income that we have been considering in detail, or indices of industrial production, or indices of consumers' expenditure at constant prices, fall into the class referred to as *volume* indices or as *quantity* indices, by contrast with the indices of these same items in terms of the current prices of each year, in which case they are referred to as *value* indices.

In exactly the same way that the index of real income or of the 'quantity' of income was seen to depend on which situation's prices were used to construct it, so an index of the change in price between two situations will depend on which quantity weights are used to construct it. Between any two years, say, thousands of prices may change. The measure of the overall

[1] Since the index of her money income would be 120 and the price index would be 110, the index of her real income would be 120/110, which equals 109·2.

change in prices, therefore, will depend on how much weight is attached to the individual price changes – i.e. how they are combined together into an aggregate index of prices. And, as with indices of real income, there tends to be a systematic bias according to which year's set of quantity weights are chosen for constructing the price index. In general, people will consume relatively less this year of the items whose prices have risen the most, and vice versa. Hence, if price changes are weighted together by means of this year's pattern of quantities consumed, the index – which will be a 'current-weighted' price index – will tend to under-estimate the rise in prices, since it will give smaller quantity weights to the goods whose prices have risen most. Conversely, if the price changes are weighted together with the quantities of the base year of the index, the resulting index (which will be a base-weighted price index) tends to exaggerate the rise in prices. Symbolically, these statements may be expressed as follows:

$$\frac{\sum P_2 Q_2}{\sum P_1 Q_2} \text{ ('current-weighted' price index)} \quad \text{is less than} \quad \frac{\sum P_2 Q_1}{\sum P_1 Q_1} \text{ ('base-weighted' price index)}$$

A series of figures of, say, national product or consumers' expenditure, *at constant prices* – i.e. corrected for price changes – need not, of course, be expressed in the form of an index number. The index number presentation is merely one in which the estimates for all the years are expressed as a quotient of some base year. But a series of values or expenditures at current prices could also simply be corrected for the change in price and then left in the form of a series of expenditure figures – in pounds sterling or dollars – at constant prices.

For example, in the following table, the first row shows the actual value of consumers' expenditure in Britain over the years indicated, in the prices that were current in each year. The second row shows the corresponding price index, which in this case is the price index of the goods entering into consumers' expenditure.[1] The third row then shows the evolution of the consumers' expenditure adjusted for the changes in price, which is obtained by dividing the first row by the price index (and

[1] The practice, in many countries, is for the price index of consumers' expenditure shown in the national accounts to be a current-weighted index. In such cases it will differ from what are usually known as 'cost of living' indices or 'retail price' indices, which are often base-weighted price indices.

multiplying by 100). Thus, for example, the 1960 figures can be interpreted as saying that although consumers actually spent

	1958	1959	1960	1961
1 Consumers' expenditure (£'000 million at current prices)	15·4	16·2	17·0	17·9
2 Index of prices (1958=100)	100	101	104	108
3 Consumers' expenditure (£'000 million at constant 1958 prices)	15·4	16·0	16·4	16·6
4 Volume index of consumers' expenditure (1958=100)	100·0	104·0	106·5	107·8

£17,000 million in that year by comparisons with £15,400 million in 1958, the rise in prices of 4% from 1958 to 1960 meant that their expenditure in 1960 was really worth only £16,400 million in 1958 prices. If, then, row 3 were to be converted into the form of an *index* of the 'volume' (or 'quantity') of consumers' expenditure (row 4), the 1960 expenditure would appear as 6·5% greater than in 1958 – i.e. with 1958 taken as the base year equal to 100, 1960 would then be equal to 106·5.[1]

Given the value of consumers' expenditure at current prices, the series showing consumers' expenditure at constant prices (whether in index form or not) depends on the price index, or vice versa. Hence, one way of arriving at the constant price series (or volume index) would have been to construct the price index and divide it into the value series. If, instead, the volume series had been constructed directly on the basis of the quantities of the items consumed, then, between them, this series plus the current price series, *imply* some price index – which, in such cases, is referred to as the 'implicit price' index. For example, many statistical sources show national product series at current prices and at constant prices, but do not show any price indices. If the current prices series is divided by the constant price series the result will be the *implied price index* for national product in that country, in the same way that if row 3 above is divided into row 1 the result would be the price index shown in row 2. Thus, given a value series (i.e. a current price series), every volume, or quantity series implies a price index, and every price index implies a quantity series (irrespective of whether it is in an index

[1] The conversion of row 3 into a volume index (base 1958) is, of course, carried out simply by dividing all the figures in row 3 by the 1958 figure and multiplying by 100.

number form with some year taken as equal to 100). This relationship between value changes, price changes and quantity changes is, as we shall see later in this chapter, quite useful for purposes of practical estimation.

Meanwhile we must investigate a little further what sort of bias the alternative quantity and price indices imply for each other. For we have seen that a quantity comparison of this year with last year weighted by, say, this year's prices tends to underestimate this year's real income by comparison with last year's real income. Hence, if the change in money income between the two years were to be divided by such a quantity index the implied price index would tend to exaggerate the rise in prices between the two years. In the numerical example of page 275, if the quantity series shown in row 3 had indicated a smaller rise in the quantity of consumers' expenditure the rise in prices in row 2 would have to be greater in order for the series to be consistent with the row 1 figures of the change in expenditure at current prices.

This common sense result can be seen more precisely with the aid of a symbolic representation of the relationship between the three concepts concerned, namely the values, the prices and the quantities. First, the actual value of expenditures in any year – i.e. at current prices – is simply the sum of all the quantities purchased in that year multiplied by their respective prices. Thus, in year 1, the value of expenditure is given by $\sum P_1 Q_1$.[1] Hence the ratio of the *value* of year 2 relative to year 1, in the prices current in each year, is simply $\sum P_2 Q_2 / \sum P_1 Q_1$. Such an index is simply expressing the actual value of the expenditures concerned in the second year divided by the actual value of the expenditures in the first year. Since there can be only one actual value of these expenditures in each year there can be only one estimate for such an index. But, as we have seen, there can be at least two estimates of the change in the quantity consumed between the two years, according to which year's price weights are used. Hence, if we wish to divide the value index by a quantity index to find the implied price index, we have a choice between two (or more) quantity indices. So the particular price index that is implied will depend on which of the quantity indices is to be used. If the quantity index used is the one that is weighted by

[1] See also footnote to pages 262 or 264.

year 2's prices (a current-weighted quantity index) then the implied price index will be found to be weighted by year 1's quantities (a base-weighted price index), and vice versa. This can be demonstrated algebraically, as follows, where it can be seen that a base-weighted quantity index has to be multiplied by a current-weighted price index in order to arrive at the value index, and, equally, a current-weighted quantity index has to be multiplied by a base-weighted price index in order to arrive at the value index.

$$\frac{\Sigma P_1 Q_2}{\Sigma P_1 Q_1} \times \frac{\Sigma P_2 Q_2}{\Sigma P_1 Q_2} = \frac{\Sigma P_2 Q_2}{\Sigma P_1 Q_1} \qquad (2)$$

(base-   (current-   (value
weighted   weighted   index)
quantity   price
index)   index)

OR

$$\frac{\Sigma P_2 Q_2}{\Sigma P_2 Q_1} \times \frac{\Sigma P_2 Q_1}{\Sigma P_1 Q_1} = \frac{\Sigma P_2 Q_2}{\Sigma P_1 Q_1} \qquad (3)$$

(current-   (base-   (value
weighted   weighted   index)
quantity   price
index)   index)

These results check with what we had already concluded, on common sense grounds, as to the bias in the price indices. For example, it was argued above that, since consumers tend to buy relatively less of the goods that have risen relatively in price, a price index weighted by this year's quantities will give greater weight to those goods whose prices have relatively declined, and vice versa, so that it will tend to under-estimate the aggregate rise in price (if any). Hence, if a current-weighted price index is divided into a value index, it would over-estimate the rise in quantity. And, as can be seen above, given the value index, it is a base-weighted quantity index that would be obtained if the value index is divided by the current-weighted price index. And we had seen earlier that, indeed, a base-weighted quantity index does exaggerate the rise in quantity. Conversely, if the change in say, consumers' expenditure at current prices is corrected by means of a base-weighted price index in order to estimate the

277

change in the 'real' volume of consumption, the resulting quantity index will tend to under-estimate the true change in the volume.

In the context of price indices, the weights are commonly referred to as the 'basket of goods'. That is, the change in the price level between any two years will depend on whether it is the first year's 'basket of goods' that is used or the 'basket of goods' of the second year. Our results have shown that a price index based on the basket of goods of some back year will tend to over-estimate the overall rise in prices, since consumers will now consume relatively less of the goods whose prices have risen relatively more.

Faced with the choice between a base-weighted and a current-weighted price index it is tempting to take some form of average, in the manner proposed for reconciling conflicting estimates of the quantity change. Whilst this procedure may be legitimate, it has to be recognised that, in the end, one no longer has a clear concept of what it is that is actually being measured. With the simple indices – whether base-weighted or current-weighted – it is possible to identify some actual basket of goods that is being priced, though the result may be limited as an indication of changes in real income (or output). With some composite index, the result may give a 'truer' impression of the change in price, and hence of the 'true' change in real income, but it is no longer possible to identify in any simple manner what prices are actually being compared with what.

5. The use of quantity and price indicators
The relationship between expenditure changes, volume changes and price changes provides a useful way of constructing comparisons of real income (or output) or of prices in spite of the fact that it is impossible to obtain data relating to every transaction involved. It is simply not possible, for most purposes, to measure the prices, quantities and expenditures for all the items to which the comparisons relate. Hence, in practice, estimation techniques consist of using indicators of volume or price or expenditure for certain items that, it is hoped, are fairly representative of some wider class of transaction.

A simple example may bring out the principles involved. Suppose that, for purposes of estimating the 'real' change in national product over the years, national expenditure is broken down into its major aggregates, private consumption, investment and so on, and that each of these is broken down, in turn, into some constituent items. One of these items might be, for example, consumers' expenditure on services. This, in turn, will cover a multitude of services, such as entertainment, medical services, transport, personal services of various kinds and so on. For many of these items it may not be possible to cover the whole of the item and some partial indicator might be used which, it is hoped, will be representative of the movements in the whole of the item concerned. For example, admissions to some kinds of entertainment may be subject to tax, so that the authorities may have reliable quantity data on the numbers admitted. These may be used as indicators of the quantity change in the whole of the item 'entertainment'. In other cases, there may be no good indicator and some 'proxy' indicator may be used, such as the number of miles run by certain types of transport vehicle as an indicator of the number of *passenger* miles travelled in that particular form of transport. In the case of private transport, the motoring component of the consumers' expenditure may be estimated largely according to data on the fuel consumed, in the hope that this partial quantity indicator is representative of movements in the other ingredients of private motoring, such as spares and garaging and maintenance.

Price indices, where these are used, are also based on partial indicators that are believed to move more or less in line with the overall price index for the item concerned. For example, one item under the heading of personal services would be the services of hairdressers. Now it would probably be impossible to estimate exactly the change in the *volume* of hairdressers' services – i.e. the number of haircuts, permanent waves, and so on – that consumers obtain. Hence, the usual procedure in such a case might be to start with information about total expenditure on hairdressers – for example, from family budget data or from returns from hairdressers for purposes of income tax declarations – and then to deflate these with the price index of hairdressers' services. But this price index would probably be based on some selected indicators, such as the changes in price of certain standard forms of haircut, shampoo, etc. These price change indicators would be weighted together into a price index for hairdressing according to some estimates of the relative weights of the different items in total hairdressing expenditures in some base year. In other words, it is assumed that the price of *all* hairdressing services moved in line with the price of those particular hairdressers' services that have been covered by the price indicators. This estimated price index would then be used to deflate the current price series of expenditures on *all* hairdressing services to obtain an estimate of the index of quantity of all such services.

For some of the items in the total picture it may be impossible to find good data on the expenditures at current prices and it may be this part of the accounts that are built up by means of estimates of the price index and the quantity index. This is particularly the case where the items concerned are goods that are produced in fairly simple homogeneous units of quantity. For in these cases quantity estimates are often more reliable than data on expenditures. For example, it is common practice to estimate gas expenditures by private households in some countries by means of direct quantity data on the amount supplied and estimates of the average tariffs used for household consumption. At the other extreme, it would be very difficult to estimate clothing expenditures this way on account of the unlimited variety of clothing. For such heterogeneous items it is more common to use expenditure data from family budget surveys of one kind or another. The implied quantity data would then be determined by deflating the expenditure series by price indices based on certain standard and selected items of clothing, since the price changes in a few well-selected items are likely to be fairly representative of the whole.

Other items fall into an intermediate band. For example, expenditures on bread and cereals are, to some extent, estimated from information of flour deliveries from mills and imported flour, followed by various estimates of the proportions used for cakes, biscuits, bread, and so on, and then adjusted by price indices for these items. Although the variety available in bread and cereals consumption might not be as great as with clothing, it is clear that this method may contain numerous errors.

But whilst the techniques may differ from country to country, as well as from product to product and from time to time, two features of all such estimates stand out, namely:

(i) since the expenditure index equals the price index multiplied by the quantity index, only two of these indices are required in order to calculate the remaining index, and which of the two will be most reliable will vary from one item of expenditure to another, and

(ii) for any one item, the statistician will invariably use some partial indicators – of quantity or price – of the movement in the whole of the item concerned.

The rationale of the procedures used in practice may be more easily understandable if we take another look at the index number formulae. We have seen that a quantity index – say, a base-weighted one – can be written as follows:

$$\text{Quantity index} \atop \text{(base-weighted)} = \frac{\Sigma P_1 Q_2}{\Sigma P_1 Q_1} \qquad (4)$$

But this formula could also be re-written in the following manner, where, it will be seen, the Q_1 cancel out in the numerator, thereby reducing the formula to its original expression. In the form shown below it is clear that one way of constructing the index would be to estimate indicators of the change in quantity of the different items (the Q_2/Q_1) for each item and to weight these quantity ratios, as they may be called, by the actual expenditure on them – i.e. by the $P_1 Q_1$ for each item.

$$\text{Quantity index} \atop \text{(base-weighted)} = \frac{\Sigma P_1 Q_1 \times \dfrac{Q_2}{Q_1}}{\Sigma P_1 Q_1} \qquad (5)$$

When the weights used to combine the quantity indicators are the expenditures in the base year, as above, then this form of the index is equal to the original version of a quantity index weighted by base year prices. If, however, the indicators of the change in the quantity of each item had been weighted by the current years' expenditure, namely by the $P_2 Q_2$ for each items, the formula would have to be adjusted to yield an index of last year's quantity relative to this year's, weighted by the current year's prices.[1] In doing this the quantity ratios would have to be expressed as the ratio of last year's quantity consumed to this

[1] The reciprocal of this would, of course, bring us back to this year as an index of last year (based on this year's prices).

year's. Then, as can be seen below, since the Q_2 cancel out, the two formula amount to the same thing.

$$\text{Quantity index} \atop \text{(current-weighted)} = \frac{\Sigma P_2 Q_1}{\Sigma P_2 Q_2} = \frac{\Sigma P_2 Q_2 \times \dfrac{Q_1}{Q_2}}{\Sigma P_2 Q_2} \qquad (6)$$

This rather abstract discussion may have more appeal if we now see what the actual operations and calculations would be, using the data already employed on page 264 for calculating the index in the normal manner. If we wished to calculate the base-weighted quantity index in the manner of equation (5), the quantity ratios, for apples and pears respectively, are 5/6 and 5/4, and the base year expenditures on apples and pears respectively, are £6 and £12. Thus, formula (5) would be as follows:

$$\frac{(£6 \times 5/6) + (£12 \times 5/4)}{£6 + £12} = \frac{£20}{£18} = 1 \cdot 11$$

Thus the same result is obtained as if the index had been calculated in the direct manner originally used on page 264 and expressed as equation (4). Similarly, as the reader can check for himself, if the current-weighted index had been calculated from the formula of equation (6), the ratio of year 1's to year 2's income would have been £34/£35 – or $\Sigma P_2 Q_1 / \Sigma P_2 Q_2$.

The quantity ratio for any single item can be looked at as a means of converting the actual expenditure on that item in two different years into the expenditures in both years valued at the prices of only one of them. For example, using the same data on the apples and pears, we have that expenditure on apples rose from £6 in the first year to £15 in the second year. The quantity of apples consumed fell from 6 tons to 5 tons, so that the quantity ratio, Q_2/Q_1 is 5/6. One way of saying what apple expenditure would be in the second year at the constant prices of the first year would be simply to multiply the £6 by 5/6, for this must show what expenditure would have been in the second year if only the quantities consumed had changed and if there had been no change in their prices. Thus, in the second year, apple expenditure at constant prices (of year 1) would be £5. The same operation performed on the pear data would yield the result that if prices had not changed expenditure on pears in the second year would have changed from the £12 of the first year to 5/4 multiplied by £12, which equals £15. The sum of the two figures of year 2 expenditures at year 1 prices is then £(5 + 15), which equals £20, which is the same, of course, as $\sum P_1 Q_2$. According to these data, the two quantity ratios for the apples and pears are 5/6 and 5/4 respectively, and the shares of each in total expenditure in the base year are £6/£18 ($= \frac{1}{3}$) and £12/£18 ($= \frac{2}{3}$) respectively. From this information the index could have been calculated as follows:

$$\text{(base-weighted) Quantity index} \begin{array}{l} = (\frac{1}{3} \times 5/6) + (\frac{2}{3} \times 5/4) \\ = 0 \cdot 277 + 0 \cdot 833 = 1 \cdot 11 \end{array}$$

Thus we arrive at exactly the same answer as by the two other methods used so far. The method just used corresponds, of course, to the common sense notion that the overall rise in, say, a housewife's aggregate consumption would be calculated by taking the increase in the volume of her consumption of individual items and combining these together by some measure of their relative importance in her overall expenditure pattern. Where the shares of each item in total expenditure are the shares in the base year, the resulting quantity index will correspond to one that is weighted by base year prices and vice versa.

Whichever formula is used for constructing a quantity index, they all boil down to the same principle in the end, namely that the total change can be decomposed into two parts. On the one hand we have indices of the change in the quantities of the individual items – which are explicitly shown in the Q_2/Q_1 ratios in equations (5) or (6). On the other hand, these quantity ratios, *which may be based on partial quantity indicators*, have to be combined together with some weights, and whether these are the actual expenditures or their shares in total expenditures, the final result is exactly the same as if the actual quantities in each year had been weighted together by the actual prices, as in the first form in which the index number was expressed.

All the above results apply, making the appropriate adjustments, to indices of price change. For example, an overall price index can be calculated by taking the price ratios for the different components of the index, and weighting them together by the actual expenditures on them in one or other of the years, or by the shares of each component in total expenditure. For example,

283

it is obvious that the following equation is true, since the P_1 cancel out,

$$\frac{\Sigma P_2 Q_1}{\Sigma P_1 Q_1} = \frac{\Sigma P_1 Q_1 \times \dfrac{P_2}{P_1}}{\Sigma P_1 Q_1} = \text{Base-weighted price index}$$

6. Methods of estimating changes in real national product

The alternative methods enumerated above of measuring the 'real' change in any flow, such as consumers' expenditure, do not, however, exhaust all the choices that the statistician faces when confronted with the task of measuring the change in the 'quantity' of national product. For, to go back to Chapter 2, he also has to bear in mind that there are three methods of measuring national product in any one year to start with, before coming on to the question of how one compares such measures in different years. These three methods, it will be recalled, comprise the expenditure method, the output (or production) method, and the income method. Thus, in addition to the question of, say, which particular form of the index should be used and which year's weights should be used, a choice has to be made as to whether the current price series that has to be deflated is the series of final expenditures – consumption, investment and so on – or the series of net output by industry or the series of incomes received.

In practice, of course, much depends on the type of data available in the particular economy concerned. It would be futile, for example, to attempt to calculate national product – let alone changes in national product – by the output (i.e. value added) method in a country where there were no good figures of production. On the other hand it would be impossible to use the expenditure method in a country lacking in the estimates of investment as well as the surveys of private consumption expenditures that this method requires. In general a mixture is used – the precise share of the ingredients depending on the particular data available in the given country for the different components of national product. For some items it will be easier to use final expenditure data – e.g. for public consumption and investment where the data are, presumably, available to the official statisticians. For other items – as with the bread and cereals example given above in connection with the methods used to estimate real changes in consumption – it may be better to build up the picture of national expenditure on them from the output and import (and export) side. Thus, although in some countries, an attempt may be made to estimate changes in real national product more or less independently by two methods – the change in final expenditures at constant prices and the change in net output at constant prices – the data used for parts of the calculation by one method are not always independent of the data used in the rival method. It should be noted that, on the whole, changes in national product at constant prices are not estimated on the basis of income data, on the grounds that only when the incomes are spent on goods and services can they be identified with any particular real flow of such goods and services.

In general, as stated in Chapter 2, national accounts are based on a variety of data devised for other purposes and so they involve a great deal of estimation. Hence, wherever the statistician can estimate some component of GNP by more than one route, he will do so as a means of checking the estimates. This means that the figure finally shown will reflect partly his view as to the reliability of the alternative sources used. This applies as much to the estimation of the components of national product in any one year as to the estimation of their changes from year to year. In fact, it is not always possible to draw a distinction between the two processes. The estimates for one year may be built up on the basis of an estimate for some back year – a 'bench mark' – adjusted by some approximative indicators of the change in the item concerned. But whatever the limitations on their precision, there is no doubt that national accounts have become the richest source of quantitative data available to the economist for analysing the structure of the economy and for studying the forces responsible for short- and long-run developments in the economy.

Summary of main concepts used

Chapter 2

Productive activities. The activities that are defined as contributing to the flow of goods and services that are included in gross national product.

Transfer payments. Payments that are not made in return for some productive activity. Old-age pensions are an example of a transfer payment. Such payments merely transfer purchasing power from some members of the community to others. Transfer payments may also be made between governments of different countries.

Final products. Of the total of goods and services produced as a result of productive activities, the 'final products' are those which are not used up in the course of further production of other goods and services. They are, therefore, desired for their own sake, either to be consumed or to be added to the economy's stock of wealth.[1]

Final demand. The demand for final products.

National product. This is what, in the end, the economy obtains as a result of its productive activities in the time period designated. It is thus an unduplicated total that excludes the goods used up in the course of further production.

Intermediate products. Goods and services (excluding exports) that are used up in the production of other goods and services. In industrialised countries, raw materials are an example of intermediate products. Purchases and sales of intermediate products are referred to as *intermediate transactions*.

Productive sector. The name that can be given to the total of all firms and establishments (including government) that are regarded as being engaged in productive activities. The same people who are employed therein may also, of course, be part of other sectors of the

---

[1] Exports net of imports add to wealth by adding to 'net investment overseas' (see below). Alternatively *total* exports can be regarded as being desired mainly as a means of buying imports (for domestic consumption or investment) and only the excess of total exports over imports as being that part of final product which is desired for adding to investment overseas.

economy in a different capacity. For example, an employee will be part of the productive sector in his capacity as an employee, though he will also be part of the 'household' sector in his capacity as a consumer.

The production boundary. The name given to the notional dividing line between the productive activities, namely those that are carried on inside the productive sector, and all other economic activities, such as transfer payments themselves. Goods and services become 'final' product (or output) when they cross the production boundary of the economy concerned.

Activities giving rise to intermediate output (or intermediate transactions) take place inside the production boundary and the intermediate products to which they give rise do not cross the boundary. The definition of the production boundary – like the definition of productive activities – is essentially arbitrary. For example, private expenditures for transport to work are usually included as part of final product though it is arguable that they represent a cost incurred by labour in making its own contribution to national product so that they should be treated as an intermediate transaction.

The expenditure method. The method of estimating national product by adding up all the components of final demand – i.e. the sum of all final products, or the value of all the goods and services that cross the production boundary in the time period concerned.

The production method (also known as the 'industry of origin method'). The method of estimating national product by adding up the contribution of each industry to national product. These contributions, which are also known as the *value added* or the *net output* of each industry, consist of the value of any industry's (or firm's) sales less its purchases of intermediate products. *Value added* is thus equal to what is available for distribution to the basic factors of production (labour and capital) in the form of wages and salaries (i.e. payments to labour) and profits which, with rent, interest and dividends, can be regarded as the payment to capital.

The income method. The method of estimating national product by adding up all the incomes received by the basic factors of production in the form of wages and salaries, or profits.

Domestic product versus national product. The former is a geographical concept, relating to the product of factors of production employed within the geographical territory of the country concerned.[1]

---

[1] Locally recruited staff of the overseas Embassies of a given country, however, are not included in the national product of that country, even though the Embassy is regarded a part of the territory of that country. *A fortiori*, repairs to Embassy windows shattered in riots are treated as an import (of glaziers' services) into the given country.

287

National product relates to the product of all nationals of the country concerned, including the product of their assets overseas (profits on overseas investments).

Net (property) income from abroad. The balance between a given country's earnings on its overseas assets and the earnings in that country accruing to assets owned by foreigners. It is thus equal to the difference between domestic and national product.

National product at market prices and at factor cost. The former is the value of national product when the goods and services entering into national product are valued at the prices actually paid on the market, inclusive of indirect taxes (less subsidies). Since net indirect taxes have to be paid to the government, however, the value added available for distribution to the basic factors of production will fall short of national product at market prices by the amount of these net indirect taxes. If national product is valued after deducting indirect taxes and after adding subsidies the result is national product at factor cost. The dividing line between indirect and other forms of tax is not very sharp, however. For example, it is debatable how far a value-added tax, or a payroll tax such as national insurance contributions, is a tax on income (direct tax) or an indirect tax.

Chapter 4

Consumption. That part of final demand or national expenditure that is required for its own sake and not for adding to the economy's stock of wealth.[1] Purchases of food and clothing are examples of consumption, as well as current expenditures on education or on law and order, and so on.

Investment. The rest of national product – i.e. that part of final output that is used to add to the economy's stock of wealth.[1]

Public consumption. The part of total consumption that is carried out by the public authorities. It includes, notably, expenditure on defence, health, education, law and order, and various public facilities (e.g. street lighting), and so on.

Private consumption. That part of total consumption that is carried out by private individuals in their personal capacities. It also includes, however, current expenditures by 'non-profit-making organisations'.

Fixed domestic capital formation. That part of investment which consists of the domestic purchase of investment goods, such as

---

[1] See, however, footnote to 'final products' above, concerning treatment of exports, which, if imports are not netted out from them, are a part of final demand that are not required for their own sake but for the sake, largely, of enabling both consumption goods and investment goods to be imported.

factories, machines, roads, houses, and so on, by contrast with the next two items.

Changes in stocks. That part of investment which consists of changes in the economy's stocks, or inventories, of goods – notably stocks of raw materials, semi-finished goods, or inventories held by the whole-sale or retail trade. Although these are not all the subject of any actual transaction, they have to be included in final demand in order to preserve the identity of expenditure on national product and value added.

Exports less imports. The excess of exports of goods and services over imports of goods and services forms the third part of investment, since it enables an economy to add to its wealth in the form of claims on other economies. It equals *net investment overseas.*

Gross and net investment. A part of an economy's capital stock is 'used up' in the course of production, and this is 'capital consump-tion', which is frequently, if inaccurately, described by the term *depreciation.* If investment is measured without allowing for that part of investment that should be put aside to cover the wear and tear of the capital stock it is said to be *gross* investment. If, however, a deduction from gross investment is made to allow for capital con-sumption, the resulting measure is known as 'net' investment.

Gross and net national product. The former is the value of national product when investment is measured gross, and the latter is the value of national product when investment is measured net (of capital consumption).

Chapter 5

Double entry accounting. A system of accounts in which, for any 'transactor', its receipts are shown on one side of an account and its payments are shown on the other side. Since any receipt must be a payment by somebody, every transaction must, with such a system, be shown twice. For any given transactor or sector there may be many types of account, such as an account showing only his pro-ductive activities, an 'appropriation' account showing *all current* receipts and payments, or a capital account showing the transactions affecting his balance sheet of assets and liabilities. For the sake of simplicity in this book we have shown, for each sector, only the one account necessary for describing the framework in which we are interested here.

Consolidated account. For any one type of account, such as a capital account, there may be many individual accounts of the same category (e.g. for individual firms). If they are all combined together in one 'consolidated' account, transactions that would appear on both sides of the aggregate account are cancelled out and deleted.

Production account. For the economy as a whole (as distinct from any sector or firm or individual) this account shows, on the credit side, the final product of the economy (consumption and investment) at market prices and, on the other side, the claims on this, namely national income (wages and profits), depreciation and net indirect taxes.

The capital account. This is a 'consolidated' account, grouping together, on the credit side, the investment of the economy (fixed, changes in stocks and net investment abroad) and, on the debit side, the sources of savings – by firms, by the government and by households (i.e. private savings).

The household account. This is a consolidated 'appropriation' account showing, on the credit side, all the income of households, whether arising from their productive activities or not. Thus it includes, in addition to wages, profits, etc., transfer payments from the government On the debit side it shows the disposal of this income in the form of private consumption, taxes or savings.

The government account. A consolidated 'appropriation' account showing, on the credit side, the receipts of the public authorities from taxation and, on the other side, its payments – for public consumption or transfer payments and its savings.

Rest of world account. A consolidated account for the 'rest of the world' showing all its transactions with the economy concerned. Thus the rest of the world's debits *vis à vis* the given country will be the given country's exports less imports, since the exports of the given country appear on the credit side of the production account of the given country (and its imports appear as a negative item on the same side). On the credit side of the rest of the world account will appear the given country's net investment overseas, since this increase in the assets of the given country must be identically equal to the excess of the given country's exports over its imports.

Chapter 6

Social accounting matrix. The presentation of the transactions linking the accounts of the usual major sectors within the framework of a matrix, in which the credits of any account are set out in a row and its debits in a column. Thus the entry at the intersection of the row and column for sectors 1 and 2 respectively represent the receipt by sector 1 from sector 2.

'Input–output table' (also known as a table of inter-industry transactions). A matrix presentation – as with the social accounting matrix – but showing also the pattern of intermediate transactions taking place within the productive sector – i.e. the transactions between different industries.

Accounting equations and behavioural equations. The former are simply the equations showing the various items that appear on both sides of an account. Since, by convention, all accounts are made to balance by including a 'balancing item' (the net savings or dis-savings of each account), balancing equations are simply identities. Behavioural equations, however, indicate the way that one item is functionally related to others – such as the way that private consumption increases as incomes increase. Such equations, therefore, are propositions about the way the economic transactors involved 'behave', and can, in principle, be found to be true or false in the light of empirical verification.

Chapter 8

'Actual' and 'planned' savings and investment. The *actual* level of savings and investment is the amount of savings and investment that actually takes place in any time period. The manner in which these are defined is such that they are always equal. But the 'planned' (or desired) level of savings and investment are the levels that the people concerned would like to carry out at each income level. Income is in short-run equilibrium only when planned savings and investment are equal.

The consumption function. This is the behavioural relationship linking consumption, on the one hand, and the variables that are believed to determine it, on the other. In the simple model being used in this book, consumption is assumed to be determined only by income.

The savings function. The equation relating planned savings to income (in the simple model used here). Thus, the savings function is related in a simple manner to the consumption function, since income is either spent on consumption or saved.

The savings ratio. The proportion of income that is saved. In Chapter 8 it has been assumed to remain constant. In Chapter 9 it is assumed to rise as the income level rises. The proportion of income that is saved is, of course, equal to unity minus the proportion of income spent on consumption which, in turn, is known as the 'average propensity to consume' (see below).

Chapter 9

The marginal propensity to consume. The amount by which consumption rises for a given rise in income. Thus, if consumption rises by £0·8 for every £1 rise in income, the marginal propensity to consume is equal to 0·8.

The average propensity to consume. The proportion of income, at any level, that is spent on consumption. Usually this proportion is lower the higher is the level of income, because very poor people generally have to spend all or most of their income on consumption.

The marginal propensity to save. The amount by which savings increase for a given rise in income. Thus, if savings increase by £0·2 for every rise in income, the marginal propensity to save is equal to 0·2. Since income is either spent on consumption or saved, when c equals the marginal propensity to consume the marginal propensity of save must be equal to $(1-c)$.

'Exogenous' and 'endogenous' items of national expenditure. 'Exogenous' items are those that are not fully determined by, or functionally related to, the variables in the model of income determination being used, whereas 'endogenous' items are so related. Thus, in the simple model used here, investment, government expenditures and exports are assumed to be 'exogenous', whereas consumption, tax revenues and imports are all assumed to be endogenous by virtue of being dependent on income.

The multiplier. The amount by which any increase in one of the 'exogenous' items of expenditure (such as investment) has to be multiplied in order to arrive at the final equilibrium change in income. It is thus the ratio of the change in income to the change in the exogenous item that induced the change in income. The size of the multiplier depends on the marginal propensity to save in the simple model in which no foreign trade is taken into account. In a model in which foreign trade and government are introduced, the multiplier will depend also on the marginal propensity to import and to pay taxes.

Chapters 10 and 11

The indifference curve. A curve showing different combinations of two goods, such as apples and pears, between which the consumer is indifferent and which may be regarded as giving him equal satisfaction.

Marginal rate of substitution. The slope of an indifference curve at a particular point; it represents the additional amount of one product, starting from a given combination of products, that the consumer would want in order to feel just as well off if one unit of the other product is taken away from him. Insofar as one is allowed to use the seven-letter word 'utility' it would equal the reciprocal of the ratio of the marginal utilities of the two goods in question.

The budget line. In graphical terms – as on the usual indifference curve diagram – it is a line showing all the different combinations of the products concerned that the consumer can buy for a given money income. The slope of the line – i.e. the rate at which he can trade off one good against the other – will therefore represent the relative prices of the goods. A parallel shift in the line will represent a change in his 'real' income since it indicates a change in the quantity of the goods that he can buy.

The transformation curve. Corresponding to an indifference curve, it is the curve showing all combinations of output of two or more products that an economy can produce with a given amount of resources, skills, etc.

Marginal opportunity cost. It is the output counterpart, on the output side, of the concept of the marginal rate of substitution that has been introduced in the context of satisfactions. It measures the cost of producing one more unit of one product in terms of the amount of the other product that has to be given up. It is equal to the slope of the transformation curve.

Change in real income. This is the amount by which income would have to change when consumers may move from a point on one indifference curve to a point on another. It can be measured as the distance between parallel budget lines passing through the two points.

Index-number spread. If relative prices differ in two situations, the budget lines corresponding to each will have different slopes. There is, therefore, no unique answer to the question of how far apart they are or what the difference in real income is. According to which slope (i.e. which year's relative prices) are used to measure the gap between the two budget lines, the measure of the difference in real income will vary. The difference between the two measures in this case is the index-number spread.

Volume index. When any two values are compared – such as values of national product or consumers' expenditure in two different years – the comparison is influenced by both the changes in the volumes (or quantities) of goods and services concerned and the changes in their prices. If correction is made for the price changes, the resulting comparison is a volume, or quantity, comparison. If the corrected figure for one year is expressed as a ratio of the other year and multiplied by 100, the resulting form of the comparisons is known as an index. For example, if *real* income in 1965 is 10% greater than in 1960, the volume index of income in 1965, taking 1960 as a base (equal to 100), is 110. Price indices are subject to index-number spread in the same way as are indices of difference in 'real income'. According to whether the basket of goods of one situation or the other is priced, the estimate of the overall change in prices will differ.

Answers to Exercises

Exercises 2.1 (page 19)

1   Value added by A=£20; by B=£20; by C=£20; by D=£20; total national product=£80.

2   Value added by A=£50; by B=£10; by C=£20; by D=£20; total national product=£100.

3   Value added by A=£50; by B=£10; by C=£70; total national product=£130.

4   Value added by A=£100; by B=£30; by C=£20; total national product=£150.

		wages	profits
5	exercise 1	44	36
	exercise 2	56	44
	exercise 3	84	46
	exercise 4	75	75

6   Private consumption equals £180; C's value added equals £100.

7   Value added in B and C respectively is £10 and £30. (Each must sell for £50 to private consumption.)

8   £40.

9   £40.

10 (a) £110; (b) £120.

11 £50 in A, £40 in B and £30 in C.

Exercises 2.2 (page 35)

1   (i) national product rises by £1,000;
    (ii) national product rises by £1,000;
    (iii) national product rises by £500;
    (iv) national product rises by £800. (But suppose the antique is a fake?);
    (v) national product rises by £8,800.

2   (i) national product at market prices=£150; national product at factor cost=£120;
    (ii) national product at market prices=£200; national product at factor cost=£120;

(iii) national product at market prices=£120; national product at factor cost=£110; (B's value added has fallen to £20).
(iv) national product at market prices=£100; national product at factor cost=£120.

3 (i) national product at market prices would rise;
   (ii) no effect; a transfer payment merely disappears;
   (iii) no effect; there will be a switch in sales of milk by the productive sector to households instead of to government. Total final sales will not be affected though its composition as between private and public consumption would change.

4 (i) national product at market prices=£197; value added: A's=£60; B's=£70; C's=£40; D's=£20; total national product at factor cost=£190;
   (ii) national product at market prices=£203⅓; value added: A's=£60; B's=£40; C's=£40; D's=£20; total national product at factor cost=£160;
   (iii) national product at market prices=£182; value added in each industry and total national product at factor cost is same as in (i) above.

Exercises 4 (page 89)
1 (i) A=£50; B=£30; C=£40.
   (ii) A=£30; B=£30; C=£40.
   (iii) A=£40; B=£20; C=£40.
   (iv) A=£30; B=£30; C=£70; total GNP=£130, corresponding to £120 private consumption plus £30 exports minus £20 imports.

2 (i) £3,000. Private consumption rises by £200 (tourism) plus £8,000 (watches), and imports rise by £200 (tourism abroad) plus £5,000 (watches at factor cost). The £3,000 corresponds to £2,000 value added by Mr A and £1,000 indirect taxes on the watches.
   (ii) £2,600. Private consumption expenditure on watches is reduced to £6,400, and there is capital formation, consisting of the increase in the stock of watches, of £1,200 since this is their cost to Mr A. In this case, therefore, the contribution to GNP is £400 less than in the previous case since this represents the unrealised £400 of A's value added on the sale of the remaining 20 watches.

3 (i) *GNP by category of final demand:* private consumption=£100; (less) imports=£30. Total GNP=£70.

GNP by industry of origin: A=£20; B=£20; C=£30. Total=£70.

(ii) *GNP by category of final demand:* private consumption=£60; capital formation=£70; exports=£50; (less) imports=£30. Total GNP=£150.

GNP by industry of origin: A=£60; B=£80; C=£10. Total=£150.

(iii) *GNP by category of final demand:* private consumption=£60; public consumption=£20; capital formation=£10; exports= =£70; (less) imports=£50. Total GNP=£110.

GNP by industry of origin: A=£10; B=£20; C=£50; D=£30. Total=£110.

(iv) *GNP by category of final demand:* private consumption=£72; capital formation=£95; exports=£50; (less) imports=£30.[1] Total GNP=£187.

GNP by industry of origin: same as in (ii), £150. The difference between this and the market price figure, namely £37, represents the indirect taxes of £12 on private consumption and £25 on C's inputs, which has been passed on to the price of capital formation.

(v) *GNP by category of final demand:* private consumption=£80; (less) imports=£30. Total GNP at market prices=£50. GNP by industry of origin is the same as in (i).

(vi) (a) The value of D's sales to public consumption would have to rise from £20 to £40; the remaining items of final demand would remain the same as in (iii) and total GNP at market prices would rise to £130. GNP at factor cost=£110.

(b) D's sales to exports would rise by five-sevenths of £20 and his sales to public consumption by the remaining two-sevenths, so that exports would rise to £64⅔ and public con-

---

[1] There are conflicting schools of thought about the correct procedure for treating indirect taxes on imports in estimating GNP at market prices. The most conventional way is to subtract imports at factor cost, which is the procedure followed here. But an alternative procedure of subtracting imports at market prices was followed until recently in Britain. It is based on considerations that have been pointed out by J.L. Nicholson, in 'National Income at Factor Cost or Market Prices?', *Economic Journal*, June 1955. One of the main ideas behind this treatment is that the market price valuation of national product should be a market price valuation of what, in fact, the 'nation' has produced, which does not include the imports. Hence, the indirect taxes on these imports should not be included in the valuation of the national product. This view appears to have some force behind it.

sumption to £25$\frac{5}{7}$; private consumption and capital formation remaining the same as in (iii). GNP at factor cost = £110.

(c) GNP at market prices by category of final demand would remain as in 3(iii), but GNP at factor cost would fall by £20, to £90, representing the £20 net indirect taxes. This fall in factor cost GNP corresponds, on the industry of origin side, to a fall in D's value added to £10, value added in the other industries remaining as in 3(iii).

4   GDP(MP) = £180; GDP(FC) = £170.

5   National income, which equals net national product at factor cost, equals £85 (i.e. £120 less £20 depreciation and less £15 net indirect taxes).

6   NNP(MP) plus depreciation equals GNP(MP), less net indirect taxes equals GNP(FC).

7   Two.

Exercises 5 (page 108)

1   *Household account*

Debits		Credits	
Household savings	6	Household income	100
Direct taxes (household)	17	Transfer payments	3
Private consumption	80	(from government)	
Total	103	Total personal income	103

Capital account

Debits		Credits	
Net investment overseas	5	Firm's savings	10
Gross domestic capital		Government savings	4
formation	15	Household savings	6
Total investment	20	Total savings	20

Government account

Debits		Credits	
Public consumption	25	Direct taxes (firms)	15
Transfer payments	3	Direct taxes (household)	17
Government savings	4		
Total	32	Total	32

Rest of world account

Debits		Credits	
Exports	30	Net investment overseas	5
less Imports	−25		
Total	5	Total	5

2 (i) household income = £180; firms' savings = £20;
   (ii) household income = £190; firms' savings = £10;
   (iii) household income = £200.

3 (a) £170;
   (b) firms' savings, equal to £30, is the only item (since capital
       formation must be equal to £30, and there are no household
       or government savings, or net investment overseas);
   (c) they would come from the production account, so that this
       would look as follows: household income = £160; direct
       taxes (firms) = £10; firms' savings = £30.

4 Private consumption = £75, so GNP = £90.

5 I = £15, so GNP = £100.

6 I = £40.

7 GNP = £125 and I = 35 (Y_h must be 100, so if Y_h = 0·8 of GNP,
GNP must equal 100/0·8, which equals 125. So S_f = 25, so I = 10 + 25,
or 125 − 90.

8 GNP = £90 (S_f = 15, so Y_h must equal 75 and C_h must equal 60).

9 Public consumption = £10; GNP = 110. (Capital formation must
be 15, namely the sum of S_h and S_g.)

10 I = 15.

11 C_g = 20; I = 20.

12 I = 20.

Exercises 8 (page 177)

1 (i) 30; (ii) 45.

2 (a) (i) 75; (ii) 100; (iii) 175.
   (c) (i) 80; (ii) 200.

3 (a) Y = 50;
   (b) 15.

4 (a) 200 and 100 respectively;
   (c) 300 and 150 respectively;
   (e) it rises;
   (f) it rises;
   (g) actual savings remains unchanged but income rises;
   (h) actual savings and income both rise.

Exercises 9.1 (page 184)

1 (a) 0·9; (b) 0·7.

2 0·2.

3 (a) $S = -5 + 0·1Y$;
  (b) $S = -10 + 0·3Y$;
  (c) $S = -5 + 0·2Y$.

4 (a) $C = 70$ and $S = 30$;
  (b) $C = 40$ and $S = 10$;
  (c) $C = 130$ and $S = 70$.

5 (a) $C = 95$ and $S = 5$;
  (b) $C = 185$ and $S = 15$;
  (c) $C = 455$ and $S = 45$.

6 (i) (a) $C/Y = 0·7$ and $S/Y = 0·3$;
    (b) $C/Y = 0·8$ and $S/Y = 0·2$;
    (c) $C/Y = 0·65$ and $S/Y = 0·35$;
  (ii) it falls.

7 (a) $C/Y = 0·95$ and $S/Y = 0·05$;
  (b) $C/Y = 0·925$ and $S/Y = 0·075$;
  (c) $C/Y = 0·91$ and $S/Y = 0·09$.

8 (i) (a) 100; (b) 180; (c) 340.
    (b) When $Y = 100$, at which level planned S and I are both equal to 10.

9 (i) (a) 110; (b) 190; (c) 260.
  (ii) None of the above is an equilibrium level, which is when
  $$Y = 150 \left(\text{from } Y = \frac{I+10}{1-0·8} = \frac{30}{0·2} \right).$$

10 (i) At income level $Y = 100$.
  (ii) When $Y = 80$, planned I exceeds S by 6 $(10-4)$, and when $Y = 200$, S exceeds I by 30 $(40-10)$.

11 (a) 10; (b) 20; (c) 50.

12 (a) 250; (b) 350; (c) 150; (d) 300; (e) 200; (f) 175.

Exercises 9.2 (page 212)

1 (a) 5; (b) 10.

2 (a) 2; (b) 2·5.

3   (a) 4; (b) 4; (c) 2·5; (d) 5; (e) 10; (f) 4.

4   (a) 50; (b) 100; (c) 25.

5   (a) 50; (b) 100; (c) −25; (d) −75.

6   (a) 1⅔; (b) 2.

7   (a) 2; (b) 1⅔.

8   (a) 30; (b) 50; (c) 10; (d) −20; (e) 60.

9   (a) −20; (b) 40.

10 (a) 90 $\left(\text{since } \dfrac{GDCF+X-a_c-a_m}{s+m} = \dfrac{10+15+15+5}{0\cdot2+0\cdot3}\right)$;

    (b) 100;
    (c) 75;
    (d) 70.

11 (a) 110; (b) 100.

12 (a) 10; (b) −15; (c) −15; (d) 10; (e) −50 (since the original income level was 110, and the new one, which has to be calculated with the aid of the complete equilibrium condition equation, is 60).

13 (a) 25; (b) 0; (c) 12·5.

Index